Playing for Overtime

The David Lee Herbert Story

Al Ainsworth

Playing for Overtime

Book cover designed by JD&J with stock imagery provided by pixelrobot © 123RF.com

Published by Family Story Legacy Publishing

Hardback ISBN: 978-0-578-53318-6
Paperback ISBN: 978-0-578-53320-9

Printed in the United States of America

To unsung small-town folks
who invest in your families and community,
who live lives of simple faith in God and mankind:
You are the heroes of this book.

Other Books by Al Ainsworth

Memoir:

Lines in the Gravel

Stories from the Roller Coaster (of a Faith Life)

Sports Fiction:

Coach Dave Season One

Coach Dave Season Two: All-Stars

Coach Dave Season Three: Middle School

Coach Dave Season Four: Travel Ball

Coach Dave Season Five: The Next Level

Contents

PREGAME

Foreword

It has been my good fortune as a sports writer to cover twenty-nine Super Bowls, several Sugar Bowls, Cotton Bowls and other major college bowl games. Those travels, those assignments have been a blessing I don't take lightly. Nevertheless, when people ask me about my favorite sports events to write about, the Super Bowls and the major college bowl games never enter the conversation. Fact is, I'd much rather cover small-town Mississippi football. Most years, the Class 1A (smallest) state championship game is my favorite game to cover.

Seems to me, small-town high school football produces the best stories. Whole towns turn out for the games. Rosters and coaching staffs are small. Players go both ways. You often see 150-pound guards blocking for 220-pound quarterbacks. And coaches? They often serve also as teachers, trainers, surrogate fathers, and bus drivers. They also wash the socks and jocks. Often, you could argue the small-town head coach, not the mayor, is the most well known, at times most beloved, and often also the most criticized citizen in town.

Fifty-three years ago, I covered my first sports event for my hometown newspaper. I was thirteen and dreaming of covering NFL championships, Sugar Bowls, and the like. My first assignment: a game in Lucedale, Mississippi, that pitted Brooklyn against Lucedale. Today, after much consolidation, that would be Forrest County AHS vs. George County.

My dad, a sports writer himself, drove me to the game fifty miles away because thirteen-year-olds can't drive. We didn't sit in the press box. No, we walked the sidelines, a practice I still enjoy to this day. You can hear the coaches barking instructions from the sidelines. You can see the players encouraging one another, emotions ranging from jubilant to despondent—and back—in a single series of downs. Turn away from the field and you see mamas and daddies and aunts and uncles living and dying with every play. Every game is its own passion play. Man, if a sports writer can't find a good story at these games, he or she is in the wrong business.

I can't remember the score of last year's Super Bowl, but Lucedale defeated Brookyn 12-0 that Friday night long ago. The coaches—Lucedale's Bill Martin and Brooklyn's Poochie Stringfellow—made an impression on me that I haven't forgotten to this day. If algebra and geometry teachers somehow could get the same attention from their students that really good high school coaches get from their players, we would have many more outstanding engineering majors at Mississippi universities.

This book is about a small-town football coach at the remote northeast Mississippi village of Tishomingo. David Lee Herbert was his name and he was a smart man who could have done most anything, but he did what he loved, which was coaching high school football. Herbert was beloved in his community, at his school, and by his players, including his son, the quarterback. This is not to say his strategy wasn't sometimes questioned. That's the life of a football coach, especially in a small town where the barber, the sheriff, and the insurance salesmen sometimes believe they know more about football than the coach.

It is quite possible that no coach ever has had his strategy questioned more than Herbert did one November night back in 1988. Now, I don't want to give away too much of the story. Suffice to say that Herbert, then a 46-year-old coach already suffering from a frightful, fatal disease, made the coaching call of a lifetime. This small-town football coach made a decision—so unusual, so against-the-grain and so remarkably brilliant—that he became nationally renowned in a matter of days.

Regretfully, I did not cover that game. But I wrote about it as soon as I heard about it. The more I learned about David Lee Herbert, the more I wanted to know about him. I thought many of the national reporters missed the real essence of Herbert's story. And I remember thinking, *Someday, this will make a good book.* I am glad Al Ainsworth finally has written it. Enjoy.

Rick Cleveland
Mississippi Hall of Fame Sportswriter

Preface

I was on the five-year college plan, starting my final year at the University of Southern Mississippi in the fall of 1988. I was preparing to coach baseball for a living, but I had long been a big football fan, too. On one of my visits home, my mother handed me an article she had clipped from the Jackson newspaper. It told the story of a coach with amyotrophic lateral sclerosis (ALS), or Lou Gehrig's Disease, at Tishomingo High School who made a call that would be repeated across the world by the end of the weekend. The first time I read the story, I was hooked.

Mom was drawn to the article because she had attended high school with Tishomingo coach David Lee Herbert. Mississippi Sports Hall of Fame journalist Rick Cleveland wrote the piece, and later, when he presided over the Hall of Fame, he posted a follow-up piece from a 2005 column on the Hall of Fame's blog. I read that post many times over the years and couldn't get away from feeling the story should be a book. A few years later, I met Rick at the Mississippi Book Festival in Jackson and asked him if he remembered the story. He did. I told him it should be a book. He agreed and told me, "You should write that book. I know the family would want their story told."

So I have written *Playing for Overtime: The David Lee Herbert Story*. There is much more to the story than just a gutsy call in a football game or a coach who got a bad break in life. It's the story of community, faith, and one family's steely determination to forge ahead no matter how much life—even God—seemed to be piling on. As I delved deeper and deeper into my research and interviewed many people who walked through parts of life with the Herbert family, I'm glad I listened to that little voice inside of me that for thirty years wouldn't let the story go.

From my first call to Linda Herbert, I encountered salt-of-the-earth people from all over North Mississippi (and a few transplants who have adapted well). Aside from being Annette's son, Linda didn't know me from Adam's house cat, to use a popular Southern idiom, but she invited me into her home time and time again to talk about all the aspects of her husband's story. She was genuine from the beginning, openly laughing and crying and telling me her family's story just as it happened, even the parts that were still a little raw. As I transcribed our interviews and wove her part of our talks into the manuscript, I found my own eyes watering and my bottom lip quivering on a number of occasions as I considered the power of a simple life of faith.

My second call was to Coach Herbert and Linda's son, Dave, the quarterback of the 1988 Tishomingo Bulldogs. His cooperation was key to delivering the football aspect of the story. We talked for about forty-five minutes on the phone that first time. He had the insight of both playing football for his dad and the perspective of growing up in a small town. It was just the insight I was looking to capture. We were ending the conversation when he casually mentioned that he had a DVD with the game film ... if I wanted it.

Early in my research for *Playing for Overtime*, I met another group of kindred spirits: some of the sports reporters who covered the story. I have covered sporting events for different media since I was twelve years old, starting with Rankin Academy football for the *Rankin County News*. Through the years I have written game stories and press releases for the schools where I have coached, been a part of radio and podcast programs as a guest, and live tweeted from various high school games. My favorite media dalliance was a three-year stint as the color commentator for the Internet stream of my older son's high school's baseball games and a recent return to the booth to call play by play. In the research for this book, I met some guys who have made a career of watching games and telling their audience about them. Their love for sports and the people who played and coached them made our time together pass much too quickly as we swapped story after story. I am particularly indebted to the sports staff of the *Northeast Mississippi Daily Journal*, who covered upward of twenty high schools in the 1980s. I was able to piece together much of Coach Herbert's six-year stint as head coach of the Tishomingo Bulldogs because of their coverage. The reporters I interviewed always pointed me to others who might fill in some of the gaps.

The biggest question I spent months contemplating was the central theme of David Lee Herbert's story. He was a common man, a hard worker with a quiet faith, and a pretty good football coach. He had never won a state championship as a football coach, though, and had a career losing record. He hailed from a Southern hill country region with racial skeletons in its closet, but his family was naive enough to see people of all colors as just people. He made a gutsy call that would win his team an important football game—as important as a school with graduating classes of less than forty would ever play—and the call may not have even been his idea. The fact that he made the call from a motorized wheelchair on the back of a flatbed truck because he had a disease that promised that this would be his last season and that his son was the quarterback caused the play to go as viral as a football play could go pre-Internet. That part of the story would make, at most, an interesting blog post or a lengthy magazine article.

The lives of David Lee Herbert and his family held more than what a magazine article covering what became known locally as simply The Play could include. Here was a man who chose to coach at small schools and live in small towns for his entire career. Aside from an ill-fated short period of time when he left coaching to make some "real money" for his family of six, he coached football and lived a simple life. The further I delved into Coach Herbert's story, the more the themes of family, community, and faith emerged. The Herbert family has proven steadfast and loyal through several generations. David Lee and Linda spent many of their forty years on the back side of their wedding vows— "in sickness," "for worse," "for poorer"—but they took care of one another until David Lee's death caused them to part. For a public figure who was at the same time intensely private, Coach Herbert's life greatly impacted the Mississippi communities of Carrollton and Tishomingo, both of which rose up to carry his burden at key moments of unimaginable grief when it seemed like life should be penalized for unnecessary roughness. Even during those moments when the world around them was nothing if not chaotic, the faith of the Herbert family remained simple and profound.

From a cool football play to something infinitely more substantial, exploring David Herbert's life has been an amazing journey. There are books that change you. This is one of those books for me. Like so many young men who grow up in small towns, I bolted for bigger options at the first opportunity. I wanted to go places and see things and experience the world. While continuing to be a lifelong Mississippian, I have expanded far beyond my hometown roots. Still, you never really escape roots as deep as mine. I notice my small-town background creeping in more by the year as I age. I never understood why my dad would take a whole week of his precious vacation time to stay home and work in his garden. My much smaller garden has often gone untended (and sometimes even unplanted) during years I didn't have time to tend it. I remember wishing I could mow my two acres at a former house in one day instead of the three (on a riding lawnmower, no less) that it took while I was coaching high school baseball. Once I left Star, Mississippi, I never wanted to live in a town that small again. My mantra was that I wanted to live a phone call away from a pizza being delivered to my house and that if I wanted a bag of M&Ms at midnight, I would be close to a store that was open and willing to sell them to me. Now, when I pull in my driveway at the end of the day, I'm happy to stay put until I have to go out the following morning.

As a coaching and sports administration major in college, I focused all my attention on coaching high school baseball at the highest level. When I stopped coaching in 2002, I had coached a state championship game, the state all-star game, and in the State Games of Mississippi, an all-star type festival. I enjoyed the success and upward movement in my life and in my career in sports. Don't get me wrong: I cared about my players on and off the field, but when I read about the lives and careers of Coach Herbert and his contemporaries who remained in the state's smallest schools by choice, I came to appreciate how selfless they were to invest in student-athletes for the joy of coaching young men. Many times, this was at the expense of their own career opportunities. Though they worked without the acclaim often afforded their contemporaries at larger schools, coaches like David Lee Herbert were and continue to be the fabric of which their small towns were made.

1

An entire coaching career had come to this.

The clock showed seven seconds remaining in a hard-fought game between division rivals Tishomingo High School and Falkner High School. The Tishomingo Bulldogs held a 16-14 lead and had possession of the ball on the Falkner side of the field. There was time for one last play. Most onlookers might have expected Tishomingo Coach David Lee Herbert to instruct his quarterback to bring his team to the line in "victory formation," take one last snap, and kneel with the ball to seal the win and cap off a winning season.

But there was a catch.

The state's division 1A classification consisted of the smallest schools in Mississippi. Two of the six teams in Division 1 1-A would advance to the playoffs the following week to complete with the state's other seven divisions for the state championship. The bottom three teams in the division were mired in dismal seasons and eagerly awaiting the end of the season. At the top of the division, though, competition had been fierce throughout the regular season. A Tishomingo win over the Falkner Eagles would force a three-way tie among those two teams and Smithville High School. The Mississippi High School Activities Association's tiebreaker system for three-way ties would come into play only if Tishomingo could hold off the Eagles. In order to secure a spot in the playoffs, the Bulldogs needed to win by four points or more. If the game were to end as it stood, Falkner would still claim the number one seed. To further complicate the matter, Smithville would advance ahead of Tishomingo as the division runner-up if the Bulldogs could not find a way to score on the game's final play.

Many of Smithville's players and coaches stood on the Falkner side on this November Thursday night in 1988. They figured they would secure the second seed with a win two nights later in a game in which they were heavily favored. Tishomingo hoped to be the fly in the ointment by upsetting the favored Falkner squad—by four or more points. Otherwise, an emotional season would end with, at best, a shared division championship that would leave them on the outside looking in at the MHSAA 1A playoffs.

With seven ticks of the clock remaining and the football sitting thirty-five yards from the Falkner end zone, Tishomingo's fine season looked like it would fall short of a division championship. The Bulldogs rarely kicked extra points successfully, much less fifty-two-yard field goals. In looking back at the game, the Bulldog quarterback, the coach's son, would say that nobody in Tishomingo County could kick a fifty-two-yard field goal. A pass play wasn't likely to produce the needed yardage either since Dave Herbert was a converted tight end who couldn't throw the ball that far.

Coach Herbert had come to Tishomingo High School six years earlier. He had run the same offensive system and used the same terminology at the junior high and high school levels since these 1988 seniors were seventh graders. His players not only knew what they were to do on every play, they knew what every other player on their side of the ball was supposed to do. With the game on the line and one play remaining to determine his team's fate, the Bulldog brain trust sent a play into the huddle that the players had never run in a game, never practiced, and never seen drawn on a chalkboard.

By the weekend—in an age before the Internet—the play went viral. So did the story of the Tishomingo coach. A year into an amyotrophic lateral sclerosis (ALS) diagnosis and coaching from a motorized scooter on the back of a flatbed truck at the thirty-five yard line, Coach David Lee Herbert created quite a buzz in the football world. Three days after The Play, Brent Musburger listed the Tishomingo Bulldogs as one of his top ten notable teams of the week on the *NFL Today* pre-game show on CBS. Paul Harvey told his story on *The Rest of the Story*. Newspapers all over the world picked up the story of the perfect call and perfect execution of a play by a little ol' 1A Mississippi high school football team.

FIRST
QUARTER

2

The Tishomingo offense operated in the first quarter of the Falkner game without any consideration of point spreads and tiebreakers. Bulldog running backs Danny Brock, Terry Enlow, Shane Hill, and Mark Blunt came ready to do the heavy lifting against a larger Falkner defense. Brock was the senior workhorse, and Hill was the sophomore speedster who could break loose on a long run at any time. Alternating carries behind senior quarterback Dave Herbert, the Bulldog backs found room to run behind their line early on.

Enlow received the opening kickoff for Tishomingo and returned it to the Bulldog thirty-seven, right in front of Coach Herbert's flatbed. Hill ran a sweep to the right for no gain. Brock ran behind left tackle for a pickup of four. Jeffery Daniel hauled in a rare Dave Herbert aerial for eight yards and a first down near the left sideline. Then, it was back to the vaunted ground game of this group of Bulldogs: Blunt ran up the middle for a gain of six into Falkner territory. A counter to Hill over the right side netted six more. Blunt took a straight hand off up the middle for sixteen yards. Hill's pickup of five on a counter sweep behind his right guard pushed the ball inside the Eagle twenty-yard line. Brock was stopped after two yards to bring up a third and three, but Enlow gained nine and a first down on a trap play to the right side of the line. Blunt carried behind the right guard for five more yards to set up a second and goal from the two. Sticking with what was working, the Bulldogs ran the same play. This time, though, Blunt met a Falkner defender at the one and coughed up the football. Falkner recovered in the end zone. An eleven-play, sixty-two-yard drive was all for naught as the Eagle offense took the field for their initial offensive opportunity.

The first Falkner drive was short lived. Three power plays behind the right guard, left tackle, and again behind the left side of the line picked up just four yards. The Tishomingo defense—mostly the same players who had manufactured the impressive opening drive—had risen to the task of stopping the Eagle offense. A short Eagle punt gave the ball back to the Tishomingo offense at the Bulldog forty-seven yard line after a fair catch.

The second Tishomingo drive of the opening quarter began similar to the first as Enlow banged into the line for no gain. Hill picked up fourteen and a first down on a counter play. Enlow's second run gained three. Brock and Hill picked up one each on successive runs the left side. On fourth and five from the Falkner thirty-four, Hill booted a thirty-three-yard punt that would be the longest punt of the game for either team, pinning the Eagles at their own one yard line.

With time running down in the opening frame, Tishomingo's offense had been unable to make good on two excellent scoring opportunities. If nothing else, though, they had won the battle of field position, which was important in the days of grind-it-out offenses. Falkner Coach Joe Horton played it close to the vest, calling a quick-hitter up the middle that gained one and an off-tackle run to the right that picked up two. As the horn sounded to end an eventful but scoreless first quarter, the Eagles faced a third and seven situation from their own four. Falkner fans had to consider themselves fortunate that the game remained scoreless as their team had given up a total of eighty-one yards on sixteen plays to the Tishomingo offense and netted just six yards on five plays themselves.

With both teams intent on running the football, the clock moved quickly. Even at the high school level, clock stoppages are regular occurrences as teams try to squeeze in as many plays as possible during the course of a game, and four twelve-minute quarters often turn into three-hour affairs. The "football time" of Tishomingo-Falkner in 1988 synchronized with "real time" about as closely as a football game ever will.

* * *

Like Tishomingo, Falkner had much on the line on this Thursday night in late November. They were the defending north half champions and looking to claim a second state championship under Joe Horton. The 1988 season would prove to be the last of eleven seasons as the head coach at Falkner for Horton, but he left quite a legacy with the Eagles. His 1983 team had claimed the state title with a 49-21 win over small-school power Weir, which would take the next two titles.[1] From 1978-1988, Horton's squads carried a 22-3 district record and a 9-4 playoff mark. However, there was much more to Joe Horton that the 71-36-1 record he amassed in eleven seasons at Falkner.[2]

In many ways the coaches on the sidelines of Falkner High School and Tishomingo High School were kindred spirits. Both had small-town backgrounds. Herbert was from Carrollton, and Horton was from Falkner. Both could have coached at bigger schools had they desired to move up in the profession. Both were reputed to be tough but fair and had reputations of caring more about their players than they did about results on the field. Both coached hard from the opening kickoff to the final whistle, as they would on this night with a single playoff berth on the line. Both small-school coaching stalwarts would also leave the profession far too young, Herbert with Lou Gehrig's disease and Horton from a massive heart attack. Horton had by then moved across Tippah County to coach at rival Walnut. In the second game of the 1990 season, he coached the first half against his old school through chest pains and was taken away by ambulance at halftime. At forty-eight years old, he was gone by the end of the game that is now known annually as the Joe Bowl.[3]

* * *

As quickly as the first quarter flitted into the cool Falkner night, the teams raced toward this final regular-season game of the 1988 slate. For Coach Herbert, the last regular-season game was a race to extend his career by at least one more game. More important to him, though, it was a sprint to reach his team's pre-season goal of winning the district and making the playoffs. He was not bemoaning a coaching career cut off in its prime or making any kind of statement; his mind and the mind of the Bulldogs' only on-field coach, Vince Jordan, were on the opportunities already lost and the onslaught of the powerful Falkner offense that they knew would offer a counterpunch to his team's dominant effort in the first quarter.

This was the first game of the season that could be the last for both groups of seniors. The story plays out on gridirons across America every November and December. Seniors who have dedicated much of their young lives to playing a sport that most will never play again after high school suddenly see the finish line of their careers. The dog days of summer workouts and two-a-day practices—think old-school two-a-days—give way to the relief of the start of school. Practices drag on until coaches dressed in the color combination that they wear practically every day during football season comment to reporters compiling their annual pre-season edition that their boys are tired of hitting each other and ready to hit someone else.

The first Friday pep rally is often when the whole high school football experience sinks in for a senior player. Mom will start crying, if she hasn't already. Oh, she'll try to hide it and he won't say anything, but that senior football player will notice the onset of her months-long battle with allergies. Dad will wax nostalgic and be unusually quiet, remembering his own senior season and battling those emotions that have never fully gone away—or maybe he'll turn up the volume, desperately trying to live out his own dream one last time by taking up the mantle of last year's dad who attempted to will the local eleven to victory by his sheer volume and determination.

For the senior player, though, the first pep rally is when he no longer follows his teammates but leads them. Sure, he has been in the front of the exercise lines since spring practice, but that's just with the guys on the team. Now, everybody sees, and the expectations are high. Nobody has played a game yet, so every team is 0-0 and filled with anticipation. Will this be "the year"? Half of the teams in the country will see their perfect seasons dissipate into air above the stadium that first night with the last of the smoke from the grill that created such a perfect setting a few hours before. Most teams have a pretty good idea of how the first game will go, but a few will fall so hard that they will never recover. A handful of others will realize that they are even better than they imagined. For most, though, during the pep rally on that first game day Friday afternoon, hope springs eternal.

After the pep rally, most senior players of the eighties entered into hours of quiet, a transition of "getting their game faces on." Most coaches of the era were methodical—some even maniacal—about Friday game preparation. Quiet. Pre-game meal. Quiet. Training room. Quiet. Pre-game walk across the field, especially for an away game. Quiet. Specialists. Stirring. Full squad pre-game. Throttled anger. Locker-room devotion and pep talk, often intertwined and almost interchangeable. Captains. Walk down. Full-blown noise and nerves. Adolescent machismo at its finest. Banner crash. Game on. First game. Don't blink. The season will be over in a heartbeat.

* * *

For Tishomingo High School, the opening game of what would be Coach David Lee Herbert's final season as a Bulldog coach came on a Friday night at Burnsville. With the usual hopes of a winning season and a spot in the state playoffs as one of the top two teams in Division 1-1A, quarterback Dave Herbert would direct his squad for this, his senior season. His had not been the typical road to playing quarterback for a coach's son. He had been a tight end on the offensive side of the ball during the previous two seasons, having only played quarterback during his final junior high season. On this night he would step under center for the first time in his high school career as a starter. Brad Howie (pronounced *who-ee*) had played all but one or two snaps during the previous two seasons, but Howie had known Dave could have taken over at any time because of his knowledge of the Wing T offense that his father had run at each of the stops on his coaching journey.

The Tishomingo roster boasted just six seniors who would lead their team through the pre-game rituals for the opening game against county and division foe Burnsville High School: quarterback Dave Herbert, receiver Bryant Southward, running back Danny Brock, linemen Grant Horn and Antony Oaks, and tight end Joe Tucker. The Tish players enjoyed no sit-down meal in the cafeteria or private room at a local restaurant before their games. Instead, they had a brief window of opportunity between the pep rally and their report time to go home for a bite if they lived in town or to grab a little something from a convenience store if home was too far from school. Some were too nervous to eat anything. The routine was all the seniors had ever known. They began their junior high football careers with Coach

Herbert and would play the 1988 season knowing it would be the last for them and for their coach.

* * *

Will Kollmeyer was the sports director at WTVA-TV in Tupelo in the fall of 1988. He remembered moving to northeast Mississippi from Wisconsin a few years earlier and discovering the dynamic of high school football in the South:

> I was raised in Madison, Wisconsin. There were seven high schools in Madison and a bunch of them in the metro area. It didn't take me long to realize how special football was down here. I went to a high school with four thousand students; we would have maybe two thousand at a game. I remember distinctly, the first game I ever went to (in Mississippi) was Tupelo at Amory, the first Friday night, 1983, and I had never seen anything like it—five and six deep around the fence and the stands completely packed.
>
> That night, I went back and told my news director that three-and-a-half minutes was not going to be enough for a high school football Friday night. He said you have three-and-a-half; that's what it is. I kept on pushing, trying to get a show, and the next year they gave me five (minutes), and then the third year we started *Friday Night Fever*. It was one of the first high school football shows in Mississippi. It went fifteen minutes, and it's still going strong today.
>
> I knew right away how special football was, and it didn't matter when I was on the air. Three hundred sixty-five days a year, if I had something on football, I would run it because people couldn't get enough.

When you combine that love for football in this area with the story of Coach (Herbert), it was like—you've got to be kidding me—this is perfect. I think that was why it wasn't just me becoming a fan; I mean, there were a lot of people talking about it. Once we ran that story (about Coach Herbert's coaching with ALS from earlier in the football season), everybody up in that part of the state knew about it. With our coverage area—we went down just north of Meridian, deep into the Delta—a lot of other people were talking about it. He was inspiring a lot more people that he probably ever even knew. His constant fight that he was doing on a daily basis—it helped, I'm sure, to inspire others to continue their fight against whatever illness or whatever they were fighting.[4]

The rites of passage for football seniors had almost all been neatly checked off for the Bulldog seniors. Now, the Tishomingo season was down to three twelve-minute periods, and they had to outscore the Falkner Eagles by four or more.

* * *

The Tishomingo football faithful could have expected a meaningful matchup in the season's final regular-season game. After all, in answer to the pressing question that small-school coaches annually ask each other—*How many y'all got out this year?*—Coach Herbert could answer twenty-six, a high-water mark during his tenure with the Bulldogs. With their head coach's decreased capacity to walk through the motions in practice, the six seniors took on the extra role of helping Coach Jordan teach the plays to the younger players. After all, the seniors knew the plays inside and out, having run them for the previous five years from a number of different positions.

The early returns of the 1988 season were filled with promise. The season opener was a district game against Burnsville, one of the weaker teams in Division 1-1A but a county rival that Tish could not overlook. The Bulldogs were scheduled to step outside of district play for their next pair of games and would not face division favorites Smithville and Falkner until the latter part of the season. Though no team finds a season-opening division game ideal, Tishomingo opened up a 12-0 lead over Burnsville by halftime thanks to Shane Hill's one-yard touchdown run and a forty-yard jaunt into the end zone by Danny Brock. Dave Herbert scored once on the ground and once through the air on a forty-five-yard catch-and-run by Bryant Southward in the third quarter to put the game out of reach for Burnsville. Brock and Mark Blunt each scored on long runs in the fourth quarter, and Herbert even tacked on a pair of extra point kicks, a rarity for the Bulldogs.[5]

* * *

Tishomingo faced a 14-6 halftime deficit in game two at home against Vina High School from just across the state line in Alabama, Brock's forty-yard touchdown run in the second quarter providing the only Bulldog points of the half. Led by the Bulldog seniors, the second half was a different story as Tishomingo exploded for thirty-six points in a 42-20 win. Herbert threw for a forty-yard score to Joe Tucker and ran for two more. Antony Oaks tallied a safety from his linebacker position, and Southward notched two scores, a touchdown run of thirty-five yards and a forty-yard interception return.[6]

Coach Herbert's troops enjoyed a bye week following their second straight forty-two-point offensive output and would have looked forward to continuing their offensive dominance against Bear Creek (AL) High School, a new opponent of the Tishomingo schedule. However, when Bear Creek officials cancelled the game a couple of weeks before the showdown, the Bulldogs faced a lengthy layoff before continuing their district schedule with Thrasher High School on the last Friday night in September.

To that point in the 1988 season, the Tishomingo Bulldogs were everything that Coach Herbert had thought they might be. Going into the fall, he knew he would lean heavily on a sophomore class of ten players that made up more than a third of his roster. The Bulldogs were coming off a 5-5 season that included a 3-3 mark in division play and a loss to Scott Central in the Little Dixie Bowl in Sturgis. However, the upcoming sophomores had sported a 7-0 mark in junior high football (which then included grades seven through nine) the previous season and had not allowed a single point.[7] Coach Herbert's optimism in the sophomores and in his son's ability to take over at quarterback for the graduated all-district performer Brad Howie (eleven touchdown passes in 1987) had thus far been well founded. The young stable of running backs was filling in nicely. Danny Brock had comfortably stepped into the role as primary ball carrier, taking up the slack for his brother, all-district back Bobby Brock, who had also graduated. Meanwhile, district favorite and defending state runner-up Falkner had stumbled out of the gate. Opportunity was knocking for Tishomingo.

3

If anyone ever seemed destined to be a small-town football coach, it was David Lee Herbert. His sixth year at Tishomingo High School marked about fifteen years in the business at three bantamweights of high school athletics. His Bulldogs played in the 1A division, reserved for the state's smallest public schools, while previous stints in Mississippi's private school division took him to even smaller hamlets than Tishomingo. The small-school culture was what he knew and the culture into which he was born.

David Lee grew up in the historic town of Carrollton, Mississippi, the county seat of Carroll County. This tiny burg sits alongside Highway 35 just south of Highway 82, seventeen miles due east of Greenwood and ten miles west of Winona. Outsiders who didn't know any better might drive through Carrollton and adjacent North Carrollton and think they were driving through one town. Local residents would quickly correct those unwitting outsiders. Though rich with historical landmarks and history—Carrollton hosts its Pilgrimage and Pioneer Days Festival each fall and even has its own walking tour app for twenty-six of its buildings[1]—the town consists of only a dozen or so streets and fewer than two hundred of Carroll County's population of ten thousand.[2] Much of the Carrollton that David Lee knew as a boy still exists today.

The Carrollton of the 1940s was more than a half century removed from an event so infamous and so buried in Carroll County history that many of its own citizens knew little about it. The Carroll County Courthouse Massacre, as labeled by the newspaper accounts of the day, occurred on March 17, 1886, and was sparked by a sequence of events that began months earlier when two brothers, half black and half Indian, spilled molasses on a white man. Though that incident was resolved, the white man told a friend about it weeks later, and James Liddell took up his friend's offense and confronted the Brown brothers. That confrontation led to shots fired on both sides; the Brown brothers then had the audacity to file suit against a white man. Shortly after the trial commenced, somewhere in the neighborhood of one hundred armed horseback riders appeared from the west in the direction of Greenwood and surrounded the courthouse. A smaller group barged into the courthouse and opened fire. The only escape route was through the windows of the second-floor courtroom. A number of blacks jumped but were met with gunfire from those waiting outside the courthouse.[3] At least ten blacks, including the Brown brothers, died either that day or later from wounds received during the massacre, though the reported number of deaths is disputed.[4] No whites were injured.[5]

The people of Carroll County were outraged over newspaper reports about the incident from as far away as New York. The townspeople remained stone cold silent about the incident. There were appeals made to the governor, to US Representatives and Senators—including

Carrollton's own US Rep. Hernando DeSoto Money and Sen. J. Z. George—and even to President Grover Cleveland. But ultimately the government took no action.[6] Few blacks or whites talked about the massacre after that, and no charges were ever filed. Aside from the work of a few researchers, the massacre is rarely mentioned. Just over sixty years later in Money, Mississippi—an unincorporated blip on the map less than thirty miles from Carrollton—a fourteen-year-old teenager named Emmett Till was brutally murdered for allegedly making crude sexual advances toward a white woman—allegations that author Timothy Tyson claims Carolyn Bryant admitted that she at least partially fabricated. The two defendants, Roy Bryant and J. W. Milam, were acquitted by an all-white jury. A few months later and under double jeopardy protection, they sold their story to a magazine, in which they admitted their guilt. Till's open-casket funeral set off a firestorm of outrage, sparking the modern Civil Rights movement.[7]

* * *

David Lee Herbert's childhood, by comparison, was more idyllic, perhaps to the point of naïveté. When David Lee was born to Cecil and Minnie Laura Herbert on March 12, 1942, he entered a world that was at war. The United States was still reeling from the Japanese attack on Pearl Harbor just over three months earlier. The first day of that year, the United States and twenty-five other nations signed a united declaration against the Axis powers. Japanese forces aggressively claimed new territory. Nazi powers met in Berlin to organize "the final solution" to exterminate

European Jews. Food and gasoline rationing began in the United States, the draft age was lowered from twenty-one to eighteen, and a Gallup Poll officially dubbed the war World War II. The United States launched air offensives over Germany, while the Battle of the Midway marked the Japanese forces' first major defeat of World War II. The Axis forces, however, surged into new territories with little resistance.[8]

The entertainment industry of the 1940s reflected the era of war. *Yankee Doodle Dandy* premiered in New York City in May, and James Cagney won Best Actor the following year for his work in the film. Composer Irving Berlin premiered his musical *This Is the Army*. In Amsterdam, Anne Frank received a diary as a birthday gift and began to document her experiences.[9]

In the year David Lee Herbert was born, Oregon State defeated Duke in the Rose Bowl, which was played in North Carolina due to the threat of Japanese attack in Pasadena, California. Major League Baseball stars Bob Feller, Ted Williams, and Stan Musial enlisted in the armed forces, beginning their service after Williams won his first American League Triple Crown (when a hitter leads a league in batting average, home runs, and runs batted in) and Musial led his St. Louis Cardinals to the World Series championship over the Yankees.[10] The Chicago Cubs dropped plans to install lights at Wrigley Field due to the war. (Ninety-one-year-old Harry Grossman would not declare "Let there be lights!" until August 8, 1988, before a game that was ultimately rained out in the fourth inning.)[11]

Near the end of 1942, President Franklin D. Roosevelt began the dismantling of the Work Projects Administration.

Begun in 1933 as the Works Progress Administration (WPA) component of Roosevelt's New Deal program, the WPA had employed 8.5 million unemployed Americans in constructing roads, buildings, bridges, parks, and airports. The program had seen its share of abuse and with the war effort virtually eliminating unemployment, the work of the WPA was set to expire during the following year.[12]

Visitors to Carrollton, Mississippi, today might notice a WPA project still in existence. The Community House—one of many such community centers constructed during the WPA era—was built from native pines in what was dubbed "government rustic" style.[13] Local contractor David Felts oversaw its construction from 1935 to 1936. Located on Lexington Street in the Carrollton Historic District, the Community House underwent a major renovation in 2001.[14] Today, it is owned and operated by the Town of Carrollton and the Carroll County Board of Supervisors.[15]

One hundred fifty miles northeast of Carrollton, the WPA was working on another project in the foothills of the Appalachian Mountains, a project that would become a part of the Herbert family's lives over forty years later. Tishomingo State Park features rock formations and plant life unique to Mississippi, a swinging bridge, a section of the Natchez Trace, as well as hiking trails and campgrounds.[16] David Lee's childhood included plenty of hiking too, but he and his friends did not need parks to enjoy the woods and rolling hills of Carroll County. David and his brother Cecil and their cousins and boyhood pals would bound out of their respective houses every day they weren't in school and run off to play sports or have adventures that most days lasted until dark.

* * *

David Lee was born into a family of five. His older brother, Cecil, and sister, Joyce, were five and three years older, respectively. When their father returned from the war, their family grew by two more girls. Janis was five years David Lee's junior, and Anne came along four years after her. The seven Herberts squeezed into a three-bedroom house with a living room, a kitchen, and one bathroom, which Joyce said was "better than an outside toilet."[17] Their narrow road leading to the nearby courthouse was known as the Cut. Two first cousins, Jo Leta and Harry Herbert Sanders, lived next door in a house so close that Linda Herbert, David Lee's wife, said, "If you threw out your dishwater, you'd hit their front door."[18] Bernard Taylor, another first cousin and a year older than David Lee, lived on the same hill, a stone's throw away. The post office was just down the hill. On some occasions when the postmaster had both the front and back doors of the post office opened for air, young David Lee would seize the opportunity to take a shortcut to town by riding down the hill and straight through the post office. That habit landed him in a little hot water with the postmaster.[19]

The Herbert home was the place where all the kids in the Cut congregated. Cecil and David Lee stayed outside most of the time, where they were joined by their sisters when the housework was finished. The yard was their sanctuary, unhindered by the adult world, or at least that's what David Lee must have thought. One day, he was playing ball in the yard and, according to Joyce, let loose an expletive during the game.

My mother thought she overheard David say an ugly word. Well, I guess he must have repeated it. Mother went outside; she brought him inside and washed his mouth out with soap. I think that cured him. I don't know whether he ever repeated that word or not, but if he did it was not in the presence of my mother. I can assure you of that.[20]

David Lee's mouth may have been cleaned that day, but it didn't stay clean for long. John Wade Herbert, David Lee's paternal grandfather, carried tobacco in a can and rolled his own cigarettes. When he discovered that his tobacco was disappearing, he told Minnie Herbert that he suspected one or more of the grandchildren was taking his tobacco and smoking. She declared court in session and elicited a confession from David Lee, among others. Her sentence included a stern warning not to take Papa Herbert's tobacco, but he was allowed to smoke grape vines. David Lee thought this was better than being sentenced by Cecil Sr., but he soon found that smoking grapevines burned his mouth, thus ending his smoking ambitions. When Papa Herbert passed away in 1951, his nine-year-old sidekick was devastated.[21]

The church adjacent to the Herbert home offered an even more expansive area for playing football, softball, or any other games requiring a bigger field. The girls joined whatever the boys were already playing, including football. Joyce says she hung in there with the boys in football and baseball, a necessity if she wanted to play. David Lee loved sports as far back as Joyce could recall, but he hated how small he was. He sometimes stuffed handkerchiefs in his back pockets to appear a little thicker until he finally began to fill out during his high school years. Perhaps a result of his small frame during his childhood, he preferred not to bother others and not to be bothered by them.[22]

David Lee's crew had the same curfew that many children of his day had: home by dark. Cousin Bernard remembered playing all over town with David Lee. "In the summer we built forts and everything else. Where we lived, right behind where David Lee lived, there were homes of six black families back there. They all had children, and we all played together. It didn't make any difference. Our parents knew where we were. We were down there in the woods or around town." At night David Lee's house was usually the hangout spot. Taylor recalled, "Uncle Cecil was a big bird hunter, and he would go out and kill a lot of birds, and we'd have bird and rice and a biscuit. We'd congregate over there, and then the adults played Rook. They'd send us in another room, and we'd play in there. We all really grew up like brothers and sisters."[23]

After dark the children in the neighborhood continued to play outside, catching fireflies or playing kick the can or cowboys and Indians or some other game. Though the Herbert children did not have an abundance of toys, Cecil Herbert did give his boys a Shetland pony, which David Lee rode all over town. He also had a BB gun that accidentally—according to David Lee—discharged on one occasion, shooting Joyce. She remains unconvinced that the shooting was accidental. Their bond was tested on another occasion when David Lee—per the usual—wanted to play football, and Joyce wanted to continue playing with her doll. David Lee resolved that quickly enough. He threw his sister's doll into a cistern. Like most of their disagreements, though, they worked it out themselves rather than tattling, which would have likely landed them both in some measure of trouble.[24]

Clint Littleton was a boyhood pal of David Lee's. His grandfather, the jailer in Carrollton, had a stroke in 1947, so Clint's family moved to town to care for him. A couple of years older than David Lee, Littleton was seven years old when his family moved into the housing unit of the jail. That put both boys within shouting distance of the courthouse lawn, where they met almost daily, along with several others, until their high school years. Littleton recounted numerous adventures the group of boys had throughout their childhood. Sometimes they played in the woods behind David Lee's grandmother's house and other times they tried to catch pigeons in the church and courthouse steeples, but one activity they did nearly every day: football on the courthouse yard. Starting with their core group of four to six boys, others always joined.

> We didn't have a football back then, so we made a football out of socks. David Lee always wanted to quarterback, and they'd have to flip coins to see who was going to quarterback. There would be several us here in town that would just get over there and play— blacks and whites played together. Nobody paid attention to it.[25]

Perhaps it was these early experiences in racially segregated Carrollton that influenced Coach Herbert later in life. One of his character qualities that his players from Tishomingo High School consistently point out is how he treated all people with the same respect, regardless of color or ability.

4

Saturdays were different at the Herbert house as the family prepared for church the next day. Sundays were about getting to church on time—though the church could be measured by steps from their house. If one of the children did not feel like going to church, that child had certainly better not feel like doing anything else that day. As a result, it was a rare occasion indeed for one of the Herbert children to miss church on a Sunday morning. Whether his regular attendance was coerced or not, much of David Lee's spiritual formation took place a mere fifty yards down the hill from his house at Carrollton Baptist Church. It was there that he chose to follow God as a young man.

After the Herbert children had finished preparing for meals and laying out their clothes for Sunday, some of them turned their attention to an entrepreneurial venture they cooked up for Saturday nights. With their daddy working late at his furniture store—the businesses in Carrollton stayed open until midnight on Saturday nights then—Cecil, Joyce, David Lee, and friends Barry and Mack Allen Smith made their way to the end of the Cut near the streetlight with an assortment of musical instruments. Two of the group would go on to hall of fame careers: David Lee in the Mississippi Association of Coaches Hall of Fame and Mack

Allen Smith in the Rockabilly Hall of Fame alongside legends like Roy Orbison, Carl Perkins, Johnny Cash, Elvis Presley, and Chuck Berry.[1]

David Lee's part of the troupe was to do the hambone—a rhythmic slapping of the thighs, arms, and chest akin to the African-Haitian Juba dance—often to the song of the same name. A bluesy rendition of "Hambone," written by Red Saunders and Leon Washington, was released in 1952 by Red Saunders and his orchestra as a rhythm and blues song; in that same year, Frankie Laine and Jo Stafford spun it as a pop single:

Joyce Herbert claims not to even know how to hold a guitar today and still cannot figure out where her brother learned to hambone, though Clint Littleton says that it was a young African-American boy named Wyatt Duren who taught him to hambone, sometimes with spoons.[2] The young troubadours even found that some passersby would drop a few coins in their open guitar case, but they mostly entertained themselves through their Saturday evening performances until Minnie Herbert called them inside. When they returned home they would doze on the living room floor, listening to the Grand Ole Opry on the radio while waiting for Cecil, Sr., to come home from his store.[3]

David Lee's love of music would accompany him for much of the rest of his life. Before he went on to become the quarterback on the J. Z. George High School football team, he played in the school marching band. Joyce was a majorette who once hit her brother's instrument as they marched in formation. He came after her, yelling, until she felt she was "going to be smeared right there on the field." When she started crying, David Lee backed off and apologized.[4] Though his high school years brought an increased focus on sports, his early experiences found a way back into his life through gospel music in his adult life. He never forgot how to do the hambone either, entertaining the adults and kids in his family in more private performances years after his early street shows.[5]

* * *

Christmas was the most memorable time of the year at the Cut for the children of David Lee's generation. In addition to Cecil and Minnie Herbert's five children and cousins Harry Herbert and Jo Leta Sanders and Bernard Taylor, some of the out-of-town cousins also spent their Christmas visits to Carrollton sleeping on pallets spread throughout the Herbert home. Christmas did not bring a bounty of presents for any of the cousins, mainly fruit and fireworks. Joyce laughed as she recalled not asking for fruit but being sure to ask for fireworks—Roman candles and firecrackers, but mostly firecrackers. For a number of Christmas seasons, the extended family of Herbert cousins and other kids near their age in Carrollton followed a similar routine:

> We would get up around three o'clock on Christmas morning. David was the first one up; I don't know that he would ever go to sleep. He would wake us all up, and we were out the door. Mom and Dad would still be asleep. We'd go around and wake up all the other kids. Well, they knew we were coming around because we put the plan together. You're talking about at least fifteen of us kids. We would go from house to house.[6]

Heralding the arrival of Christmas through fireworks became a tradition with the Herberts when David Lee was about six or seven years old. Taylor smiled when he thought back to signaling the arrival of Christmas all over their small town. "Really, getting up and shooting fireworks was more important to us, more exciting to us, than what we were going to get for Christmas." The cousins had plenty of fireworks in addition to the small bag they each received for Christmas because Jo Leta and Harry Herbert's family owned Sanders Grocery Store in town and could contribute big bags of fireworks that had not sold at the store. Just down the hill—about where Carrollton's post office currently sits—the county maintenance barn made for a memorable first stop. Taylor recalled, "They had all these big culverts down there. We would take these firecrackers and these TNT bombs, and we would put 'em in those culverts and light 'em, three or four, and it sounded like an atomic bomb down there." From there, the kids systematically made their way through town announcing that Christmas had once again arrived well before dawn in Carrollton.[7]

The tradition continued into the group's early teenage years, when David Lee and his cousins decided that sleeping in on Christmas Day was more important. Taylor recalled, "As time grew on, I guess people got tired of it. They asked us—you don't need to do that—but that didn't deter us a whole lot. We went right along. When they would come out and say something to us about it—now, you boys and girls need to get back home or whatever—they knew we were having a good time and that there wasn't anything malicious going on." Thinking about their holding those cherry bombs in their hands until the fuse was almost gone, he added, "It's a thousand wonders we didn't blow our hands off."[8]

Joyce remembered outfoxing the sheriff one year as he attempted to bring a premature end to their fun:

> We were where the old post office was, and he was sitting there waiting for us. He caught us and sent us back home. It was three o'clock in the morning. Well, we went back to the hill and waited until he got home. We gave him about thirty minutes and went back and started all over that town shooting firecrackers. There were so many of us; he never did catch us.[9]

* * *

When David Lee and his friends reached working age—ten or eleven years old—each of them took jobs with one of the four small local grocery stores in Carrollton. They would pull grocery items from lists that residents called in, place them in baskets on the front of their bicycles, and deliver goods to the customers' homes, which were always left unlocked for the boys. They would place the refrigerated goods in the refrigerator or ice box and stack the rest of the order on the customers' dining room tables. After delivering all of the orders, the boys would congregate at the courthouse lawn—still on the clock, Littleton added—to play football until one of the owners beckoned them for another delivery.[10]

The close-knit group often visited one another in their respective stores, all within easy walking distance of one another. David Lee, known throughout his life as an aggravator, particularly liked to joke around with Bobby

Gee Beckwith, a meat cutter at Paul Tardy's grocery store where David Lee worked. Beckwith was wielding his meat cleaver one day when some of the other boys dropped in to visit. Littleton shook his head at the memory of what happened next:

> David Lee was in there aggravating him while he was cutting. He'd stick his finger up there and tell Bobby Gee to hit it with that meat cleaver. Well, one time David Lee stuck it up there at the wrong time, and he cut the end of his finger off and it fell on the floor. We gathered it up and took it to the doctor's office next door to the grocery store—Dr. Holman was in there. We carried his finger in there and then called his mama and told her what had happened.[11]

Bernard Taylor was there when it happened and confirmed Beckwith never intended to actually cut David Lee's finger but was playing along with his coworker. "David Lee loved having fun, which was very typical of his daddy. In his daddy's family—my mother and her sister and the other two brothers and so on—they were just a fun-loving family. David Lee was one of those. He was just sticking his hand up there; he didn't think it would happen, but it did."[12] The finger never healed right and David Lee's pals kidded him that he threw a football so well because his finger was bent just right to hold the smaller end of the football.

Littleton remembered David Lee's learning another lesson the hard way behind the jail one day during their teenage years:

A bunch of the men here in Carrollton would get in the back of the metal building that used to be there by the jail. They'd play card games back there—drink beer and gamble. So we all decided that when they left, we were going to go in there and get us some of that beer. So we did; we waited until they left and raised the window and got us some Jax beer. We went down behind the old jail down there. We sat down there all afternoon drinking that beer, and we thought we were something. David Lee got so sick he threw up all over himself, all over his clothes and everything, so he stripped all the way down to his shorts, slipped around—back then, it wasn't populated like it is now—and got home and changed clothes before his mama ever knew anything about it. I don't guess he ever drank any more beer.[13]

* * *

David Lee arrived in high school in the fall of 1957, already with quite a few life lessons under his belt. He finally began to fill out a little, no longer requiring the handkerchiefs in his pockets to look the part of a star athlete. He started at quarterback by his senior year and loved being on the field. This was where he decided he wanted to invest his life, teaching the game and investing in the next generation of young men. His sister Anne, nine years younger than the senior quarterback, remembered watching both her brothers play quarterback for their high school team. "We would park at the goal post at J. Z. George School. The whole family would be in the car, and we would watch it from there. Now, Dad would get out and go to the stands, but we never did because Janis and I were too young."[14]

During his adolescent years, David Lee became very active in Delbert Edwards' 4-H club at J. Z. George, raising a calf that he showed in Greenwood at 4-H shows. Still, sports dominated David Lee's thoughts throughout high school, from the football field to his eventual assignment as sports editor of the school paper. For his senior quote in the school yearbook, David Lee chose "Life is itself but a game of football" from Sir Walter Scott. The quote is from the poem "Football Song" and although it referred to soccer, it could not have been more appropriate to frame the remainder of David Lee Herbert's life. It foreshadowed the victories and defeats that lay in front of him—in athletic completion and in life—and the renown that he would achieve nearly three decades later.

SECOND
QUARTER

5

alkner faced third and seven on the first play of the second quarter. From his team's own four yard line, Coach Joe Horton played it safe and called a quarterback keeper around left end. The play netted just four yards and brought up fourth down and a punting situation. The Eagle punter stood in his own end zone, ready to kick the ball back to Tishomingo. When the snap sailed high over his head, both teams scrambled to pounce on the loose ball which bounced through the end zone for a safety and a 2-0 Tishomingo lead two plays into the second quarter.

By rule, when a team gives up a safety during regulation, they must then kick the ball back to their opponents from their own twenty yard line. This kick can be from a tee like a regular kickoff or a punt. Though a ball kicked from a tee typically travels farther, most teams opt for the punt since it allows more time for the kicking team to run down the field and hold the receiving team to fewer return yards. Falkner's punt was downed by sophomore Shane Hill at the Tishomingo forty-two yard line.

The Bulldog running game took advantage of the good field position. Danny Brock carried four times in succession—over left tackle for two and three consecutive times around left end for five, ten, and three yards. Sophomore Terry Enlow picked up eleven running behind the left guard for another first down. Hill swept around the right side for two more. Facing a second and eight, Dave Herbert threw incomplete to set up a third-and-long situation. His screen pass to Brock near the right sideline was complete, but as Brock neared the Falkner fifteen yard line, he was hit by an Eagle defender. The ball popped loose, and Falkner recovered, taking possession at their own thirteen. Three Tishomingo offensive drives in the first half had now netted nothing but frustration and field position.

The Tishomingo defense shut down the Falkner offense yet again after the turnover. The Eagles managed a single first down run on the first play of the possession but were unable to keep the drive alive and prepared to punt. This time, the Eagle punter received the snap but shanked the punt to the right sideline, advancing the ball only nineteen yards. The Tishomingo offense took possession on the Falkner forty-seven. Another golden opportunity stared them in the face.

Enlow tried the middle for three yards. Sophomore Jeff Daniel made a sliding catch of Herbert's wobbly pass along the left sideline for a gain of nine and a Bulldog first down. Brock ran a counter play over left tackle for a pickup of eight, and Enlow gained another first down with a four-yard run behind his left guard. Brock's twisting, turning run up the middle picked up twelve more yards and a first down at the Falkner eleven. Brock gained eight more behind left tackle to push the drive to the Eagle three. Herbert ran a quarterback sneak to the one and plunged over the goal line for a touchdown on the following play.

The touchdown pushed the Tishomingo lead to eight and set the stage for a two-point conversion. Few small schools of the 1980s had players that today are known as specialists. Today's college and even larger high school rosters are routinely dotted with the positions *K* (placekicker), *P* (punter), and even *LS* (long snapper). Players on small schools regularly played both offense and defense. A coach's idea of giving a star player a break was not playing him on one of the special team plays: a kickoff, kickoff return, punt, or punt return. Kicking extra points was a rarity for small schools, and field goal attempts were practically unheard of. On this night as on most other nights during the 1988 season, the Tishomingo offense stayed on the field to attempt a two-point conversion from the Falkner three yard line. Herbert's pass to Daniel fell incomplete, and the score remained 8-0.

Falkner returned the ensuing Tishomingo kickoff to their own thirty-eight yard line, by far their best field position of the night. With the clock winding down toward halftime, the Eagles put together their best offensive effort of the first two periods. A pair of quarterback option keepers around right end pushed the ball into Tishomingo territory, where the Eagles attempted their first pass of the night. Though quarterback Tyrone Gaillard's pass landed harmlessly ten yards short from his intended target, Coach Joe Horton undoubtedly took note that receiver Stacey Edgeston was wide open on the play. The Tishomingo defense stiffened after that, and Falkner's drive ended at the Bulldog thirty-three yard line when the horn sounded to end the second quarter and send the teams into the locker room.

Coach Herbert's team had dominated the first half, both offensively and defensively. His offense had piled up 171 yards, mostly on the ground, in thirty-two plays. The Tishomingo linemen—or hawgs, as Coach Herbert was fond of calling them—had played close to a flawless first half. Center Junior Russ, guards Vince Stanley and Antony Oaks, and tackles Grant Horn and John Moore counted on their technique and finesse more than brute strength against the bigger Falkner defensive front. The misdirection in the backfield of the Wing T allowed them to create angles on their opponents and open up running lanes again and again for the Bulldog backs. What could have been a three-touchdown advantage at the half, however, was just a one-possession lead. In the locker room, the Bulldog linemen celebrated their first-half dominance. However, blocking the bigger Eagles on offense and playing defense against those same bigger players was taking its toll on the Tishomingo line.

Falkner had run just fifteen plays and mustered only forty yards. They had surrendered a safety and set up the only touchdown of the game with a short punt. Still, on a night with playoff positions at stake for both teams, a one-possession lead hardly felt safe for Tishomingo. The Bulldog coaches went into halftime looking to finally break through the Falkner defense with scores instead of turnovers and to keep the dangerous Falkner offense at bay. In the other locker room, Coach Joe Horton made adjustments of his own to stop the potent Tishomingo ground attack and to give his team better field position in the second half. Like their opponents, the Falkner side knew the importance of playing mistake-free football for the final twenty-four minutes.

* * *

When Buzz Bissinger published *Friday Night Lights* in 1990, football fans across the country were invited behind the scenes of high school football on its biggest stage—Texas football at its highest classification. It was around this time that the landscape of Mississippi's smallest football programs was changing. School consolidation across the country was nothing new. Beginning around the turn of the twentieth century, improved roads and access to transportation reduced the number of school districts across America. Consolidation began in earnest in the 1930s, moving students from single-teacher schoolhouses and schools run by just a few employees to larger buildings that served many more students. The number of consolidated school systems had been on the uptick since the turn of the century.[1]

From 1932 to the 2010-11 school year, the number of schools in the United States dropped from 259,000 in 127,000 districts to about 99,000 schools in 13,000 districts.[2] People were divided over the new trend. Some liked the efficiency and opportunities that came from larger districts. Others favored a more localized approach to educational decisions. Though the early movements of consolidation seemed to be driven more by educators and citizens genuinely concerned about the quality of education available for all students, politicians and courts have typically driven consolidation efforts over the past few decades. For example, in Mississippi, court orders have created many new school districts in order to satisfy a decades-old desegregation order.

The Mississippi Professional Educators' December 2016 report "School District Consolidation in Mississippi" echoed much of the historical data and conclusions on consolidation. Though the two primary reasons lawmakers give for merging school districts are financial savings and increased performance, multiple reports cited by the study question whether either is actually accomplished. As school districts grow, central administrative growth often gobbles up any savings. The report also questions whether increased educational opportunities lead to better performance, especially in impoverished areas. One example of a unique consolidation is the 2015 merger of the successful, predominately white Starkville school district with the failing, mostly black Oktibbeha County schools. Because of significant community involvement, the new Starkville district has drawn positive initial reviews on the education side. In the efficiency part of the equation, though, the $2 million annual savings from the merger will potentially be offset by the need for a new school building estimated at $20 million. Including the new Starkville district, eleven consolidations were set for 2014-2019: one in south Mississippi, one near Jackson in the central part of the state, and nine in the northern third of the state. In all but one of the cases, the small-school athletic programs lost their identities. Ironically, the MPE's final conclusion in its report was, "Community engagement is critical to the success of any consolidation. Legislators should continue to seek and respond to input from local communities."[3]

* * *

Regardless of the purpose for the creation of new and larger schools or the opportunities that consolidation may provide, the net result for small communities is a loss of identity along with the loss of their schools. Sports, especially at smaller schools, are often the focal point of a town. Ricky Black is one of the winningest active coaches in the nation and has spent his entire career coaching in the state of Mississippi. The long-time head man at private school powerhouse Jackson Prep in Flowood spent eleven years building the program at 6A Tupelo High School and six years on Jackie Sherrill's staff at Mississippi State. His roots, though, run deep in smaller programs. His head coaching debut came at Kosciusko High School, but he grew up and played football at Ackerman High School in Choctaw County, which is about twenty-five miles southwest of Starkville at the edge of the Tombigbee National Forest. Ackerman has a storied football history that includes a pair of state championships, including the 1997 squad under Coach Ricky Woods that outscored their playoff opponents 117-0 en route to the title. Many of the school's forty-three winning seasons, including those from Black's playing days, predated the playoff era.[4]

Black recalled that in the late 1950s, the Ackerman football field was only ninety yards long. The ground rules called for either the offense or defense to declare when they wanted the extra ten yards marked off, though long touchdown plays stood. During his time as a high school athlete prior to segregation, both the white and black schools in Ackerman shared the field and attended one another's games. Unlike the communities of east-central Mississippi, though, many small towns in northeast Mississippi centered around basketball. Black remembers going to a high school basketball game at a 1A school and being struck by the age of many of the spectators, who represented generations with ties to the program. When he moved to Tupelo, Black remembers someone's inviting him to a party on Friday night in the fall. That would have been unheard of when he was at Ackerman or Kosciusko. He had to decline, saying that his job required his presence on Friday nights. When Black spent a number of seasons at Mississippi State and was a part of some big wins for the program, he said a call to his dad after a football weekend would result in a five-minute conversation about a Bulldog victory and thirty minutes about the Ackerman game.[5]

Like so many of the schools mentioned throughout this book, Ackerman High School's storied history fell victim to consolidation. Ackerman consolidated with perennial 1A juggernaut Weir High School to form 3A Choctaw County High School in 2013. In their first six years as a new school, the Chargers have competed in the playoffs more often than not. More telling from a community standpoint, though, is their longest-running rivalry in football: six years against Choctaw Central High School. At its closing after the 2012-13 school year, Ackerman had suited up against Eupora sixty times.[6] Weir had tangled with Noxapater fifty-seven times.[7] Fathers, grandfathers, even great-grandfathers shared in those transcendent rivalries. Playing sports for the small schools that still exist often means the athletes do not just represent their moment in time but they also represent the community, whose citizens have been closely tied to the school and its athletic programs for generations.

During the 1990s and into the 2000s, many 1A high schools closed the books on storied football programs. Whether or not the small-school programs thrived in the state's smallest classification, their tales were passed down from generation to generation—and likely growing larger or stranger or funnier as they were retold—because the schools were the center of out-of-the-way communities like Ecru and Durant in the north and Clara and Dexter in the south.

One story that Black has often retold is about Thomastown High, near Kosciusko in central Mississippi. According to Black, the school's football program faced financial adversity at least as far back as the 1970s. The principal at one point told the football coach that he couldn't afford to buy chalk for the lines on the football field. The coach was faced with quite a dilemma since his team was scheduled to play a home game that week. The principal suggested that the coach visit the cafeteria and take some of the excess evaporated milk. In typical small-school fashion, the coach used the milk to line his field, which looked just as good on game day as if he had used chalk—until the rain set in.[8]

Thomastown High played its last football game in 2010. In contrast to some small schools remembered for their success on the gridiron, the Bulldogs lost every game over its last three and a half years, including twenty shutouts in those last thirty-eight losses. The program's last two wins came versus county rival Edinburg, with whom they merged along with Carthage to form Leake Central in 2011.[9] When Leake Central was formed, the other school in Leake County changed its name from South Leake to Leake County. Both schools share the same mascot and colors, intimating further consolidation.

Looking back on generations of football with programs large and small, public and private, Ricky Black understood the argument that consolidation might make schools more efficient, but he also recognized the price of consolidation in some of those towns:

> Consolidation has destroyed a lot of communities in Mississippi because the community pride—let's take a city like Weir, one of the greatest football schools ever. Man, you took the identity of the city away. Heck, even [Major League Baseball pitcher] Roy Oswalt said people in Weir are so obsessed with football, they thought he had a summer job in Houston.[10] Where's Roy? Oh, he's in Houston working this summer. Everybody in Weir went to the football game. Everybody in Ackerman went. Everybody in Eupora went. Everybody in Sturgis—all of those communities—that was the event. It was a community pride. Everything you did—people in the community heard about it. It was essential that you played sports in those small communities, that you contributed. People knew if you didn't play. Basically, if you played for a small school, you were a soldier for the community.
>
> Whatever you did on Friday night—well, Saturday morning at the barber shop, you're gonna hear about it. Word on the street, wherever it was. Sunday, you're going to church. All the people that went to the football game went to the different churches. And then, Monday, you go back to school and you got to share all that with your students—you were held accountable. You don't hear that much in the larger

schools today, but you had to explain yourself for Friday night's performance all the way through the weekend into Monday, and you couldn't wait until the next week to play again if you lost.[11]

Black recalled conversations about football before, during, and after his haircut at the barber shop in Ackerman as a kid. "If your son happened to play and he fumbled the ball, if wasn't the best day to get your hair cut; you might want to wait until he threw a touchdown pass or something." The same is apparently true for coaches. Even through his successful forty years of coaching, Ricky Black's wife has always cut his hair.[12]

* * *

David Lee Herbert maintained his childhood connection to small-town life throughout his coaching career. His son Dave's childhood mirrored his father's upbringing in many ways, one full of riding bikes and playing sports in the yards big enough for games in Carrollton and North Carrollton; Marvell, Arkansas; and finally in Tishomingo, where the fields were bigger and came with stripes. At Carroll Academy as a young team manager, Dave marveled at how everyone in town knew the players and what positions they played. It took him less than a year to adjust to playing at Tishomingo because he was used to moving around. After he began playing high school football in Tishomingo, Dave remembered running down to the Sunflower grocery story, one of a handful of businesses in town, to pick up a few items for his mother on Saturday mornings during football season. "A lot of people would be down there talking about the game, especially if you did good. That's just the way it was back then."[13]

The younger Herbert also remembered the community aspect of his father's being the coach for the team that the locals were talking about on Saturday mornings at the grocery store. He recalled hearing very little criticism of his father back then. "These days, everybody expects you to win no matter what. Then, sports were more recreational. You always wanted to win, and you always played to win, but I don't think that winning was everything like it is now. Coaches weren't fired after one bad year. Winning was expected. Every time we played, we expected to win. Being in a small school, though, sometimes you're limited in what you've got, and sometimes you have to have a bad year to get to the next good one."[14]

* * *

Coaches enjoy plenty of positive aspects of coaching at a small school. They maintain closer bonds to their players since they tend to coach many of them from seventh grade all the way through high school. Life happens at a slower pace, and the pressure to win is often less than for their large-school counterparts. The resourcefulness of coaches at smaller schools, though, is born out of necessity, like Thomastown's coach using condensed milk to line his field when the budget would not allow for chalk. At Tishomingo High School, David Lee Herbert did not have the budget to paint the lines for his football field either. As a result, every summer he and his football managers would outline the football field with string, a wooden template, and cans of diesel fuel. Even the diesel fuel that would kill the grass and form the lines to the field was carefully sourced. Chris Moss and Benji Luttrell were two of Coach Herbert's managers in his early years at Tish. Moss said that Herbert would send his two managers to the store to get four gallons of diesel fuel. They would inevitably run out. He would send them back for two more gallons and when that didn't quite finish the job, one more. Only years later did Moss realize that Herbert was so careful in rationing the amount of fuel he bought because he was paying for it out of his own pocket.[15]

Derrick Brock was an offensive and defensive lineman for Tishomingo during the 1985-1987 seasons. He laughed at the thought of his team's riding in a charter bus to games a couple of hours away like some schools do today instead of riding in a regular school bus. He also remembered that the Gatorade never tasted quite right.[16] Brock's quarterback, Brad Howie, offered a theory: "We were so poor that instead of five scoops to get the Gatorade like we wanted it, Benji would just put one in to give it some color."[17]

Even the flatbed truck from which Coach Herbert coached the road games during the 1988 Bulldog season was a multi-use vehicle. Jeff Holt was a manager on that team. He remembers loading the truck, which had panels on the sides and on the back, with helmets, shoulder pads, and other team equipment for the away games. Once the truck arrived at its destination, the managers would unload the gear so that the driver could move the truck to the closest spot they could find near the sidelines. A group of men would then hoist Coach Herbert and his mobility scooter onto the truck. After the game they would set him down so that the truck could be used to haul the equipment back to Tishomingo.[18] It fit with the nature of small-town football.

* * *

Another difficulty for schools in the state's smallest classification is scheduling out-of-conference games. In all the other classifications between the smallest and largest classes, football coaches have the ability to frame their non-district games around their teams' perceived ability levels. Weaker 3A teams, for example, have the latitude to schedule early games against 1A and 2A schools to put a few wins on the board before division play, while strong teams in the same classification can play up against 4A and 5A teams to better prepare for games that count toward the playoffs. What is a 1A school to do? The better teams in the 1A classification could take on 2A and 3A teams; indeed, early season rankings of Mississippi 1A schools often include top-five spots for teams with losing records because of "good losses" against bigger schools. Like other small schools situated near the borders with other states, Tishomingo had another option: play the smallest of schools from Alabama and Tennessee.

Schools like Vina and Waterloo from Alabama and Middleton from Tennessee, along with county rivals Iuka and Belmont (both 2A schools) and weaker larger schools Mantachie (2A) and Alcorn Central (3A), regularly helped fill the Bulldogs' out-of-conference schedule. Bear Creek High School from northwest Alabama made its first appearance on the Tishomingo schedule for the 1988 season. Like Vina and Waterloo, Bear Creek was located in the

Freedom Hills area, a region known historically as a place to hide. Escaped slaves, Civil War draft dodgers and deserters, moonshiners, and even outlaws Jesse and Frank James reportedly hid in and around Freedom Hills.[19]

A couple of weeks before Tishomingo's week three matchup with the appropriately nicknamed Bears, Bear Creek abandoned its commitment to play Tishomingo, taking with it the early-season momentum of a Tishomingo team preparing for a dogfight in division play. Meanwhile, Falkner took on 3A opponents Ripley High and Alcorn Central and 2A North Pontotoc in its early non-district slate.[20] Smithville took the same approach, loading its early schedule with 3A Hatley and 2A foes Mooreville and Hamilton.[21] Tishomingo, on the other hand, endured three weeks between opponents due to the Bear Creek cancellation and their already scheduled bye week, not the best formula in returning to district play against Thrasher. However, the Thrasher Rebels were still winless. Mantachie and Walnut, the next two Tishomingo opponents, were also without a win at that point in the season. The Bulldog offense, so effective against Burnsville and Vina at the beginning of the season, would have a favorable schedule to get back on track.

* * *

The Bulldog offense proved to be as rusty as Coach David Lee Herbert had feared against Thrasher. With a 20-19 Tishomingo advantage coming down the stretch, the game came down to a thirty-yard field goal attempt on the last play of the game. Tishomingo's defense blocked it to keep their team undefeated in league play. Though their play had been shaky, they had been able to finally get back on the field without taking a hit in the district standings. Having two more winless opponents next up on the schedule could not have been planned any better.

Dave Herbert remembered preparing for the non-district clash with Mantachie the following week: "They were a 2A school at the time, but we usually handled 'em pretty well. They were not very good that year." It turned out they were good enough. Mantachie running back Dean Cates rolled up 168 yards on the ground to lead his team to the upset against Tishomingo.[22] Recalling the 13-0 loss, the Bulldog quarterback said, "We were off but should have beaten them anyway. But coming off those two weeks without a game was tough. We came out flat."[23]

Falkner was attempting to get on track in a key matchup with Smithville. The Eagles were still struggling, carrying a record of 2-3 and needing a goal-line stand and a fourth-quarter length-of-the-field drive to defeat winless Walnut (6-0) in their first division game. The Smithville Seminoles, meanwhile, came in at 4-1 but had not beaten Falkner in six years. The Seminole offense would be put to the test by the Falkner defense, the Eagles' strong suit.

Coach Joe Horton's young Falkner team, which returned only a handful of key contributors from the previous season's 1A North champions, turned in a solid performance to beat Smithville, 16-14. Smithville held an 8-0 lead from midway through the second quarter until late in the game. A personal foul penalty on a Falkner defender aided the initial scoring drive. After an eight-play, forty-nine-yard drive for a touchdown and a two-point conversion, the Falkner defense made the play of the night. Michael Prather blindsided Smithville quarterback Eric Spann, causing a fumble that David Prather picked up and returned thirty-four yards for a go-ahead score. Eagle quarterback Tyrone Gaillard completed a pass for the two-point conversion and a 16-8 lead. Smithville was not finished yet, though. The Seminoles drove to the Falkner two-yard line with four minutes to go in the game but could not get into the end zone. Two and a half minutes later, though, they scored on an eleven-yard run to pull within two, but the Eagle defense stopped a sweep play on the two-point conversion attempt to preserve the Falkner victory.[24]

After the Falkner-Smithville game, Eagle Coach Joe Horton felt confident about his team's playoff chances: "Confidence-wise, this is a big lift for us, because this is the best team we've beaten. But we've got Tishomingo and Thrasher left, so we aren't out of the woods yet." Smithville Coach Dwight Boling reflected on an opportunity missed but still saw hope in his team's future: "We've got a shot to win the division, depending on what Tishomingo does against Falkner and us. If nothing else, we've got a shot at second place and that will get us in the playoffs." When both coaches learned of Tishomingo's loss to 0-5 Mantachie— even though the Bulldog loss meant nothing in the division standings—they must have felt a boost of confidence that their teams were sitting pretty for those two playoff spots.[25]

6

When David Lee graduated from J. Z. George High School in 1960, the shy eighteen-year-old left Carrollton (population: about five hundred) to attend Delta State University in the booming metropolis of Cleveland, Mississippi (population: ten thousand). Even there, though, David Lee enjoyed family support. He lived with his sister Joyce and her husband, Bill, during the first semester of his freshman year at Delta State. Joyce recalled David Lee's pursuit of a college degree with an older sister's motherly perspective: "He tried so hard. He expected so much out of himself. He was an average student, but he gave it everything he had."[1] Still, his freshman year was a struggle, a hill that seemed too steep to climb.

David Lee reached his breaking point later that first year. He called home to Minnie Herbert and told her, "Mama, come get me. I just cannot do this. I'm coming home." Minnie brought David Lee's youngest sister, Anne, to Cleveland, where her son was crying and upset. He said, "I just can't do it; I just can't do it."

Anne saw her mother's steady hand with her brother that day. "My mama sat on that couch with him and encouraged him and told him that he did not need to quit college, that he could do it. She hugged him and said, 'Anne and I are going back home, and you're staying right here until you graduate from Delta State.' And that's what he did."[2]

* * *

While the pep talk from his mother kept David Lee in school after his freshman year, the practical impetus for his academic improvement had not yet arrived in Cleveland. David Lee had been in seventh grade when Linda Staten's family moved to the country between Carrollton and Greenwood. He was a year ahead of her in high school, and she said he didn't know who she was because she was skinny. Her twin brother, a grade behind her in school, was on the football team with David Lee, though, and often went home with him after school on football Fridays when he didn't have time to travel to the Staten home and back for the game. Even with that connection, she still claimed that he wouldn't have known her if she had walked through the door.

For his part, David Lee had not dated much, if at all, before his high school prom. That's when his little sister Janis spread the rumor that David Lee was going to ask a certain girl in his class to the prom. Janis described her as "a real pretty girl, a good little girl." Janis couldn't recall what made her spread the rumor back then, but she had it in her mind that her brother needed a date. David Lee felt that the gentlemanly thing to do was to squash the rumor, so he took the young lady to the prom.[3]

A year after David Lee graduated from high school and went to Delta State, Linda graduated from J. Z. George and continued her education at Holmes Junior College in

Goodman. When she returned home after finishing at Holmes, she received a phone call that would put her life on a path she never could have imagined.

"I bet you don't know who this is," said the voice on the other end of the line.

"Yeah, I think it's David Lee."

"Yeah, would you like to go to the show this weekend?"

"Yeah, I guess I would."

And just like that, David Lee and Linda's courtship began. According to Linda, David Lee had passed only physical education in his first year at Delta State. That was about to change. Linda recalled their courtship days in the Mississippi delta:

> We didn't have any money. We couldn't go to a movie. He didn't have a car, and I sure didn't have a car, so we'd just go to the library. So he started studying. I think it was Western Civ that was always so hard for him. He had failed it—I don't know whether he took it more than one time or not, but then he allll-most had an A at the end of the semester, so I was a good influence on him.[4]

After that stressful beginning at Delta State, David Lee began to recover his typical good humor as he continued to pursue his degree and an opportunity to coach. Near the end of one fall semester, David Lee received a Christmas present that he left unopened for a few days. At that time he was living in the dormitory where he had relocated after Bill and Joyce moved away. The gift from his cousin Jimmy Herbert aroused his dorm mates' curiosity, and they finally drove David Lee to open the sizable package. He unwrapped the box and began to pull out paper and then more paper and more paper until finally in one corner of the bottom of the box he found a single lemon. Understanding that revenge is a dish best served cold, David Lee waited a full year to mail a Christmas package to his cousin in nearby Shaw. Jimmy was excited to get a call from the Shaw post office telling him that a Christmas package had arrived with his name on it. Burrowing through a box full of paper, Jimmy uncovered a single lemon, allegedly the same lemon from the previous Christmas.[5]

Fast-forward a couple of years and after many meetings in the library, David Lee and Linda were set to graduate on the same day. David Lee had finished his class requirements at the end of the first semester and taken a basketball coaching job at nearby Silver City, where the basketball coach had passed away earlier in the school year. He spent the spring coaching at Silver City and waiting for the May matriculation to receive his hard-earned college degree. Linda finished her course work during the spring semester, and the couple decided to marry on the Saturday before graduation. Neither wanted, nor could afford, a big wedding. David Lee did not tell anyone in his family except his mother of his wedding plans, preferring that the rest of the family learn of his and Linda's marriage after the fact. He swore Minnie Herbert to secrecy until after the ceremony.[6]

David Lee and Linda concocted a plan to drive over to Alabama—where there would be no waiting period after their blood test as there was in Mississippi—but, alas, their destination closed after lunch on Saturday. With his mother sworn to secrecy about their marriage and thus unable to explain their absence, David Lee's main concern turned to appearances. He sped back to Carrollton so as not get people talking about his bringing Linda home after dark. Linda walked back into her house that evening and said matter-of-factly, "Mama, we couldn't get married; couldn't get our blood test."[7]

Two days later, David Lee drove to Carrollton from Silver City to pick up Linda and take her to Belzoni for their blood test. By Wednesday they were set to get married. When David Lee arrived at Linda's house, her mother was at work at Baldwin Piano Company in Greenwood, and Linda could not leave her youngest brother—seven or eight at the time—at home by himself. So David Lee and Linda and Andy piled in the car and drove first to Greenwood to drop off Andy and then to Belzoni, where a friend of David Lee's would join them at the church. Linda recalled the next few hours of her wedding day:

> We went out to the church. It was David Lee, me, the preacher, his wife, and Larry David—that was five of us. We got married; David Lee gave him ten dollars, I think, and we went down to I think it was called the Pig Stand or something and got us a hamburger basket and that was our supper. Then we went back to Silver City. No honeymoon. That was it. I bet that ten-dollar wedding lasted longer than some of these ten-, twenty-thousand dollar weddings. It was fine with me and fine with him.[8]

A couple of days later, David Lee and Linda graduated from Delta State and began to figure out where their lives would go from there.

The newlyweds began their married life together both teaching at Belzoni High School, and David Lee also coached football. They stayed two years in that town of about four thousand. It would be the biggest town in which they would live for the entirety of their careers. From there, they spent three years in Itta Bena, a Mississippi Delta town in Leflore County about half the size of Belzoni. David Lee once again assisted with varsity football, adding ninth grade football and track to his responsibilities.

With the integration of public schools in full swing across the Deep South in the late 1960s, private academies began to pop up all over Mississippi. In Carroll County "a survey conducted by concerned mothers in the area . . . showed there was sufficient interest to start a private school in Carroll County," according the Carroll Academy website.[9] For a young football coach eager for an opportunity, it was the perfect chance to get a head coaching job—and a chance to go home. David Lee's cousin Bernard Taylor was the school's first headmaster, and Herbert would be able to spread his wings not only as the head football coach but also as a coach of multiple sports since he was the school's *only* coach during its initial school year. Taylor is quick to point out it was the lure of coming back home and the opportunity to be a head coach that fueled his motivation to join the staff at the segregationist academy. Referring to their childhood in Carrollton, Taylor said, "We all played together; race was not a factor. David Lee was interested in education. It really didn't make any difference whether students were white or black or whatever. He was interested in kids; he was interested in their learning; he was interested in their athletic ability, in building that. Wherever he was, whether it was public school or private school, he gave it all he had."[10]

Delbert Edwards was the president of the school board of the fledgling school when he discovered that Carrollton's native son was open to a move home. "I say I recruited him, but he recruited himself. When we found out he was looking to come back, we were glad to get him."[11] David Lee's assignments included varsity football, junior high football, girls and boys basketball, and girls and boys track; he also taught four social studies classes. A math teacher by training, Linda taught a multitude of subjects, including science, where she stayed just ahead of the students with all of the preparations she had as a teacher. Lest he feel outworked by the teachers and coaches under his direction during the early years of Carroll Academy, Taylor filled the roles of headmaster for elementary, junior high, and high school; taught three classes; directed the music program; and did the guidance counseling.[12]

The first year in the life of the high school was a season of making the best of each situation. The football games were all played on the road for lack of a field. Basketball home games were played at an old armory at Greenwood that had been converted into a gym. With no gymnasium, the basketball teams practiced on an outdoor dirt court. A gym was a non-essential for a talented group of girls and their young coach, though, as the girls notched championships in basketball and later in track under Coach Herbert in Carroll Academy's first year as a high school.[13]

David Lee's childhood chum Clint Littleton remembers the reassurance of Herbert's coaching his children. "We were already real close friends, and it made it that much better knowing that he was coaching your daughter and your son because we knew what he was like, how he grew up. Growing up, he never did get into any kind of trouble. We were doing devilish things but nothing bad or anything like that. He was always a good person."[14]

David Lee's priority after that first year as Carroll Academy's football coach was to make sure he had a field on which his team could play. Like many initial preparations in the first-year school—the paint color for the school's first building was a mixture of hundreds of gallons that volunteers brought from their household surpluses—the completion of the football field before the first game was a race against the clock. Edwards and the school board dispatched a dirt mover from Winona to level and crown the pastureland that would become the football field. He recalled that the first action of the man hired to move the dirt was to move all the engineering stakes already put in place (and paid for). "Boy, we got after him, big time," Edwards said. "He said, 'I don't need any engineering stakes; I can fill this thing in and get it right.' Well, when he got through, he had it right except for one little puddle in it."[15]

With the dirt work for the field completed, the calendar was getting ready to turn over to August when the Carroll crew spread fertilizer and Bermuda seed on the field. Even though football seasons did not begin until September in those days, they faced the problem of not having running water with which to irrigate the newly seeded field. Edwards recalled how the innovative crew tackled that problem by installing a pump and running pipe from nearby Big Sandy Creek adjacent to the field to water it. "We're talking about late July now, and David Lee said he wasn't going to put his team out there on it unless it was serviceable by the time of our first game. Every afternoon, we'd go down there and lay down to see if there was a cast of green anywhere."[16]

Herbert's football team eventually played on the spanking new football field that year but not before one last adventure. When the football field was just about ready to go, the school hired a Mississippi Power and Light employee out of Winona to put up the stadium lights. Taylor recalled a mystifying situation with one of the lights in the southwest corner.

> We tested every one of them before they went up. When the MP&L guy climbed that pole and put that light up, it would not burn, so he brought it back down, plugged it back up, and it burned. He climbed that pole and put it up on the pole—it would not burn on that pole. He checked all the connections on that pole; they were all hot. He said I'm not going back up that pole again. We had bought those lights in Greenwood at one of the electrical companies. I went down there and got another light, brought that light out here; he climbed that pole, put that light in, and it burned. I told them, "this light is jinxed somehow." I don't know what it was, but we never had any more trouble.[17]

Though his stadium was ready, David Lee still depended on old-fashioned ingenuity and perseverance to make sure that his players were prepared. He spent his own money for the needs of his team and his players, a habit he would carry with him throughout his career. He drove many of his players to and from practices, so they would have an opportunity to play, another practice that he would never abandon. Though he and Linda barely made enough to get by, the life of a small-school coach who did a little bit of everything seemed to fit David Lee.

7

L auriann Herbert was born in 1967, followed by Dave in 1970, Stacie in 1974, and Hollie a year later. For a family of six surviving on two schoolteachers' salaries in their little house next to the North Carrollton United Methodist Church, most of America would have said they were barely getting by. David Lee's sister Joyce Bowman remembered it differently:

> We stayed very close. We started our family; he started his family. They were on a limited income; we were on a limited income. About the only thing we could do was visit each other. We lived in a trailer. It was small. They would come over; we would just make pallets on the floor. We would go to their house, and it would be the same thing. The kids, we'd just let 'em run wild. I hate to say it, but that's the truth. They just enjoyed playing outside. We had a roof over our heads and running water. We had a garden, and we canned everything; we had a freezer, so we ate. We were fine. We didn't hurt for anything.[1]

As David Lee and Linda's family grew, so, too, did their extended family. Cecil and Minnie Herbert had moved to some property outside of Carrollton that the family referred to as the Place. David Lee and Linda's children, along with their cousins, spent many memorable hours at the Place with its cows and fishing ponds and land to hunt. The family enjoyed picnics and time with one another there. Still a part of the family today, the Place was also the location of the memorable mud hole scene in the 1969 motion picture *The Reivers* starring Steve McQueen.

Like it had been a generation earlier, Christmas was always a big time for the growing circle of Herbert cousins, albeit without the fireworks. As one generation turned over to the next, Lee, Dan, Rainey, Mandy, Ashley, Shane, and Matthew joined Lauriann, Dave, Stacie, and Hollie around the kids' table. David Lee's sister Anne remembered visits by Santa Claus at her mother's house:

> Lauriann, the first granddaughter, was still a baby. Percy Boy Bryant played Santa Claus. We would have all the grandchildren there, and he would come every year until he died. That was one big thing that I remember about all our children. That was something unique to a little town like Carrollton. He looked just like Santa and sounded like him.[2]

Even with the swirl of his growing family and his responsibilities at school, David Lee committed to teaching Sunday school at Carrollton Baptist. While the church didn't have an outlet for his hambone skills, he did find an avenue to rejuvenate his passion for music. Bernard Taylor, the director of music at Carrollton Baptist Church for fifty-six years, slotted him in the church choir and often called on his "quality voice" for solos. Taylor remembered that David Lee was never quite sure of the timing of the songs he sang but would come to his house to practice an upcoming solo over and over.

He was very conscious about getting everything right. It used to tickle me because when he would sing—if it was a note he had to hold out for, say, four counts—he always sang with his hand behind him. Sitting behind him on the pulpit, I could see his fingers behind him counting off the timing. He would say, "That's the only way I can do it." And he wanted to do it right.[3]

Beverly Taylor was a high school classmate of David Lee's at J. Z. George. She agreed with her husband that the Coach Herbert at Carroll Academy was hardworking and responsible, which was quite different from the David Lee that she remembered from English class. The self-confessed Miss Goody Two-shoes of their class, Beverly sat on the front row, just in front of David Lee and his cronies Bruce Heath and Clint Gee, who were as fun-loving as he was. In a day before most students had watches, David Lee and his buddies regularly passed notes to Beverly, inquiring of the time. She soon figured out that their ultimate aim was to cause her to pay attention to them and get in trouble with the teacher. "They just loved to have fun—weren't as interested in becoming good students."[4] Though he never lost his playful nature and likable personality, David Lee had matured into a responsible adult who was trusted not only with the students of the next generation but also with leadership within the church.

Despite all of his activities and responsibilities, David Lee kept his family as a high priority. Anne recounted his love for Linda and his children through her mental picture of David Lee's driving the kids around in his Datsun truck. When he sensed his wife's angst rising due to four young children running around the house, he would corral them and drive them to his mother's or one of his aunts' houses in Carrollton. Anne said, "When we would see 'em coming, we would say, 'Well, David Lee's giving Linda a break.' It never failed—he wasn't there ten minutes with those children, and she was calling him wanting to know how long he was going to stay there. She had gotten her break."[5] The responsibility David Lee felt toward his family led him to ponder another career move.

* * *

After a few years coaching at Carroll Academy and in the midst of completing his family, David Lee began to feel the itch that so many small-school coaches do—the urge to make more money. For him, that meant leaving teaching and coaching and helping his father with the local furniture store. However, Linda claimed, "You don't do too good when you're working for your kinfolks."[6] Cecil Herbert, she said, had a heart of gold but was not a businessperson. He was the type to extend credit to try to help someone from the community. Clint Littleton remembered going to his friend's father in need of help:

> When I first got married, I didn't have a penny to buy furniture or anything else. Why I got married, I don't know. I went down to his daddy's store. Of course, I was just like one of his kids. He said, "What all do you need?"
>
> I told him I didn't have a refrigerator, stove, couches—I had to have everything.

He said, "I'll tell you what you do. You gather up everything you need, and I'll deliver it for you. You pay me twenty dollars a month until you get it paid for."

That's what I did. I bought every lick of furniture I had from him that day.[7]

Littleton wondered how many others like him Cecil Herbert Sr. helped through his furniture business, recognizing now that there must have been quite a few who never fully paid their debts.

Life was hard for the young, growing family. "Dave was born, and I wasn't teaching that year," Linda said. Cecil Herbert's willingness to help the members of his community who couldn't pay cash up front or keep up regular payments led to strain in his son's household as David Lee and Linda struggled to pay their own bills. "We were eating peanut butter and crackers some meals. Some weeks, David Lee would have to tell his daddy that he needed to get paid some that week."[8]

David Lee didn't work for his father long before deciding to make some "real money" by opening a United Dollar Store. "Well, that was a mistake," Linda recalled. "He didn't have that but maybe two years, or three." Those are the days that she referred to as the time "when we were making our millions." Dave's reminders through the years would not let her forget the matching shirts she sewed her children for Christmas one year. "Well, David Lee had the dollar store," Linda recounted, "and you had to take whatever you didn't sell. He had some material to sell, and it wasn't selling so I got it. I made all of them a shirt, and with what scraps I had left over, I patched up my couch." While daughter Hollie sat a few feet away laughing at the shirt story, Linda continued matter-of-factly, "I thought it looked real good."[9]

When the dollar store ultimately failed, David Lee's banker chalked up the venture as a lesson learned, though Linda was quick to point out that the bank still expected to be repaid. Delbert Edwards remembered the end of the dollar store era for the Herberts from a different perspective:

> Things just didn't go well down there. The popular thing to do when you get in trouble like that is file for Chapter Seven bankruptcy and liquidate all your assets and start all over again. They owed a ton of money, but they didn't declare bankruptcy. They worked and worked and paid and paid until they paid it off. That tells you something about their character.[10]

For years after David Lee's dollar store days, Linda continued to refer to the time "when we made our millions" as a defining time that turned their family back in the direction where they would make their greatest impact.[11]

David Lee returned to Carroll Academy for a short second stint pursuing his real passion, coaching. Football for the Herberts became a family affair. Dave helped out as a football manager, Linda sponsored the cheerleaders, and Stacie and Hollie were the unofficial cheerleader "mascots." One interesting football game for Carroll Academy during that time was illustrative of small-school football. Football coaches know that the best referees go to the bigger schools, and small schools are often assigned officials who are either inexperienced or not very good, or both. One night when Carroll was supposed to play East Holmes Academy, though, the referees did not show up at all. By the time officials could be located, kickoff was pushed back to 10:45

p.m., and the game concluded at 12:50 on Saturday morning. Since the game began on September 30 and ended on October 1, a newspaper article claimed two state records: latest starting time and the only game played over two months.[12]

* * *

No one was ever more groomed to be a coach's son than Dave Herbert. Dave had just finished third grade at Carroll Academy in the spring of 1980. His childhood was in many ways a mirror image of his father's. He likened his childhood to the movie *The Sandlot*:

> Small towns—everybody knew everybody. You could hop on your bike and go play and everybody kind of looked out for everybody. We had our meeting spots. In Carrollton, it was right around the corner at this lady's house who had the biggest yard, where you played football, baseball, whatever you wanted to play. She'd come out and watch sometimes. She was older, a grandmother-type lady.[13]

He also recalled that the town revolved around the football team, that everyone in town seemed to have a stake in the team as a relative of a player or as a booster. The locals knew the players and what positions they played, the score of the latest game, and every game on the schedule. For a starry-eyed manager whose dad was the coach of the team, there was no doubt he would one day play the game himself.[14] However, he would not play for his hometown team. Before the fall of 1980, Coach Herbert accepted a head coaching position at Marvell Academy in eastern Arkansas.

* * *

The Herberts moved to Marvell—a town of slightly more than 1,500—as a family of six. Lauriann was thirteen; Dave, ten; Stacie, six; and Hollie, five. They kept their family home in Mississippi, returning to it during breaks from school, but lived in a mobile home behind the Marvell Academy campus when school was in session. Like most small-school coaches, David Lee coached virtually year-round. After football in the fall, he coached girls' basketball during the winter and track in the spring to finish out the school year. His daughter Stacie recalled having her father as her physical education teacher, as well, and how much he loved putting together field day activities for the elementary students at Marvell. Mike Reans, whose house trailer stood end-to-end to the Herberts' on the Marvell campus, assisted in football and was the head coach in boys' basketball and baseball. Reans had been at the school a year already when the Herberts arrived and cherishes the three years that they spent together as colleagues and neighbors.

Stacie remembered her daddy working one or two summers driving a truck during harvest time and coming home every day with his face covered with dirt. Mostly though, he did what football coaches do during the summer: prepare their practice and game fields for the fall as they lead their charges through summer workouts. The Herbert siblings helped their father prepare his football field at Marvell. The above-ground sprinkler system used to irrigate the field was an enormous metal configuration that took hours for the coaches and the Herbert children to construct. The Herberts and Reans sometimes borrowed the contraption to irrigate the large garden they cultivated between their mobile homes.[15]

The two families shared a number of other memorable experiences. One night, as a thunderstorm brewed in the Mississippi delta and threatened to spawn tornadoes, Mike Reans urged his wife, Beverly, to go with him to the school to take refuge in a small vault that was available to both families in such occasions. With the wind howling and the rain beating against their trailer, the Reans finally dashed to their car and made for the school. With visibility limited from the force of the rain, Mike and Beverly made their way up the little road to the school, almost running into the Herberts, who were also driving to the school in a last-minute rush to safety. Other than the near miss on the road, everyone escaped the storm unscathed.[16]

On another day, David Lee was rattled by a loud blast that he had heard in the direction of the school and called it to Mike's attention. Reans opened his door and BOOM! another blast from the direction of the school. The two called their headmaster, who lived in town about a half mile away. Mr. Burks arrived a few minutes later with several hunting dogs in the back of his station wagon. By then Reans and the others were on edge, standing around outside as the dogs ran loose through the building, searching for the source of the blasts. "You'd be looking in the window and see one of the dogs jump up on the inside. That was scary."[17]

David Lee carried a gun as the amateur investigators continued their search for the source of the volleys behind the elementary school. Suddenly, they heard a tremendous noise emanating from one of the air-conditioning units behind the school. David Lee spun around and trained his gun on the air conditioner. Reans said that it was a wonder that Coach Herbert didn't blow that air-conditioning unit to smithereens.[18]

The most memorable incident of the Marvell era, however, was when the Herberts and the preacher's son loaded in the family's Pinto station wagon for a drive to Carrollton. Linda asked David Lee if he had given their dog his heartworm medication. He couldn't remember and thought it might be good to take some Tylenol himself before beginning the two-hour drive, so he went back inside so that both he and the dog would be properly medicated. He tossed his jacket on the table and took his medicine before searching for the dog's pill. Not finding it, he went back to the car and confessed to Linda, pale faced, "You know what I did? I just took that dog's heartworm pill. What do I do?"[19]

Linda told David Lee to try to make himself throw up, but he was unable and returned to the car to try to leave. Driving around the loop toward the front of the school, where a large crowd was gathering for a basketball game with rival Helena, he stopped when he began to feel sick. Panic-stricken, Lauriann and Hollie began to cry. David Lee felt sicker and sicker, and the only doctor in Marvell was out of town. He had Linda call the closest hospital to see what he needed to do. Linda called and told someone at the hospital that her husband had just taken a dog's heartworm pill by accident and needed to know what to do. After a pause in which she heard laughter in the background, the person on the other end of the phone responded that they did not need to follow up... unless, of course, David Lee had heartworms.

Suddenly feeling much better, David Lee rose from the couch and grabbed his jacket to try for the third time to leave for Carrollton. When he picked up the jacket, he exposed the dog's pill that lay underneath. He snatched it up, walked to the door, and flung it as far into the yard as he could. Settling back into the car, David Lee turned to the preacher's son and said, "Don't you tell anybody about that pill."[20] Whether or not the preacher's son spilled the beans, that story has been told and re-told by family, fellow coaches, and friends for nearly forty years.

8

Beginning as a fourth grader, young Dave Herbert had the run of the Marvell Academy campus, playing basketball in the school gymnasium with his friends and using the school's sports fields as his personal playgrounds. Life in Marvell was not unlike the small-town from which his family had come. While the Herbert's next-door neighbor took care of their home in Mississippi, they spent the next three school years in Marvell with David Lee's doing what suited him best and Dave inching ever closer to playing the game he had dreamed of since starting school. His debut, however, would not come in Arkansas. Three more years of coaching and teaching at a small, private academy with its accompanying small paychecks and minimal benefits set David Lee and Linda thinking about a move back to public education.

Coach Herbert's first interview was with Burnsville High School in Tishomingo County in extreme northeast Mississippi. His coaching mentor from Carrollton, Bobby Tackett, was the principal at neighboring Tishomingo High School at that time. After David Lee's interview at Burnsville, Tackett called and wanted to know why he would interview at one of his rival schools. Tackett had spent a good number of years in Carrollton and knew the likable Herberts were just what he needed to counterbalance his strict leadership style. He wasted no time hiring David Lee as Tishomingo's head football coach and social studies teacher and Linda as a junior high and senior high math teacher. In the summer of 1983, the Herberts moved their mobile home to the Tishomingo High School campus, settling between the football field and the road that ran parallel to it. David Lee likened the surroundings at his new school to a college campus with all its big, pretty trees.[1]

Danny McClung was the basketball coach at Tish when Coach Herbert came to the school as its head football coach. He had grown up in Tishomingo, played basketball and baseball in high school, and gone on to play both sports at Northeast Mississippi Junior College in Booneville, where he was named all-state. He had a couple of offers to play basketball at smaller colleges, but he had met his wife by that point and decided not to pursue basketball any further. A semester before obtaining his degree from Memphis State University, the principal at Tishomingo High School called and asked if he was interested in coaching basketball at the school. He said no at first. He didn't think he wanted to, but Mr. Strickland continued to pursue him until he finally came back to his alma mater as a basketball coach. He coached basketball, baseball, and a little football, though he considered his football coaching role that of a "go-fer," helping whoever was coaching football at the time. After Mr. Strickland retired, Bobby Tackett took over as principal and brought with him a football coach who stayed just a year. Coach McClung's brother, Ben, took the reins for a year before moving up Highway 25 to become Iuka's baseball and, eventually, basketball coach. Tackett coached the team himself in 1982 before luring his friend David Lee Herbert to Tish.[2]

McClung took no official role on Herbert's staff but continued to help out. Their sons were the same age and would play basketball and baseball together. Coaches McClung and Herbert worked well together, sharing athletes and respecting one another's seasons. McClung told of one player whom Herbert concluded just wasn't built for football, so he released him to start practicing basketball, where he could better help the school succeed. All of the coaches worked together to cover bus routes, with each coach taking morning routes during his season and afternoon routes when it was over.[3]

* * *

Stepping into a new school with a big family can be daunting in a town of less than four hundred people, but the Herberts were becoming accustomed to the life of a coach's family, moving around every few years, so the transition to Tishomingo was smooth. The agriculture teacher, who also lived on campus, had a son Dave's age and a daughter close in age to Hollie and Stacie, and the girls' basketball coach also had a son Dave's age. Paul Whitlock was a member of the school board when Coach Herbert was hired. He and his wife, Phyllis, had two daughters, who became friends with the younger Herbert daughters, which drew the two families together. Phyllis Whitlock had been one of Tishomingo High School's first homecoming queens, and Paul was the public address announcer for the football team's home games. He likened the Herberts' first year in Tishomingo to Mayberry R.F.D.[4]

Once inside the close-knit community—a process that Dave says took less than a year—the Herberts considered life in Tishomingo just like being back in Carrollton. Coach Herbert could set about the task of teaching his high school and junior high football players the Wing T offense, and Dave could finally suit up and play football. Like several other kids at the school, the Herbert children could take classes under their parents every year from seventh grade until graduation. For the three youngest Herbert children, when asked what they consider their hometown—even with all the moves—they claim Tish.

Tishomingo, Mississippi, is a tiny blip on Highway 25 between Highway 30 and the Natchez Trace Parkway, just a few miles from the Alabama border and just a hop, skip, and a jump from the Tennessee line as well. Named after Chief Tishomingo of the Chickasaw Nation, the town bearing his name was chartered in 1908. The area where the town would one day be located was used as a camp by General Andrew Jackson during his march to fight the Battle of New Orleans in the War of 1812. The water source that Jackson and his troops called Good Springs later was named after the general and is still the source of most of the town's water.[5]

In March of 1913, just five years after Tishomingo's town charter was issued, a tornado destroyed many of its six buildings and personal residences. The tornado displaced one house from its foundation. The savvy homeowner attached a cable to one end of the house, ran the cable through the house, and attached it to a tree to stabilize the house. Both the house and the cable still stand in Tishomingo today.[6]

Five miles to the southeast is the well-trafficked Tishomingo State Park. Tishomingo County has the rare distinction of having two state parks, with J.P. Coleman State Park in Iuka also within the county borders. Tishomingo State Park, located in the Appalachian Foothills, is known for its unique rock formations and is popular with hikers and rock climbers. Featuring Mississippi's only rock canyon, Tishomingo State Park's 1,530 acres boasts thirteen miles of foot trails that include a swinging bridge and a multitude of native stone steps developed by the Civilian Conservation Corps in the 1930s as one of Franklin Roosevelt's most popular New Deal programs.[7]

Tishomingo's biggest link to outside culture for many years was the opening music to *Prairie Home Companion*, a weekly public radio variety show hosted by Garrison Keillor. "Tishomingo Blues" is a jazzy tune written in 1916 by Spencer Williams, who spent some time in the town. Author Elmore Leonard, whose epitaph reads "The Dickens of Detroit," titled his thirty-seventh novel *Tishomingo Blues*.[8] The story is set in Mississippi but not Tishomingo specifically, though the author did once pose for a photo at the city limit sign.[9] The town also claims a few mentions in the movie *O Brother, Where Art Thou*.

For David Lee Herbert and his family of six, in 1983 Tishomingo was just another small town in a lifetime of small towns that afforded an opportunity to fit into a new school and to enjoy a new town where outsiders rarely came to live. Tishomingo High School's football team was coming off a 6-4 season and a third-place finish in Class B District 1 behind small-school powerhouse Hamilton and Smithville.[10] Hamilton came into the 1983 season as the defending state champion and was in the midst of what would become a then state record fifty-one-game winning streak. Hamilton Coach Jimmie Moore spent sixteen seasons with the Lions, winning state titles in 1981 and 1982, the first two years of the Mississippi playoff system. He certainly would have won more, as his teams put together an astounding eighteen-game run between the 1976 and 1978 seasons in which Hamilton was unscored upon. Moore's 1977 squad outscored their opponents 375-0 but did not have a state championship for which to compete.[11] The good news for Coach Herbert's Tishomingo Bulldogs of 1983 was that Hamilton was moving up a classification to BB and would no longer be a district menace.

One aspect of the new Tishomingo team that would give the Bulldogs' division opponents fits was the offense that Coach Herbert brought to northeast Mississippi: the Wing T. Also known as the Delaware Wing T, the offensive scheme depends on misdirection in the backfield and angle blocking. The offense can cause such chaos for defenses that offenses with less talent can still be successful moving the ball. In that way, it rivals the Notre Dame box offense for creating mischief for defenses. Long-time Mississippi sports journalist Rick Cleveland wrote about legendary coach Ed Reed's misdirection offense in a piece about the Notre Dame box offense:

> What follows is a part of Mississippi football legend: Reed's South Natchez team was about to play a bowl game and the coach of the opposing team called Moss Point's inimitable coach/philosopher Billy Wayne

Miller to ask him for advice on how to prepare for Reed's offense. Billy Wayne said this: "Well, see, you tell your boys to get a good night's rest and then you feed them a good pre-game meal. And then, when it's game time and they tee that ball up at the 40-yard-line, you tell your boys to take a good, long, hard look at that football. You tell them to look at it good, because they aren't going to be able to find it the rest of the night."[12]

Similarly, the Wing T—with three running backs behind the quarterback in a line parallel to their linemen—can cause confusion on the defensive side when the backs began moving in several directions at once at the snap of the ball. The beauty of the Wing T offense—designed by Tubby Raymond of the University of Delaware and chronicled in his seminal work, *The Delaware Wing T: An Order of Football*— is that even though the wingback mostly contributes to the running game, the defense must honor him in the passing game. This causes the defense to often have one fewer defender at the point of attack. It is an offense that requires a great deal of discipline by every player on the offensive side of the ball to execute properly and an equal or greater amount of discipline by the defense to stop it. More recently, Gus Malzahn installed a modernized version of the Wing T at Auburn University.

Coach Herbert learned the Wing T from Bobby Tackett back in their Carrollton days. Tackett was generous with his knowledge of the Wing T, mentoring a number of up-and-coming coaches in the intricacies of the offense. Chief among these was Willis Wright, who won state championships at several different schools in Mississippi and Alabama and is considered the architect of the program at Mississippi juggernaut South Panola High School. Mike Reans remembered learning the Wing T working with Coach Herbert at Marvell Academy in the early 1980s. Reans was most impressed with how schooled Herbert was in the science of the offense. "It was a disciplined offense, a lot of pulling, lot of trapping. Coach Herbert believed in it, he made it work, and he had people who could run it."[13]

Assistant coach Kenneth McClain served as the link between Tackett and Tishomingo's new coach. A former head coach himself, McClain saw offensive innovation in Tackett and Herbert he felt that he had lacked earlier in his career. He spent three years with Herbert, coaching defense while his head coach guided the Wing T offense. McClain attributed Coach Herbert's ease in acclimating to the program at Tishomingo to the groundwork that Tackett had laid for football in a basketball-rich region, to Herbert's knowledge of the game, to his fairness with all of his players no matter their race, and to his fortune in arriving at Tish for Eric Powell's junior and senior seasons.[14]

9

After moving to Tishomingo for the start of the 1983 football season, Coach Herbert began to meet the players whom he would expect to master his version of the Wing T. Derrick Brock and Ronny McKee were eighth graders then, big linemen Herbert would dub his "hawgs" after the acclaimed offensive line of the Washington Redskins of that era. "We were like, who is this guy?" Brock admitted. "He would come in with those glasses on."[1] McKee chimed in, "He looked like a foreigner."[2] Derrick's cousin Danny Brock was in seventh grade when he met Coach Herbert in the cafeteria, where he shook his hand before signing up for football. Even then, Brock remembers, he thought he was "a cool guy."[3]

The bigger, older Brock remembered Herbert's first impression of his junior high team was that they didn't look like they knew what they were doing.[4] The new coach brought continuity to the Tishomingo program, having his teams run the same plays from seventh grade through their senior seasons. The key to the entire offense, according to all of the members of the various teams gathered in Coach Herbert's former classroom in the summer of 2018, was simple: "post drive near backer" (or *back-ah* in Herbert's middle Mississippi hill country twang that his players enjoyed mimicking). That basic building block of the offense was a directive as to who would block the nearest linebacker in the trapping offense's blocking scheme.

A new head football coach typically has a season or two to fully implement his offensive and defensive schemes before locals begin to raise their expectations. Even though David Lee Herbert was stepping in at Tishomingo High School when Eric Powell—likely the best athlete he would ever coach—was a junior quarterback, Herbert's system took some time to take effect. Even as the Mississippi High School Activities Association (MHSAA) was pursuing an expansion of its classification system to five classes,[5] Herbert was guiding his team to a 22-14 win over county rival Burnsville in his debut as Bulldog head man.[6] A loss to Blue Mountain the following week, however, was more indicative of the way his first season would go. Future district rivals were going in other directions. Falkner—who would not become a district mate until the 1987 season—was favored to win its district, as usual. Thrasher began its football program during the 1983 season and pulled off its first win, an 8-0 decision over Mooreville in the season's third week.[7]

A pattern of early leads with an inability to hold on late in the game became a common theme for Coach Herbert's Bulldogs during that first season. Powell notched two early touchdowns against Hatley on a long run and a long pass, but the Tigers came from behind for a 38-30 win.[8] Tishomingo limped into homecoming with a 1-4 record after the loss to Hatley. Always a high-spirited week at Tishomingo, the players considered every year's homecoming contest a must-win game. On the same week that New Hope ended Hamilton's fifty-one-game winning streak, Powell's three-touchdown performance highlighted a 342-yard rushing attack as Tishomingo beat Mantachie 21-6.[9]

Meanwhile, the big sports news in Mississippi was Marcus Dupree's dismissal from the University of Oklahoma's football team and potential return to his home state, where the Philadelphia native is still widely considered the greatest player the state has ever produced.[10] While the Dupree news dominated the headlines of sports pages around the state, Tishomingo limped toward the season's finish with losses to Iuka and Alcorn Central, though the Bulldogs closed to within a point late against the Golden Bears on a trick play before a missed extra point sent them to a 14-13 defeat.[11] The Tish players begged their coach to go for the win, but Coach Herbert played it safe. It would perhaps play into a much riskier decision a few years later.

Even with a 2-6 record, Tishomingo still had an opportunity to make the state playoffs as District 1-B had only two teams in the 1983 season: the Bulldogs and Smithville. The winner of that game, regardless of their record, would advance to the playoffs. Powell and Ronnie Ryan led a strong running attack in the first half against Smithville, but the Seminoles matched both of the Tishomingo touchdowns, adding a pair of two-point conversions for a 16-14 halftime lead. Smithville controlled the second half, allowing the Bulldogs just thirteen offensive plays, in a 22-14 win that eliminated Tishomingo from playoff contention. Coach Herbert's first season, though competitive, ended with a disappointing 2-7 mark.[12]

* * *

For the seniors of 1988 and the classes behind them, Herbert's first impression was something different from the players who were already in high school when he arrived. "He's the only coach I ever had. It's really hard to compare playing for him to anything," said Joe Tucker, a tight end and safety on the 1988 squad.[13] Shannon Edmondson, a few years younger than the seniors from that year, "thought a lot of him in the classroom and in football," but could not understand why he was not receiving the playing time that he wanted on the junior high team.

> I didn't realize at that time how small of a kid I was, so I always thought he didn't like me and that was the reason I didn't get to play. I can remember one day hearing him get onto an assistant coach for putting me on defense during practice. Back then, we had to run half-lines because we didn't have enough to have eleven on both sides. If you had a helmet, you had to play in practice; that's all there was to it. I remember hearing him getting onto the coach for putting me at linebacker: "You're gonna get him hurt, and I don't want him hurt." I always remember that. He was watching out for me more than I realized as a kid.[14]

Perhaps remembering his own angst over his size at a youngster, Coach Herbert looked out for all of his diminutive players. Of the twenty-one sophomores, juniors, and seniors listed on the 1988 roster—with roster weights usually trending between generous and very generous for undersized players—nine checked in at 150 pounds or less.

Coach Herbert took care of his big guys too, beyond his affection for them on the practice field. Grant Horn was a big senior tackle on the 1988 team. His parents had divorced about the time the Herberts arrived in Tishomingo for the start of Horn's seventh grade year. His father did not come to watch him play until his senior year, and Horn never recalled a family member bringing him to summer workouts or giving him a ride home. Coach Herbert always made sure he had a ride, even when he was spending summers with his dad in neighboring Itawamba County, at least twenty miles away. Dave Herbert and assistant coach Vince Jordan continued to make sure their big right tackle had a way back and forth to practice even after Coach Herbert was later no longer able to drive.

Eddie Blunt badly wanted to play football for Coach Herbert when he was in junior high. He talked to his parents and begged for their permission in spite of a genetic eye disorder that causes retinal detachment. They finally consented but with the stipulation that they had to tell his coach about the possibility that a collision could cost him his sight. When Coach Herbert heard the details of Eddie's condition, he sat behind his desk with tears in his eyes and said, "Eddie, if something happened to you that caused you to lose your eyesight, I could not live with myself, so I can't let you play." Eddie recalled: "I told him I would be pulling for them from the bandstand as much as I could. *That* is the kind of man Coach David Lee Herbert was.[15]

John Moore met Coach Herbert on his first day of seventh grade when Moore came to school feeling a little under the weather. He felt worse as the opening assembly wore on. Coach Herbert approached him and asked him what was wrong. Moore responded that he felt nauseous. On their walk together to the office to call Moore's dad, Herbert paused while his future offensive tackle lost his breakfast. Once they arrived at the office, Herbert held young Moore's head and wiped his face until help from home arrived.[16] Four years later, Moore would repay that initial kindness with the blocks that helped make David Lee Herbert's name known around the world.

One aspect about their coach's demeanor from the very beginning of his time at Tish that still stands out to his players three decades later is how he did not play favorites. "He really beat sportsmanship into us," Horn recounted. "The way you carried yourself in school and on that field and anywhere you went, it reflected on him. And you were going to receive your just reward out there on that field." Horn remembered several teammates caught smoking in school had to do tumbles on the field until they gave up smoking for good. "Coach Herbert was a good man. He taught us history, and I got my tail whupped quite a bit. He may have made sure I got home, but he didn't play favorites."[17]

* * *

As empathetic as the new Tishomingo football coach could be with his players, he commanded discipline and respect both on the field and off. In the days of corporal punishment as standard discipline, he used extra running and the paddle to keep his troops in line. Dave Herbert and Joe Tucker recalled one time when he spanked their whole class. "There was one time he assigned us some homework," Tucker said. "We didn't hear. I don't know if he assigned it or not, but nobody had it done." The younger Herbert added, "He was going over the stuff, and nobody was answering his questions. So he said, 'Who in here has done their homework?' I think one girl raised her hand. It was like, everybody out. He got us all out in that hallway. He didn't hit hard." Tucker and Lance Hollingsworth remembered Herbert and his assistant coach taking care of other teachers' classrooms at times when they deemed it necessary too.[18]

As Coach Herbert became familiar with his players—and they with him—his humorous side made its way onto the football field. He particularly liked joking around with his big linemen, but no one was immune. One player remembered a slightly off-color hint of favoritism on one occasion though, when Dave was hit in the mid-section during a running play in practice and was slow to get up. When some of the other players suspected the younger Herbert of milking the situation and joined forces to "encourage" him to get up, his daddy called them off. "Y'all boys just leave him alone. He's like his daddy; he's got a pair of big ones."[19]

Eric Powell was a junior when the new head football coach arrived. He remembered the fun that the players had mimicking their coach's Carrollton drawl: "We would always come up to the line of scrimmage when we were doing three on three or seven on seven, and he would always say, 'Give me a cent-ah. Give me a cent-ah. Give me a cent-ah.' And it was like he was asking for a sinner. Scott McClain was the team's center. "Oh my goodness, he would say, 'Give me a sinner.' And the other coach's son was a center," Powell cackled.[20] Other players remembered responding, "We're all sinners, Coach."

An admitted class clown, Powell also had fun with Coach Herbert in the classroom. One day, Powell decided to play a little game of hide-and-seek with his coach in economics class. The student desks were lined up in traditional classroom fashion, from wall to wall on the sides and about five deep with Coach Herbert's desk in the front of the class. Powell slipped in and hid on the floor among the desks in the back corner of the room farthest from the door. Not one to stop with so simple a prank, he proceeded to risk testing Herbert's biggest annoyance. "First of all, you weren't allowed to chew gum in class. But second of all, you better not pop it if you had it. That was one of his pet peeves." Powell popped his gum from his hiding place and then again five or ten minutes later as Herbert's blood pressure steadily rose while he searched for the culprit. As Herbert continued his lecture, Powell popped his gum again after another ten minutes or so. "It upset him so bad. The third time I popped that gum, he came and stood in the direction he was hearing the sound. You had the wall and the desk and Coach Herbert standing right there beside the desk because he knew it was coming from that direction. He stops teaching and there's probably twenty minutes left in the class." Still undetected, Powell stood when the bell rang and filed out with his classmates. He passed by his teacher and said, "Hey, Coach." Herbert responded, "Hey, Eric."[21]

Powell laughed at the thought of Coach Herbert's wondering, *where did Eric come from*? He knew that punishment was coming as soon as Herbert pieced together the source of the infernal gum popping.

> It was worth it. Everybody in the class was sort of laughing under their breath because everybody knew

I was back there except for him. I don't know, maybe an hour went by, thirty minutes went by, and he found me. He wiggled that finger, and he said follow me. He said, "Now, Eric, you were sitting in the corner of that classroom popping that gum, and you know I don't like it. And you sat back there in that corner. Now bend over that desk." He gave me about three licks. It did hurt, but we all had a big laugh out of it.[22]

Jay McGee—who went by his first name, Orville, during high school—told of the time Coach Herbert needed to step out of the classroom for a few moments. The class turned their desks around in the opposite direction and moved his desk to match. When he walked back through the classroom door, McGee said Herbert was totally oblivious and continued as if nothing had changed. Perhaps drawing from his own experience in the classroom as a long-time teacher and coach himself, McGee reconsidered and added, "He either didn't know or just played along."[23]

No one was immune from Coach Herbert's good-natured ribbing or occasional prank. Jeff Holt was a seventh-grade manager walking from his last class toward the football field, where the team was already running plays in practice one day. Holt exited the building at the same time as classmate Hollie Herbert, and the two walked together toward the field house—very innocently, emphasized Holt. Dave Herbert remembered being in the middle of running plays on the field when his daddy saw Jeff and Hollie walking together. "He said, 'all right, guys, when I say go, y'all go monkey pile him,' something like that. I remember Jeff's eyes were big because he had no idea." Holt didn't know why the players were sprinting toward him, and he couldn't get away once they reached him. "They dropped me down, and everybody got me right there. Ever since that time, he always kidded me about that. 'You ain't gonna be walking my daughter no more, are you? '"[24]

* * *

On the football field, Coach Herbert demanded discipline from his players. Chris Moss was the team manager for a number of years. He wanted to play, but he was too small. One of his memories of Coach Herbert was before practice as the players transitioned from the classroom to the football field. He wanted them on the field as quickly as possible with no *lollygaggers*. With mostly two-way players on his team, he conditioned them for the long season ahead, and the linemen particularly hated all the running. He did not want them taking plays off during a game. Once Herbert came to Moss and told him to watch one particular lineman. After a few plays, he walked back down the sidelines and asked Moss what he saw.

"Honestly, Coach, he's just standing up."

"That's what I thought," Herbert replied, walking off without another word. That type of effort often precipitated a Saturday practice as it revealed a lack of conditioning, for which he took personal responsibility.[25] The running backs were not immune to their coach's high expectations, either. When they would give less than full effort running the ball, he would admonish them to "stop tip-toeing through the tulips."

Moss found himself often serving as a liaison between his classmates and their coach. He knew the players who were nursing injuries, the ones who had been in trouble with their teachers during the school day, and those who were having difficulties at home. Coach Herbert had a way of pulling out of his players their best effort, but did not compromise his personal relationship with them. He was a coach his players did not want to disappoint. Moss remembered that he would raise his voice but not in anger. If he really needed to make a point with an individual player, he would come up really close to the player and say what he needed to say, and the player would get the message. He might let an "ugly word" slip on occasion in practice, but he would not stand for that type of language from his players, especially if ladies might be around.[26]

The Herberts' extra-long trailer was nestled among a small grove of hardwoods in the southeast corner of the campus just a couple of first downs from the football field. Moss and others frequented the Herbert home, where they were always welcome. "Linda, fix these boys some sweet tea," Coach Herbert would say when they came to visit. While he was on the field, though, he had another habit that he did not want Linda to discover. One of the managers would get an occasional visit from Coach Herbert, looking for a dip of snuff. "Now, don't tell Linda," he would always cajole.[27]

Coach Herbert's players recalled his away-from-home tobacco habit, which Linda did know about despite his best efforts to keep it from her. He never seemed a natural at the spitting part, though, and his players still imitate his technique. "And then we had to get down on the grass and roll in that stuff," Derrick Brock recalled with upturned nose and furled lip.[28] For her part, Linda Herbert admitted that not only did she know about her husband's occasional tobacco use, she regularly scolded him for taking what belonged to those boys.

Derrick Brock was determined to repay his coach for years of relentless ribbing, even after he graduated. During one game, Brock stripped the ball from a running back's arms from his defensive tackle position and returned the fumble for a touchdown. "Seventy-two yards," he remembered specifically. Coach Herbert rode him mercilessly about his speed—or lack thereof—in scoring what would be his team's only points of the game in a loss to Belmont, informing Brock that he was "fixing to go the snack bar and come back" before his big hawg crossed the goal line. A year after he graduated, Brock saw the opportunity to get one over on his old coach. Upon seeing Brock at one of his team's practices, Herbert pointed him out on the sidelines, telling his linemen that they had to be better than "that big old hawg over there." Returning his greeting with a smile, Brock said, "Hey, Coach, Mama said to make sure you bring home some milk when you get finished," to which Herbert turned a deep shade of red and acknowledged, "Good one, good one."[29]

Third Quarter

10

Falkner and Tishomingo returned to the field for the second half after making necessary adjustments. Only two twelve-minute quarters remained to paint the Division 1-1A playoff scenario. Many of the Smithville coaches and players watched on this Thursday night ahead of their expected win two days later. Falkner fielded a squib kick and returned it to their own thirty-five yard line to open the second half. The option game that had been stymied for an entire half by poor field position and the Tishomingo defense suddenly came to life. Dive, pitch, keeper—first down. Quarterback keeper, reverse option pitch, dive, quarterback option to the Tishomingo thirty-three. Facing a fourth and two, Coach Horton never hesitated in calling option left. Bulldog linebacker Terry Enlow was in position to make the stop behind the line of scrimmage, but the shifty Falkner running back slipped through the tackle and picked up nine yards and a first down at the Tishomingo twenty-four. Seven plays later, the Eagles were in the end zone after a punishing sixteen-play, sixty-five-yard drive that consumed seven minutes of the third quarter. Quarterback Tyrone Gaillard's option keeper on the two-point conversion attempt tied the game, 8-8. Falkner had held the ball for more plays on their opening drive of the second half than they had managed during the entire first half.

Tishomingo began its first drive at its own thirty-seven. Enlow pounded the right side for a yard. Danny Brock picked up five on a counter play over left guard. The same play netted only two on third down, two yards shy of a first down. Facing fourth down on their own side of the field, Tishomingo's Shane Hill punted the ball back to the Eagles.

Falkner continued its relentless rushing attack on its next possession. Bruising running back Steve Plaxico carried left for twelve yards and a first down. Plaxico over the right side for fourteen. Plaxico up the middle for seven. Plaxico to the left for two. Gaillard keeper up the middle for four and another Eagle first down.

When the scoreboard clock ticked down to all zeroes, Falkner had reached the Tishomingo twenty-eight yard line. The Eagle offense had stayed on the field most of the third quarter, piling up 104 yards—all on the ground—on twenty-two plays. Tishomingo had managed eight yards on three plays and would start the fourth quarter backed up in their own territory still trying to figure out how to stop the suddenly potent Falkner ground game.

* * *

Ask almost any experienced high school administrator, and he or she will tell you that the success of the football team is the key contributor to school harmony each fall semester. When the team is doing well, school life tends to flow smoothly from one Friday night to the next. Especially at a small school where such a large percentage of students and teachers are involved in football in some way, a successful football team results in positive feelings all around. School spirit can carry almost all the way to Thanksgiving, at which time the school calendar moves very quickly toward exams and Christmas break. On the other hand, a disappointing football season can drag a school through the fall semester.

For the Tishomingo High School football team of 1988, expectations coming into the season were about the same as they had been throughout Coach Herbert's six-year tenure. Even after much turnover at the skilled positions, the senior-led squad had set their sights on winning the district and making the playoffs, and the two season-opening triumphs had done nothing but fire up the entire school. Though Dave Herbert had three touchdown passes in the first two matchups, it was the running game that produced most of the firepower, producing eighty-four points in those two games. The bye week in the third week and then the Bear Creek cancellation seemed to put the season—and the whole semester—on hold.

The stretch of three consecutive games against then-winless teams seemed an opportunity for a reboot to the 1988 season for Tishomingo. However, the Bulldogs had barely nipped Thrasher in a district game and fallen 13-0 to Mantachie a week later. Suddenly, the division clash with 0-5 Walnut took on added importance. Coach Herbert's state of the team address was simple: "The two open dates hurt us. We haven't played really good ball offensively since."[1] With district matchups with favorites Smithville and Falkner still to come, the Walnut game had the makings of a game that could define the season if the Tishomingo offense couldn't get back on track.

The Walnut Wildcats had given Falkner all they could handle earlier in the season and came ready to put Tishomingo to the test, as well. Walnut scored first on a short run early in the game, but a failed conversion left the score 6-0. Dave Herbert tossed a sixteen-yard touchdown to Bryant Southward for the tie, and Danny Brock added a conversion run for an 8-6 Tishomingo lead. The Bulldogs scored again on Brock's twenty-yard run to increase their lead to 14-6. The Wildcats answered with another short touchdown run to edge within two. That was as close as they would get, however, as Tishomingo's offense returned at last to its early-season form in the second half. Shane Hill ran for a pair of touchdowns, and Brock and Herbert each found the end zone in Tishomingo's 41-12 romp that improved their overall record to 4-1 and their division mark to 3-0.[2]

The road to the playoffs would become much more difficult for the Bulldogs in their final two division matchups. High-flying Smithville had the most potent offense in Division 1-1A, averaging nearly thirty points a game, so the Tishomingo offense would be called on to outscore the Seminoles. Smithville's only division loss had come at the hands of Falkner. The Eagles had started slowly after almost tripping up against Walnut early in the season but was rounding into shape and had the division's best defense. Tishomingo to that point had piled up wins against the weaker teams in the division and remained unproven against its quality opponents.

* * *

Mississippi's high school playoff system began in the 1981 season with four classifications: B, BB, A, and AA. The state's smallest schools were Class B and the biggest schools were Class AA. Three years later, the Mississippi High School Activities Association (MHSAA) revamped the system and redistributed its member schools into 1A-5A classes. The state's current largest current classification, 6A, was added for the 2009-10 school year. At present, the state's thirty-two largest schools by enrollment make up 6A, and the next thirty-two largest comprise 5A. The smallest thirty-six schools are classified 1A for the 2019-2021 classification cycle.[3] The rest of Mississippi's high schools are divided evenly among 2A, 3A, and 4A classifications. This makes getting into the playoffs easier than ever. The top four schools from each of the state's four regions advance to the playoffs, meaning that half of the schools in 6A and 5A advance to the playoffs and almost half of 1A teams play postseason football.

Making the playoffs in Mississippi has been possible only during about a third of the years since Meridian High School played Mobile Military Institute to a 0-0 tie in 1908 in the first game involving a Mississippi high school. The Wildcats' fledgling program was followed by Columbus Lee in 1910, and Laurel in 1914. Five years later, after the resolution of World War I, a bevy of Mississippi schools trotted out teams for the first time: Clarksdale, Corinth, Greenville, Greenwood, Grenada, Moorhead, and Winona. Gulfport entered football competition in 1920, followed by Pascagoula and Perkinston in 1921 and Hattiesburg and Picayune in

1922. Others—like Jackson Central—also may have played earlier than available records indicate. By the 1927 season, Jackson Central's schedule was made up completely of other Mississippi schools: Forest, D'Lo, Yazoo City, Hattiesburg, Vicksburg, Laurel, McComb, Gulfport, and Meridian. That same season—while Babe Ruth and Lou Gehrig were leading the most famous of the New York Yankee baseball teams to another World Series title—Mississippi high school football took its first step toward today's playoff system with the formation of the Big Eight conference.[4]

While high school football was slowly coming into its own in Mississippi, the physical landscape in parts of the state was suffering through one of the greatest natural disasters in United States history. The Great Mississippi River Flood of 1927 caused approximately a thousand deaths in the Mississippi Delta alone. Over twenty thousand buildings gave way to the flood, and more than sixty thousand others were damaged. Hundreds of thousands of farm animals drowned, and the yield of the 1927 crop year was nil.[5] Heavy rains in the Upper Mississippi in the fall of 1926 had set the stage for the flood, so by the time spring rains moved in, levees up and down the Mississippi were feeling the strain. Prior to this devastating flood, local municipalities were responsible for protecting their own towns from Old Man River, who visited the Delta fields on a regular basis.[6] However, nothing had prepared the eleven states affected by the Great Mississippi River Flood for what besieged them in the spring of 1927. Rains pounded day after day, and the river continued to rise at historically swift rates—sometimes a foot or more a day—and to heights never before recorded. The river did not begin to subside until August, and the devastation was catastrophic. In addition to the losses in terms of life and property, racial tensions in the Delta during the disaster and recovery efforts sped up the Great Migration to the North, bringing further change to the region.[7] Passage of the National Flood Control Act of 1928 and the handing of responsibility for flood control on the Mississippi over to the Army Corps of Engineers was like locking the barn door after the horse had escaped.

As Mississippi recovered from the Great Mississippi River Flood of 1927, the Big Eight Conference began with charter members Biloxi, Brookhaven, Gulfport, Hattiesburg, Jackson Central, Laurel, McComb, and Meridian—all in areas not directly affected by the flood. Vicksburg, Clarksdale, Greenwood, Greenville, Columbus Lee, and Tupelo joined in the 1930s, making the no-longer-aptly-named Big Eight a statewide conference of the state's largest schools. Many schools came and went from the Big Eight during its long history as Mississippi's premier high school football conference. The loosely knit organization expanded to as many at twenty-five schools by 1978 and played its last season in 1980 with twenty-one teams.[8] Other competitive groupings like the Little Dixie, Chickasaw, Tallahatchie, Apache, Choctaw, Pontotoc Ridge, Big Black, and Mid-Mississippi conferences gave many other schools of various sizes the opportunity to play for a championship. Bowl games like the Red Carpet Bowl in Vicksburg, the Shrimp Bowl on the coast, and the Little Dixie Bowl in Sturgis gave teams potential postseason rewards for a good season. Not until 1981—with the advent of the state football playoff system—could teams stake claim to the incontrovertible title of state champion. Sturgis (B), Hamilton (BB), Rosedale (A), and South Natchez (AA) raised those first gold balls.[9] Of those 1981 champions, only Hamilton remains as an unconsolidated high school.

In the thirty-eight years from the beginning of the MHSAA football playoffs through the 2018 season, only twenty schools have won Class B or 1A football state championships, with eight schools winning multiple titles. That number would likely be significantly smaller if not for consolidation. Consider that Weir, which leads the pack with six state crowns, has not existed since 2013. Hollandale Simmons won three straight championships between 2015 and 2017[10] but dropped from 2A to 1A after a number of 1A stalwarts went the way of consolidation to make Simmons— a 3A school as recently at 2000[11]—one of the smallest high schools in the MHSAA.

Consolidation has spread all across Mississippi over the last thirty years, but northeast Mississippi and the Delta regions have been affected more than others. Of Tishomingo's old district rivals, only Walnut, Thrasher, Smithville, and Falkner remain. Still, north Mississippi dominates the Class 1A landscape. Of the thirty-six smallest schools in the 2019-21 alignment, only seven are located south of Interstate 20, which bisects the state near its geographical middle.[12] Like Hollandale Simmons, many current members of the smallest classification have spent much of their histories at 2A or larger. While the likes of Simmons (three titles), Puckett (three), Mount Olive (three), Mize (four), and Stringer (four) continue to chase Weir's standard of six 1A championships, one has to wonder if the most significant opponent of these burgs of Piggly Wigglys and Dollar Generals in their quest for state football championships is not one another but consolidation.

* * *

The 1981 Mississippi high school football season marked the beginning of its playoff system, but the real story of that autumn was Marcus Dupree. A senior at Philadelphia High School that year, Dupree was still considered by many as the greatest high school athlete the state had ever produced. Compared to the likes of Herschel Walker and Bo Jackson, Dupree entered his final season as a Tornado within sight of Walker's high school record eighty-six touchdowns. While Coach Herbert was still several years away from making his mark on the Mississippi football playoffs, the extended season offered the potential of extra games for Dupree to chase Hershel's record.

The significance of Marcus Dupree's senior season extended beyond the myriad college recruiters descending on the red-clay soil of the county seat of Neshoba County and the heart of Choctaw Nation. Less than twenty years earlier, Neshoba County was the scene of the murders of three civil rights workers—Andrew Goodman, James Chaney, and Michael Schwerner—investigating the burning of a black church in the county. The Freedom Summer of 1964 that originally drew the three to Mississippi was a massive campaign to register black voters in Mississippi in response to the Ku Klux Klan's intimidation tactics. The FBI's investigation into the murders led to seven convictions among the eighteen accused in the trials that ended in 1967.[13]

One key figure in the murders was Cecil Price, then a young deputy sheriff in Neshoba County. He was the deputy who had arrested the three, violating their due process rights in the process. He tracked them down after their release and served them up to the Klan mob awaiting them. Price was one of the seven found guilty in the subsequent trial and served four and a half years of a six-year prison sentence for conspiracy to violate the civil rights of the three victims, though his part in the murders and his ties to the Ku Klux Klan made his role more dubious than his sentence indicated. Six years was the longest sentence meted out for any of the guilty parties.[14]

That Dupree played alongside Price's son cannot be understated as Mississippi moved from the troubled 1960s to a generation of blacks and whites attending school together in integrated public schools. Dupree ultimately broke Herschel Walker's high school touchdown record as blacks, whites, and Native Americans cheered him on. All over Mississippi fully integrated classes graduated from the state's public schools in the early 1980s and in the years following, with change occurring more quickly on the athletic fields than anywhere else. There, on the simulated battlefields of sport, blacks and whites practiced together, blocked and tackled one another, and tossed the ball to one another. In the process they laughed together, fought one another, celebrated together after victories, and mourned with one another after defeats. What Vietnam did to force racial harmony among American troops in the late 1960s, football fields did for young men coming behind them. Just as at least three races rallied around native son Marcus Dupree as he broke a record some thought unattainable, other communities around the state found the formidable idea of racial reconciliation as easy as uniting under shared school colors—at least on Friday nights.

* * *

Coach Herbert's move to Tishomingo in 1983 set the stage for a step forward in racial reconciliation in his new community, though to be fair, northeast Mississippi was never known as a hotbed of racial unrest in the first place. After the first year of coming to like their new coach, Coach Herbert's players and others in the community grew to love and respect him. As for his attitude toward his black players, Linda Herbert pointed to an overnight football camp at Mississippi State that Dave wanted to attend between his seventh and eighth grade years. David Lee was a protective father who would allow his son to go to the camp only if he roomed with Eric Powell, his African-American running back.

A gospel singer in duos and quartets at his church in Tishomingo, Coach Herbert was occasionally a guest at the African-American church at Carter's Branch, just outside of Tishomingo. His daughter Hollie, reminiscing on how she and her sisters and brothers were reared explained, "We didn't see a color, we just saw a person. That's how we were raised. Were we just naïve or what?"[15] Year two of David Lee's Herbert's tenure at Tish would further blur the lines between white and black and change the lives of many in that small Mississippi burg forever.

11

After the 1983 season, with a year of familiarity with their new coach under their belts, the Tishomingo Bulldogs looked to take a giant leap forward in their second season together. Triumphs over Burnsville and Mantachie were the only wins the Bulldogs were able to muster en route to a 2-7 finish in 1983,[1] but hopes were high for 1984, as Coach Herbert and his family continued to find favor with the Tishomingo community. The returning roster had a season and an off-season of experience running the Wing T and were poised to make a run at the school's first playoff bid. Linda Herbert was excelling as a high school math teacher and quickly becoming a favorite among her students. Dave had a year's experience on the junior high team and would be playing tight end as an eighth grader. Lauriann, an upcoming senior, would be co-captain of the cheerleading squad that hoped to cheer their team all the way to the school's first playoff appearance.

The 1984 season carried different expectations than the season prior because it would be Eric Powell's senior year. Any small-school program that has ever enjoyed any success in football in Mississippi has that one athlete whose athletic feats become the stuff of legend. Powell was that transcendent athlete of small-town lore. When interviewed, no one in Tishomingo with any depth of knowledge of the Tish football program wasted any time bringing up the name of Eric Powell. Still beloved by his teammates, they believed there was nothing Powell could not do on the field.

In the decade before consolidation changed the landscape of the 1A classification, rivalries ran deep, and competition was fierce among neighboring small schools. Athletic families in those communities shaped rosters and, in turn, expectations from year to year. In Tishomingo, the more Brocks, Powells, and Southwards that appeared on the roster, the better the opportunity for a winning season. The 1984 edition of the football Bulldogs featured Derrick Brock at center and all-everything quarterback/running back Powell in the backfield, among others from the three dominant athletic families. A game changer on offense and defense, Powell roamed the field from his free safety position, causing nightmares for opposing coaches. Defensive coordinator Kenneth McClain coached Powell and remembered:

> He was the type of athlete that you basically left alone and let him use his natural talents. I did some coaching as far as how to read the offense—what they were doing, the people to read, knowing when to come up and when to drop back. But basically, thank goodness, I stayed out of his way so that he could be a great athlete. He had the speed that if you couldn't cut him off, you couldn't catch him. Eric was very easy to coach. If he hadn't hurt his knee [in a playoff game later in the 1985 season], he could have played pro ball.[2]

Powell could also be a handful for opponents while returning kickoffs and punts for the Bulldogs. He rarely left the field for even a single play.

During Powell's senior season, Brad Howie and Ronny McKee were among the freshman who were called up to the varsity team when their junior high season reached its conclusion. Howie said, "Anybody could have picked him out. He was the focus of every game from the time he was in ninth grade. If you stopped Eric Powell, you were going to stop the team."[3]

McKee was a lineman, a big 'ol boy who told Coach Herbert one day during practice that year that he thought he could take Powell in a one-on-one drill. Herbert waved his hand toward his star running back and said, "Get him." McKee was braced and ready when Powell approached him carrying the football. Or so he thought. "Son, he run over me like I wasn't even standing there. I believe that's the hardest I've ever been hit. There was no stopping Eric Powell. He was a legend around here."[4]

School board member Paul Whitlock called Powell's name many times during his stint as Tishomingo public address announcer. However, his bond with the Bulldog superstar goes farther back than Powell's days on the gridiron and deeper than that of a fan of high school football.

> Eric is like my son. Eric lived at my house—when I say lived there, he stayed there enough till I told him I claimed him as a dependent. Half the football team would be in my den floor. I would have to leave to go to work at night—working third shift, eleven to seven—and they would still be on my floor in my den watching TV when I left. Sometimes, he'd be there the next morning, just part of my family. Everybody loved everybody; this is what the good life is about.
>
> Color didn't matter. I grew up with their fathers. We worked together. We were close—the Powells, the

Brocks, the Southwards, all of those in that black community. They were just part of me and still are today. Eric became part of my family. My nine-year-old daughter worshiped the ground Eric Powell walked on. It was a unique thing. That raised some eyebrows in some people's minds, but not mine because I was blind to our differences; I grew up with their parents, and we had been friends for years. He's like my son and I would do anything in the world for him.[5]

Phillip Whitehead and Eric Powell also have a special bond that goes well back into their days as teammates. Whitehead was the team's starting quarterback by the end of the 1984 season after spending some time as a receiver while Powell played quarterback. "If he decided he wanted to be a golfer tomorrow," Whitehead said, "he'd be a scratch golfer within a week. Just a talented guy—incredible." The one part of football that Powell detested, according to Whitehead, was practice:

Coach would call practice to order, and Eric was always clowning because he could. What are they gonna do, throw him off the team? He'd do whatever he wanted. Eric hated practice and would do anything to get out of practice. The only thing worse than fall practice was spring practice because there wasn't any point to it.[6]

Nevertheless, Powell could put the team on his shoulders, and he had to at times during the 1984 season in order to lead the Bulldogs to the school's first playoff berth.

Whitehead claimed it was Coach Herbert's good spirit that helped him connect with all of his players, no matter their personalities or abilities or race:

> Most of the time your football coaches in high school... are easy to hate because—at least in that era—they felt like they had to make a man out of you. Around here, most of the kids grew up on a farm of some type; we'd already been exposed to some hard living. The toughening up thing almost seemed fake. Country kids take that as a projection of insecurity.[7]

When Coach Herbert arrived and gave his players a measure of respect for the life that they had already experienced, they gave it back to him in far greater measure.

* * *

The headline of the Tishomingo football capsule in the *Daily Journal*'s annual pre-season football insert said it all for the Bulldogs' 1984 season: "Tishomingo must have more than Powell." Coach Herbert's quote for the article was simple as well: "We can't depend on one athlete, even if he is a good one." With more concentration on defense and conditioning during spring practice and summer workouts, Herbert expected more from his team. They were undersized, with defensive ends that weighed 155 and 170 pounds and a starting defensive lineman listed at 155, not much more than the defensive backs playing behind him.[8] Always, though, there was Powell, the offensive and defensive standout. The only game from Tishomingo's two-team district that counted toward the playoffs in the newly minted 1A classification was Smithville, the regular season's last tilt. Falkner, meanwhile, was coming off a state championship, was favored to win its district, and would not cross paths with the 1-1A winner until the postseason.

Burnsville was first on the 1984 schedule. The Bulldogs won that one handily, 32-14, behind the strong running of Powell and Ronnie Ryan, both of whom eclipsed the 100-yard mark.[9] Tishomingo continued its momentum by beating Blue Mountain in week two. Powell scored on a seventy-six-yard reception from Whitehead, and Ryan added a forty-yard touchdown run to highlight the win.[10] Tishomingo passed the ball more than normal that night, but its receivers dropped quite a few passes. Assistant coach Kenneth McClain kept Whitehead and Powell after class the following Friday, the day of the Belmont game. He reminded Whitehead that although he spread the ball around to all of his receivers against Blue Mountain nobody could catch it.

"I know, Coach. I wasn't happy about it, either."

McClain then instructed him to pass to no one else but Powell that night against the hated Cardinals. Whitehead and Powell responded. "I threw the ball eighteen times that night," Whitehead recalled. "In '84, that was like fun 'n' gun, Jim Kelly stuff. I think I was like thirteen for eighteen; twelve of 'em were to Eric." Whitehead's other completion that night was to a wide open receiver over the middle. "I pumped about three times before I threw it to him. I thought, I'm probably about to get in trouble." Whitehead and the other receivers almost got in a fight on the bus home because of his singular focus in the passing game.[11] As successful as the passing game was that night, Tishomingo could not take down Belmont, falling 26-6. The only points

Tish scored that night came on a touchdown pass from Whitehead to Powell in the third quarter.[12]

Year after year the Bulldogs were never able to beat their 2A county neighbors to the south. The Cardinals were simply bigger and better, or something always seemed to happen to turn the game in Belmont's favor. Brad Howie's ninth grade team came within two points of beating Belmont, and he remembered Coach Herbert telling him after the game that they would get them as seniors. By Howie's senior year, though, Herbert dropped Belmont and Iuka from the Tishomingo schedule. With the physical intensity of those games and the short rosters with which he was already working, their coach decided that having his players healthy for district play and, potentially, the state playoffs was more important than county rivalries.[13]

The series may have ended, but the deeply ingrained animosity toward Belmont still exists. Today, at the end of their eighth grade year, students from Tishomingo Middle School are able to choose between Belmont High School and Tishomingo County High School. One former Bulldog revealed how that process unfolded in his family:

> Most of the kids get together with their buddies and go to Belmont, most of the decent players. Not when my son graduated from eighth grade. My wife said there ain't no way in hell you're going to Belmont. That's how my wife felt about it. She's from Iuka, and there was no love lost from those county rivalries back then. She was like, you may do a lot of stuff in life— you may marry a stripper—but you ain't going to Belmont High School. And she meant it.

They were fighting about it. All of his buddies—there weren't but about two or three of his middle school team that went to TC with him. I said, that's fine. If y'all can't figure it out before it's time to enroll at the end of May, then I'm going to send him to a private school up in Tennessee; I've got a couple picked out. They figured it out, and he went to TC. He played linebacker over there and had a great time doing it.[14]

* * *

Frustration set in for Tishomingo on the last Friday night of September against Biggersville as the Bulldogs moved the football up and down the field but could only manage one Powell-to-Whitehead touchdown pass in a 12-6 defeat. The Bulldogs dominated the stat sheet but couldn't find the end zone, even after Coach Herbert moved Powell back to quarterback, where he had often played during the 1983 season.[15] Herbert's team took it on the chin again the following week at Hatley, 35-12, by giving up exactly 148 rushing yards to two different Tiger running backs. Two more touchdowns from Powell to Whitehead were not nearly enough for an offense that had sputtered for three straight weeks.[16] During the week before the Mantachie game, Herbert called on his sophomore-laden offensive line to "grow up" and learn to handle their blocking assignments.[17]

* * *

When the football season reached its mid-point, a distinctly northeastern Mississippi phenomenon crept into the area's sports coverage. For schools without a football program, basketball season could begin on the first Friday night in October, a full three weeks before their football-playing brethren could join the fray. Those mostly 1A schools could begin basketball practice as soon as school started, about the time other schools were finishing up two-a-day football practices. In 1984, seventeen schools in northeast Mississippi began their sports season with basketball rather than football, including legendary programs like Wheeler, Ashland, Hickory Flat, Ingomar, Tremont, and Jumpertown. Citing lack of interest and the financial burden of beginning a football program, most of the basketball-focused schools were content to focus on roundball.[18]

Will Kollmeyer did a freelance piece on Wheeler High School basketball back in the 1980s for the Jefferson Pilot Southeastern Conference Game of the Week halftime show. Called "The Hoosiers of the South," the piece focused on the Prentiss County school's willingness to take on all-comers, no matter the size of the school, and was the only piece Kollmeyer ever remembers the Charlotte-based group running about a high school program.[19] Coach Ricky Black remembers going to Wheeler for a basketball game and sensing a unique community:

> The first time I went to a game in Wheeler, I said there's something that's different here in that old gym. I got to looking around at the average age of people attending that game—must have been sixty-something. Everybody in that community came to that basketball game that was played at Wheeler. That place was covered up with old people.[20]

* * *

Halftime of the Mantachie game proved to be a turning point both for the game against the Mustangs and for the 1984 Bulldog season. Trailing 6-0, Coach Herbert made some changes, not the least of which was moving Whitehead back to quarterback and Powell back to tailback. The two then put on a show far beyond the confines of the offense in rallying their team. Whitehead blocked a punt that Sidney Bennett returned for a touchdown and then intercepted a pass on Mantachie's next play that led to Orville McGee's twenty-two-yard touchdown run. For his part, Powell scored on the ground and on an eighty-eight-yard punt return in Tishomingo's 32-12 win.[21]

Tishomingo hosted the 2-A Iuka Chieftains from a few miles up Highway 25 in their next game, looking to upset their county rivals and build on their momentum from the second half against Mantachie. With a TD pass from Whitehead to Powell and Powell's one-yard run, the Bulldogs trailed just 14-12 entering the fourth quarter but could not get over the hump in a 21-12 loss.[22]

Against Thrasher the following week, though, the boys from Tish were able to get back into the win column. Powell ripped off a sixty-three-yard touchdown run on the game's first offensive play. Thrasher matched the Bulldog touchdown with a long drive to knot the score at 7-7. The next significant threat in the game was a field goal attempt by the Rebels in the fourth quarter. After blocking the kick to preserve the tie, Tishomingo drove twelve plays to eat up the rest of the time on the clock. Powell plunged into the end zone from the two-yard line on the game's last play, his bookend scores giving the Bulldogs a 13-7 win.[23] The defining moment of their high school careers—most of them called it the pivotal moment of their lives—stood just two weeks away after a bye week.

12

As a small-school football coach, David Lee Herbert did not limit any of his players to a single position in his offense, knowing that his needs might be different from year to year. Between seventh grade and his senior season, Dave Herbert played tight end and quarterback at different times. Eric Powell played quarterback and running back. Shane Hill and Terry Enlow played guard and tackle, respectively, in junior high but moved to running back for their sophomore seasons. Coach Herbert tried to find a spot for all two dozen or so players on his roster, even if they just played on special teams. With class sizes usually hovering around forty students, fewer than eighty made up the entirety of the male population at Tishomingo High School in most given years.

With the rapid changes that many of the boys' bodies went through between the time they began playing football in junior high and the time they cracked the high school roster, Coach Herbert stressed the importance of every player knowing his assignments and everyone else's because graduation and injuries meant each player could be playing another position if that was the best move for the team. Brad Howie first played for Tishomingo in the spring of his eighth grade season, getting a crash course in the Wing T that his teammates had already spent a junior high season learning. He remembered the importance that Coach Herbert placed on teaching the young players who were often overlooked in other programs as they paid their dues on the way to more significant roles with the team.

> Coach Herbert's theory was, he was going to take these seventh graders—these whippersnappers, he called them—treat 'em like they're on the team, and teach them how to run Wing T. And you just start beating that into their heads until they get to tenth grade and they know it.[1]

The 1984 Tishomingo Bulldog varsity football team already had a firm grasp of the Wing T. With Eric Powell back at running back and Phillip Whitehead directing the offense, the potential of the talented team finally seemed to be falling into place. With two games to go in the regular season, Tishomingo stood 3-4 with an open date before a non-conference game with 3A Alcorn Central and a division matchup with Smithville that would determine both teams' playoff fate. A natural progression for a coach taking over a program is to teach his system in year one. This often means a rough season as players and coaches work toward being on the same page with one another. In a coach's first year, success usually comes first in non-conference action against weaker opponents. The defining threshold for up-and-coming programs in Mississippi since 1981 is playoff success—first, making the playoffs and then winning games in them. With Tishomingo High School's first appearance in the state playoffs just a win away, the Alcorn Central game became a tune-up for the most important game in David Lee Herbert's brief stint at the school.

Powell remembered how the stars aligned, quite literally, on Friday night, November 2, on County Road 254 in Glen, Mississippi, seven miles southeast of Corinth. "The guys that I played with often talked about that particular night we played Alcorn. There was a bright star in the sky. I don't have a clue which star it was. All I know it was one lone bright star that stood out among all the stars. Everybody saw it."[2] Whether or not a big win over a larger school had any connection with an astrological phenomenon, everything seemed to work for the Bulldogs that night. Powell had the best game of his career, scoring seven times in Tishomingo's 47-21 win over the Golden Bears.[3] "Everything we called that night in the huddle worked. Everything we ran worked. Whatever we wanted to do, we could do it on the field. It was one of those games."[4]

Teammate Orville McGee used the word *awkward* to describe the Alcorn Central game. Relating it to the butterfly effect—where every small event can have larger effects later—McGee described a number of incidents outside of the norm for a football Friday night. He, Powell, and Ronnie Ryan made a tackle near the sidelines in which an Alcorn Central player twisted his leg around a pole in the fence behind the Tishomingo sideline. His leg was broken, and the game was delayed for several minutes while those assisting him untangled him from the fence. The lights went off at one time, the scoreboard malfunctioned through much of the game, and a pair of dogs ran onto the field on several occasions. "And, of course," McGee added, "Eric scored all those TDs on punt return, kick return, interception, offense. Just an MVP night."[5] Assistant coach Kenneth McClain called it the longest football game he had ever witnessed in his life.[6]

* * *

Right up there with pep rallies and pre-game meals and crash signs and locker-room speeches, post-game rituals are part of the Friday night high school football experience. Home games usually mean a meeting after the game at a coach's house, local restaurant, empty parking lot, or even the home team's locker room. After establishing *Friday Night Fever* at WTVA, Will Kollmeyer saw a change in how home teams spent Friday nights so that they could catch a few highlights of their own games and others in the WTVA coverage area:

> There were a lot of coaches who realized that they couldn't get home in time after the game. More and more, I would hear stories through the years that the booster club would buy a TV for them. So they'd bring the pizzas or whatever in for the post-game meal, and the team would stick around and watch *Friday Night Fever*.[7]

Teams like Tishomingo High School on that Friday night in Alcorn County had one priority above all others after the game: to get those hungry football players something to eat. For fast food restaurants, that meant a busload of players and coaches and their accompanying caravan descending on their establishment not too long before closing time. Most 1A towns in Mississippi in the 1980s—and many municipalities several times their size—were home to, at most, a mom-and-pop cafe that only served lunch. Fast food for a small-town child of the eighties was a treat, especially after an out-of-town sporting event. Corinth had a number of fast-food options just fifteen minutes from Alcorn Central, including McDonald's, the destination for the Tishomingo troupe on November 2. The team and its fans were riding high after their big win and looked forward to continuing their celebration in Corinth.

Eighth-grader Dave Herbert pouted when his dad turned down his repeated requests to ride to Corinth with Linda, Stacie, and Hollie after the game, instead pointing him toward the bus on which he rode to the game. Instead, Hollie's friend Kimberly Whitlock and Kimberly's four-year-old sister, Amy, rode with the Herberts while their mother followed directly behind, getting a head start on the busload of starving football players.

Powell was still on cloud nine after his and his teammates' nearly flawless performance and enjoyed the bus ride to McDonald's. He remembered the team's celebration was suddenly cut short when the bus topped a hill and everyone saw the devastating evidence of a wreck about fifty yards ahead. Powell and his teammates did not recognize the vehicles at first.[8] Driving the bus, David Lee Herbert soon knew as he pulled up close to the scene. Speaking through tears even thirty-five years later, Kenneth McClain related how the events played out from his seat at the front of the bus:

> We came over the hill. Coach Herbert was driving. He pulled over and said, "I'm going to go down and see what's happening." We couldn't see straight down the hill. He came back up and said, "Coach, it's my family." We got off behind the bus and prayed. After

that prayer, he said, "It's peaceful now." I don't know how he could have said it, but he said it. After that, he went back down, and I went back down. I remember seeing the wreck, and I think they had already gotten his wife and the children out, but Lauriann was still there. I kept thinking, we need a miracle, Lord, but it didn't happen; she was already dead. I don't remember a lot after that. Coach Herbert went with his family to the hospital, and I drove the kids back to the school.[9]

* * *

While Lauriann had been driving east on Highway 72 toward Corinth—near where the two-lane highway widened into four lanes—two teenaged boys who had just left their jobs at a grocery store were racing in the other direction. One driver lost control of his vehicle and came across into the far right lane where Lauriann was driving, smashing into their Mercury Zephyr head-on. Linda was riding in the front passenger seat and remembers very little about the wreck. Stacie saw the car coming over into Lauriann's lane and thought *LOOK OUT!* but did not have time to get the words out.

Stacie was the first to come to after the accident, and the one who remembered the most about it, though her memory of the night of the wreck is still fuzzy. She remembered the headlights coming down the highway and a little concern from Linda and Lauriann. Her next memory was waking up at the accident scene:

Some man had picked me up off the side of the road, I suppose, because from what I understand, I was ejected from the car. He had picked me up before anybody else had gotten there; I don't know who he was. I don't know how close he was because I was kind of in and out of consciousness. I remember the little girl's mother—hearing her—because she was the first car behind us. I remember seeing Dad when they were loading us up in the ambulance. I was in and out the whole ambulance ride. I remember waking up in the emergency room. That's about as much as I remember.[10]

Other family members recall Stacie's telling them that the man who held her assured her that she would be okay, then kind of disappeared from the craziness of the scene after help arrived. Many suggest that he was an angel, and Stacie doesn't argue the point: "I had no recollection of where he came from or who he was. I just remember waking up with somebody holding me. I could have sworn we were in front of his car, or *a* car, but I have no idea how."[11]

* * *

Brad Howie and Bobby Brock were freshmen on the 1984 team, traveling to their first road game after being called up to the varsity team for the last few games of the season. They were sitting near the front of the bus when they topped the hill and saw the accident scene. Howie remembers that the accident had obviously just happened and that the players knew only that it was "someone from Tish" at first. He watched Coach Herbert walk around the car, looking in all the windows, as some of his older teammates tried to extricate the passengers as they awaited the arrival of emergency personnel.[12]

Howie and others remembered seeing Coach Herbert walk to the edge of the highway, shaking his head.[13] When his coach walked back onto the bus, McGee was taken aback at his calm. *Why was Coach not yelling and screaming?* McGee had earlier needed to be calmed himself for Dave's sake. He later realized that Coach Herbert was in shock.[14]

Emergency workers were quick to the scene, but Lauriann was pronounced dead on arrival at the hospital.[15] The driver of the car that struck the Herberts' car passed away the following day, and Kimberly Whitlock died on that Sunday. Stacie, Hollie, and Amy Whitlock were admitted to various hospitals, as was Linda Herbert, who suffered head trauma and extensive damage to her legs and remained in intensive care through the weekend.

* * *

Coach Herbert's sister Joyce Bowman was living in Michigan when she received a call from her brother late on a Friday night.

> Bill and I were getting ready to go to bed, and I had a phone call, and it was from Dave. I thought he was going to talk to Bill about a ball game. And then I noticed that he stopped talking and didn't say anything, and I said, "Dave, what's wrong?"
>
> He told me there was an accident and he said, "Joyce, I don't think Lauriann's going to make it." After that point, he couldn't talk to me at all.

David Lee handed off the phone to Powell, who calmly filled in Joyce on the details and urged her to come as quickly as possible. "I told Eric to tell his coach it would take us a little while because it takes about fifteen hours for us to get there." She remembered thinking how her brother was being well taken care of by his players and his community.[16]

Powell, a close friend of the Whitlock family, recalled the girls' mother—who had been driving right behind the Herberts and had to swerve to avoid the wreck herself— banging on the door of the bus and frantically calling his name. He exited the bus, at first unaware that the Whitlock girls had been in the car that was barely recognizable at the scene. He rode in the ambulance while law enforcement officers tried to locate the girls' father, who was at work over an hour away. When Powell arrived at the hospital, Coach Herbert was already there. Powell vividly remembered the scene over three decades later:

> They wheeled this lady in—we're in the emergency room and there were people everywhere. This lady comes in—she's covered in blood. She was covered in so much blood that I did not recognize her. Coach Herbert asked, "Who is that?"
>
> Somebody said, "That is your wife." He spent much of the rest of the night saying, "The kids need their mama. The kids need their mama. The kids need their mama."[17]

Phillip Whitehead was sitting with Powell on the bus on the night of the accident, their practice since first moving up to varsity together at the end of their ninth grade season. Later than night, he found himself behind the emergency room doors at one point—he didn't remember why. He saw Lauriann's body on a gurney in the hall, and since emergency personnel were not working on her, he knew she had not survived.

Whitehead remembered Coach Herbert's coming up to him and saying, "Phillip, I need to know what's going on."

"Coach, they don't know yet," he lied.

Decades later, Whitehead said,

> I knew—and I felt bad afterward. I didn't know to what degree [the others were injured]. I knew it was just bad. That whole night was like a blur. After that we had the week of the funeral and that was just a horrible thing. One week, you're with somebody on the cheerleading squad; the next week, you're going to a funeral in Carrollton.[18]

David Lee Herbert leaned hard on his Christian faith on that Friday night, both at the scene of the accident and later at the hospital when he knew Lauriann had passed. Howie's father, Royce, was among a group of men who arrived at the hospital to pray for all involved in the wreck and for their care. What he experienced next served to strengthen his own faith going forward:

> The thing that stood out in my mind all these years was that we had gotten to the hospital; Coach Herbert had gotten there. There was a big room full of people. We were going to have prayer for the family, and Coach Herbert said, "Fellas, I feel like I need to pray." He was holding himself together and he said that. When he prayed, the part I remember so well is, he said, "Dear God, thank You so much for not taking *all* my family away from me today. I thank You for your goodness and your kindness." He said something

about, "We need you more now that we've ever needed you."

He didn't pray long, but that's what he said. Part of his family was dead, and it looked like everything that was going to happen wasn't going to be good, but David Herbert was praying praises to God. I will never forget being in that room with that man. I don't know if I could be that strong.[19]

Coach Herbert's faith, always a part of the life that he modeled to his family, his students, and his players, had in a moment become front and center for the unassuming coach of the Tishomingo Bulldogs.

13

E ven in the initial shock of the accident David Lee had the presence of mind to reach out for a dependable lifeline: his family. His youngest sister Anne had just put her boys to bed when her cousin Jo Leta called. "David Lee and them have had a bad wreck." Word had spread throughout the family after David Lee's initial call to his mother. He was crying and said that he needed help and needed it quickly.

Anne and her husband, Mike, drove first to Carrollton to pick up other family members and then to Corinth, three hours away. "That was a long, awful ride. When we got there, David Lee was down in the chapel praying. The nurse came out and told me, "Somebody's got to come in here and talk to Ms. Herbert because if they don't, she probably will not make it." When Anne entered Linda's room, she remembers thinking she was looking at a mummy. Linda was dressed in gauze from head to toe and bleeding through all of it. Anne spent the better part of the night in Linda's room, talking to her and asking her questions and also in Stacie's room, picking glass from her niece's face.[1] Though her injuries were not life-threatening, Stacie had sustained multiple breaks from her eye sockets to her jaw and had lost her front teeth.[2] When Anne rotated back to Linda's room and asked her name at different times during the night, Linda responded each time with math equations. The nurse said that was fine, though, as long as her brain remained active.[3]

By the time Bill and Joyce Bowman arrived in Corinth from Michigan, their mother, Anne, and Mike were already attending to the Herbert family. David Lee knew that Lauriann was dead by then but made his family promise to keep it from Stacie and Hollie until they found out whether or not Linda was going to come out of her coma. When the Bowmans arrived at the hospital, they were amazed at the number of concerned friends and neighbors from Tishomingo and Carrollton who filled the waiting room.

Joyce, who had been charged with keeping the news of Lauriann's death from Stacie and Hollie, made sure that the televisions in the girls' rooms remained powered off so they wouldn't see news coverage of the accident. She and David Lee kept the crowd from visiting the girls, but people sent back gifts to keep them busy. Hollie was discharged before Stacie, and the ICU nurses arranged for her to stay in Stacie's room and sleep on a pallet beside Stacie's bed. As a nurse herself, Joyce was used to telling her patients the truth, even when it was hard to hear. When Stacie pleaded with her to see Lauriann, Joyce said, "Well, you can't see her right now." When Stacie persisted, Joyce responded, "She's in another room and you can't go in there. You've got to stay in here, and she's got to stay in her room." Though she may have stopped short of total deception, Joyce nevertheless called the situation the "hardest lie I've ever told in my life."[4]

David Lee asked Anne to prepare a Sunday funeral for Lauriann, a next-to-impossible turnaround. While his sister was taking care of the funeral arrangements, David Lee used the hospital chapel to beg God for his wife's life. The

McClains had already picked up Dave and kept him with their family through the weekend. When the time came for Lauriann's funeral, Linda had not yet come to, so David Lee and Dave were the only immediate family members to attend.[5]

* * *

Anne handled the funeral arrangements from the gravesite to reserving the church to contacting the pastor, even down to writing Lauriann's obituary. Her first stop after accepting the charge to plan the funeral was the Herbert mobile home. She looked for a suitable dress in the room that Lauriann shared with both sisters but could not find one. She remembers sitting back on the bed and crying, overcome by grief and the size of the task of pulling off a Sunday afternoon funeral.

> About that time, there was a knock at the door, and it was Danny McClung's wife and her daughter. I said, "I am so glad y'all are here. I've got to get Lauriann a dress; they don't have one."
>
> She held up a pink dress and said, "Lauriann just wore this to church there on Sunday, and she just loved it." It was her daughter's. We were ready to leave, fixin' to go out the door. God took care of it. And then, I just happened to look, and Lauriann had just gotten her album of senior pictures in that Friday. I went back and grabbed them.
>
> I got all her makeup and her hair rollers. When we got to the funeral home in Winona, the funeral director said, "Anne, I hate to tell you this..." He looked at

Mike and said, "I can't stop her from going back there, but she does not need to."

I said, "Mr. Land, of course I'm going to do all this for David Lee and Linda."

Mike said, "You're just going to have to tell her why."

He said, "I'll take these clothes, but it's got to be a closed casket." I laid that portfolio of all her senior pictures on top of that casket. You can't tell me that wasn't the work of the Lord.[6]

Mike Reans, who had coached with David Lee at Marvell Academy, was then coaching at Kossuth, forty-five minutes away from Tishomingo. He drove David Lee, Joyce, and Bill to the funeral in Carrollton on the Sunday after the wreck. It was the same day that Mississippi football coaches all over the state were turning their attention to a rare televised game between two of Mississippi's historically black universities—Mississippi Valley State, with their record-setting quarterback-receiver tandem of Willie Totten and Jerry Rice, versus highly ranked Alcorn State. Reans recalled the sadness of driving to the funeral while Linda was undergoing an hours-long surgery back in northeast Mississippi and driving back soon after the funeral was over.[7]

* * *

Lauriann Herbert was remembered as a quiet, sweet girl who was a member of the Beta Club and was academically minded (unlike Dave, who considered any grade of *70* wasted, according to his mother). Lauriann had been a second mother to Stacie and Hollie, seven and eight years her junior. Hollie remembered that Lauriann could not stand to hear her siblings smacking gum and would make them spit it out.[8] Stacie recalled one day not long before the accident, Lauriann was doing her little sister's fingernails and preparing her for the following year, when she would leave their home for college and find Stacie "somebody's little brother for a boyfriend to have there" on visits to her older sister.[9] Linda remembered that Lauriann was good at "wagging around" her younger sisters.[10]

Lauriann had just turned seventeen and had myriad friends in Tishomingo and back home in Carroll County. After her death, Carrollton Baptist Church set up a scholarship in Lauriann's name that is still given to a senior from the church who lives up to the characteristics of her life. The church makes the decision as to who receives the scholarship, and if none of the seniors in the church live up to the qualities of the name on the scholarship, they give it to a deserving senior in the larger Carrollton community. In the beginning many of the recipients were personally aware of the attributes that defined Lauriann's life. Over the years some of the recipients have been children of those who knew her. The back of the scholarship award lists the characteristics of Lauriann's life as a way to honor her memory perpetually: integrity, character, faithfulness, church participation, and academic excellence.[11]

A day or two after Lauriann's funeral, Linda regained consciousness. David Lee asked his pastor to break the news to Linda and his girls. However, feeling that it was something he should do as the leader of the family, David

Lee took control and broke the news himself. Joyce had told many families about the passing of a loved one in her experience as a nurse, but she confessed that when it came to being a part of that conversation, she chickened out. "They had the pastor in there, and I thought, that's all they need." David Lee, Dave, Stacie, Hollie, and the pastor gathered around Linda's bed when David Lee told her what happened. Linda, still barely recognizable from her numerous injuries, was overcome with grief. Joyce could hear her wailing from far down the hall.[12]

* * *

Linda did not learn until several years later about the outpouring of love for her daughter, her heart still too heavy to talk about Lauriann's funeral. Though Carrollton is not a town built for heavy traffic in the first place, every street within a mile or so of the church was lined with cars and buses and people from Tishomingo and Carrollton who came to pay their respects to the senior cheerleader. Thousands signed the guest book. Hundreds brought food. Anne took a week off from work to write over a thousand thank-you notes. After a number of years, Linda was finally able to look through the guest book for the first time.[13]

No one recalled David Lee's talking about how he felt as he drove up to the scene of the accident on the fateful Friday night. What everyone remembered, though, is how he kept insisting that his kids needed their mama and begging God for her life. Joyce never heard him talk about his grief. She knew he had seen Lauriann in the car after the wreck that night and did not want to cause him to relive the scene.[14]

Perhaps he was able to release some of the burden he carried to George Smith, the pastor of the church in Carrollton, with whom he talked often after the accident and during Linda's recovery. Perhaps he also gained some solace by sleeping in Lauriann's room with her little sisters until their mother returned from the hospital.[15]

* * *

Meanwhile, another Tishomingo family was grieving the death of their own daughter. The Herberts and the Whitlocks remain inextricably linked in the legacy of Tishomingo High School and the Tishomingo community at large. Phyllis Whitlock was imbedded in the community, having graduated in 1969 in one of the school's first few classes. The former homecoming queen spent fall Friday nights rooting for the boys in black and gold with the rest of her town. On the night of the Alcorn Central game, she outfitted nine-year-old Kimberly and four-year-old Amy with their pom-poms and drove to Glen, Mississippi, to watch Eric and the rest of the team play. Paul had to work at his railroad job about thirty-five miles away in Muscle Shoals, Alabama, that night.[16]

After the game, Kimberly and Amy Whitlock were as excited as anyone else about a stop at McDonald's with the team. Riding to the restaurant in nearby Corinth with Stacie and Hollie Herbert made it even better. Their mother drove alone behind the Herberts' car. When the car racing in the other direction crossed the median, she had watched hysterically and helplessly as it smashed into the car carrying her girls, barely avoiding the wreck herself.[17]

An acquaintance of the Whitlock family lived across the road from where the wreck happened and called Paul to inform him. Without many specifics, she told him that he needed to get to Corinth in a hurry because there had been a bad wreck involving some of his family. The urgency of Paul's drive to Corinth from fifty-five miles away took its toll on his car engine, which gave out about the Alabama-Mississippi state line. A law enforcement officer who was driving in the other direction looking for him pulled up about the same time that his motor gave way and drove him to the hospital in Corinth. His thoughts were all over the place as he imagined the worst. He didn't learn any details until he reached the hospital.[18]

Eric Powell and a couple of other football players were sitting with Phyllis when Paul arrived. A few minutes later, hospital officials made the decision to transport both of the girls to Le Bonheur Children's Hospital in Memphis, Tennessee, almost a hundred miles away. Hospital officials gave the couple little hope that either of their girls would survive. Nine-year-old Kimberly was brain dead upon arrival, but both girls were taken to Le Bonheur for the best pediatric care in the region. Amy was to be flown via medical helicopter, but in an effort not to separate the sisters, the teenager who drove the other car in the accident was airlifted instead.[19]

Shortly after Paul made it to the hospital in Corinth, his brother arrived and followed the ambulance across Highway 72 to Memphis. About halfway to Memphis, near Highway 7, the right front tire of the ambulance blew. Paul's brother scurried under the ambulance to retrieve the spare tire only to discover that it, too, was flat. The call went out for a local ambulance to finish the transport while paramedics in the back of the ambulance worked to keep Kimberly and Amy alive.[20] The moments of waiting must have seemed endless to the frantic Whitlock family, but they finally arrived at Le Bonheur, where the prognosis for both girls matched their initial outlook.

On Sunday, a Le Bonheur chaplain and an intensive care doctor asked the Whitlocks to meet with them in a private room. One of them opened the conversation by asking if the couple could still have children. "That was kind of an odd thing, but it told us where we were going," Paul recalled. Kimberly was pronounced dead, never having had any brain activity after the accident. Paul and Phyllis made the long drive back to Tishomingo to plan her funeral, not knowing whether or not Amy would still be alive when they returned to Le Bonheur. Her head was swollen, and officials described her condition as touch and go.[21]

Paul remembered the surreal conversation he and his wife had on the drive back to Tishomingo County that afternoon:

> We've got to plan a funeral. Who are the pallbearers? Both of us said we want Eric Powell toting the head end of that casket, and then we filled in the rest of it. The funeral was going to be in the Baptist church in Tishomingo—really never been a black in the Baptist church in Tishomingo up until that time. I thought— well, I wonder what the deacons are going to say.
>
> To be honest with you, there wasn't anything. He was the pallbearer at the head end of that casket, and he was black, and he was in the Baptist church in Tishomingo. Now, that doesn't seem like a big thing

now, but it was one of those things that changed everything. It changed the relationship between the town and Carter's Branch, the black community. That has just gone on and on and on and grown. There were a lot of things that came out of that. It took it another step. To me, the black-white thing never was an issue anyway.

After burying Kimberly, it became a time of healing in the community. But that wreck changed that whole community. I'm sure it all was there before, but everything—the compassion, the caring, the loving, hugging the necks—I'm talking about everybody. The community just rose up and by doing that, gave comfort to both families. It was little things but more than just bringing food and other things. People's attitudes changed. The attitude in that community became more loving, caring, compassionate.[22]

* * *

Paul Whitlock and David Lee Herbert never considered suing the other families involved in the accident. Both had been raised with the mentality that money gained in that matter "would basically never do you any good."[23] There was, though, another consideration that the two friends discussed, one that Paul Whitlock points to as one that defines the character of his friend:

We're also dealing with the fact that the young man that hit 'em, he was dead, so we knew his family was grieving. So we talk and we decided we need to do something. We need to reach out to that family, which to me said volumes about both families because Mrs. Herbert was in the hospital and in bad shape, and

Amy was still in Le Bonheur. Two dead. We took time to think about that other family. We talked. What do you want to do? We need to at least send something, some flowers or something to the funeral home with a card expressing that we're sorry for their loss. And we did that. We never got a response, but we never really expected one. We did it because we wanted to. That was Coach Herbert's nature. In the midst of all that was going on, he was still mindful that there are other people that are hurting, too.[24]

The Whitlocks attended Kimberly's funeral with their car already packed, ready to return to Memphis. As soon as the service was over, Paul and Phyllis drove to Memphis, hoping against hope that they would arrive to good news. Hospital officials met their questions at the door: How is Amy? Has there been any change?

Paul recalled their response: "'We're going to let you be the judge.' They took us back there. They told us to put our fingers in her hand. They said, 'Amy, squeeze your daddy's hand.' She squeezed. "That started the long, long road to recovery."[25]

Amy Whitlock stayed in a coma twenty-one days. The Whitlocks took her home with the prognosis that their daughter might never walk again and might easily never talk again, either. They were informed to be happy with whatever they got in her recovery. Phyllis undertook Amy's recovery as her personal mission, daily propping up Amy with pillows opposite a mirror in the same den where the football players had gathered just weeks before. She called her name while pointing to the mirror. One of the only signs of Christmas for the Whitlocks in 1985 was several visits from Eric and other members of the football team during their Christmas break. Months passed with Phyllis pointing into the mirror, saying "A-my" until one day, her parents heard what seemed like a grunt at first. It progressed into their daughter's looking at herself in the mirror and repeating, "Aaa-my."[26]

Amy Whitlock still carries scars, some physical disabilities, and a mild limp from the collision. As for the voice that she might have never used again, her daddy said, "She can outtalk me." Today, Amy has a younger sister who shares a middle name with Kimberly and a younger brother. A great deal of her mother's recovery from her own trauma from that November 1984 night in Alcorn County has been due to Amy's convalescence.[27]

14

ishomingo's 1984-85 senior class numbered fewer than forty and was hit hard with the loss of one of their most popular students. Lost in the priorities of life in the week following the accident, the Tishomingo football team prepared to face Smithville in the game that would decide whether or not they made the playoffs for the first time. Coach Herbert tried his best to juggle caring for his wife and daughters in the hospital and later at home, preparing for a funeral in Carrollton almost three hours away, taking care of Dave, and keeping up his family's house. The most important football game for which he had prepared took a precipitous drop on his priority list. A monumental team effort by his extended family and his community kept everything moving forward. Brad Howie would later say that forward was the only gear that the Herbert family had.

Phillip Whitehead remembered being approached by the school's administration, who asked whether or not the football players wanted to continue their season. He and the other seniors did not know the right thing to do, so they followed the lead of their coach, who felt like they needed to keep playing.[1] Perhaps Coach Herbert thought that the game, that football, would allow him and his school to escape their pain for a short time. Coach Kenneth McClain was Herbert's only assistant coach, and he prepared the team the best he could for their game. With as heavy a heart as he would ever carry on the sidelines, Herbert joined

McClain on the sideline to coach their team against Smithville the Friday night after the accident, trying to earn that first-ever berth in the playoffs for Tishomingo.

As so often happened in the Tishomingo-Smithville rivalry, the game came down to one key play. With Tishomingo players and fans wearing yellow armbands in Lauriann's honor, the Bulldogs took an early lead when Whitehead hit Powell with a twelve-yard touchdown pass. Chris Clay's extra point put Tish up 7-0, but Smithville countered with a touchdown and two-point conversion to take an 8-7 lead. The Bulldog defense prevented another score just before halftime with a fumble recovery deep inside their own territory. *Daily Journal* columnist Bill Ross noted that as the game progressed, Herbert was "getting more and more into the game."[2] For the whole team, it seemed, getting back on the field proved therapeutic, if only for a couple of hours.

On Smithville's first possession of the second half, the Seminoles again coughed up the football, and Whitehead recovered at the Smithville twenty-nine-yard line. Ronnie Ryan and Powell gobbled up the yardage on the ground, with Powell scoring from four yards out. Clay's extra point gave Tish a 14-8 lead in a game that earlier in the season seemed to mean much more than it did after the tragedy. Powell's interception return and Ryan's subsequent touchdown in the fourth quarter provided a little cushion, but the Seminoles struck back with a sixty-four-yard pass play to cut the Tishomingo lead to 20-14.[3]

Whitehead remembered getting the call from the sideline that Coach Herbert hoped would keep a late drive and last opportunity alive: "We were fourth and long. We had a play called to the short side of the field, an option-type play out of that Wing T. There was no place to go. Eric was playing tailback, and I pitched it to him. It was set up as a run play, but for some reason Lee Hollingsworth sprinted across the field. Powell saw it and threw it to him for a first down."[4] The converted quarterback's completion set up his four-yard touchdown run that gave Tish the 27-14 win and the school's first playoff berth.[5]

Even in the depths of the town's collective grief, football had provided a temporary balm. Coach Herbert continued to take time away from the practice field over the next week to care for Linda, who was released in time to travel to the playoff game that was played in Okolona. The night was cold and the field muddy, and she watched the best she could from the comfort of her car parked near the field.[6] In many ways, the 40-7 loss to Vardaman in the first round of the playoffs—a game that Powell dominated early on the defensive side of the ball before he exited the game with a knee injury—was a relief to an entire community trying to shoulder a piece of their coach's pain.[7]

* * *

When the 1984 football season came to an end, David Lee was able to focus all of his efforts on helping Linda recover. Even though she was in the clear as far as survival, her recovery would be long, and the doctors doubted she would ever walk again. Coach Herbert faced what promised to be a long, difficult winter. Months before he had made a commitment to his principal that he would take over coaching girls' basketball. Prior to the 1984-85 school year,

Danny McClung had been coaching boys' basketball, girls' basketball, and junior high basketball. When football season drew to a close, McClung approached him about finding another option.

> He just lost his daughter who would have been playing. I realized how difficult that would be for him. I asked him, 'Coach, do you feel good about doing this? We can work something else out if you don't feel good about doing it.' He said, 'No, I need to do it.' So he coached basketball that year.[8]

Grieving would not take its full effect on the family as a whole until they returned to their home in Carrollton for Christmas with their extended families. In the daily struggle to take care of the next thing in front of them for the better part of two months, the reality of the empty place at the table hadn't really set in until that Christmas. David Lee confided in his pastor some but kept most of his thoughts to himself. One person he spoke to was his old friend and cousin Bernard Taylor.

> He said that that was one of the most traumatic experiences he had ever had. Dave was with him on the bus and when they pulled up to the wreck, he didn't have a clue as to who it was until he saw the car. After that, he was just in total shock. He said he was always so thankful that Dave was with him because if Dave had been in the car, he would have been sitting between Lauriann and Linda and probably would have been killed too.
>
> David Lee handled that as well as anybody possibly could, I think. I remember after that happened—of course, Linda was still in a wheelchair—they came

home for Christmas. Our church always goes Christmas caroling, and we went down there the night that they came home for Christmas and caroled there. He was so appreciative of that. All of that time, David Lee was in a sense putting on a front for Linda, keeping her spirits up as much as he could. He was grieving so inside—I've always thought that was possibly one of the onsets of the ALS.

I never shall forget he said, "I've got a song that I want you to help me with because I want to sing it in church while I'm here." It was "He Was There All the Time." He sang that several times in the church. He always said that song meant a lot to him because it took him through that period of time that God was with him because he had a daughter who was dead, a wife in the hospital—who he didn't know would live or not—and two younger daughters in the hospital. He had to have Lauriann's funeral and burial, not knowing whether Linda was alive or not. As soon as we had the funeral and burial, he went right back. That was really a traumatic time for him.[9]

The Herberts stayed in their trailer beside the football field until the end of the spring semester of 1985. David Lee's mother had come to tend to the family's cooking and housework, so he could take care of Linda. Jase Melvin, the ag teacher, built a ramp on the concrete slab in front of their mobile home for Linda's wheelchair.[10] Others in the community continued to bring food. By the second semester, Linda was back in the classroom, parking her wheelchair by the overhead projector that she used to teach her math classes. David Lee wheeled her across the parking lot to her classroom and back every day as they continued to do what needed to be done.[11] In the course of Linda's rehabilitation, her injured leg grew back shorter than her other leg. After surgery to remove the rod in her leg, she depended on crutches for about a year. Melvin came to the rescue again, devising a wooden wedge to fit inside Linda's shoe to aid her balance.[12]

David Lee also did his due diligence as the girls' basketball coach. With only six or seven girls on his roster, he didn't win the state championship by any means, and McClung does not remember him talking about his emotions during the season. His actions, however, spoke volumes about his commitment to his word as he worked through his grief the best way he knew how—by continuing to move forward, however painful it might have been. "That was one of the things that said a lot about him," McClung said.[13]

In late spring following the accident, David Lee moved his family into a rental home in the Paden community between Tishomingo and Booneville. The house came complete with a pool, but Linda learned that her kids would rather travel back down through Tishomingo to the state park because that's where the other kids swam. That summer, Tishomingo High School's principal left the school, and McClung took over as principal. He already owned a house in Tishomingo, so he didn't need the one in the center of the school's campus provided for the principal. He offered it to the Herberts, and they moved back to town just months after they had left.[14]

David Lee's stress level continued to be off the charts for months after the accident. He cared for Linda, took on more responsibility at school, and moved his family twice, causing his sister Joyce to speculate, "You know with all that adrenaline circulating in his body for so many days, there's no telling what it did to his system."[15] Her brother would start showing initial signs of amyotrophic lateral sclerosis (ALS) less than two years later.

Fourth Quarter

15

Mike Talbert wrote a weekly preview of the 1A schools in the *Daily Journal* in 1988. On the Thursday before the Tishomingo-Smithville game, his headline read, "Key 1-1A Game May Turn into Shootout." Smithville faced elimination with a loss, but they entered the game with extreme confidence. Seminole quarterback Eric Spann had thrown for fourteen touchdowns in seven games and was coming off a five-touchdown game against division doormat Burnsville the previous week. Smithville was also carrying the momentum of a 44-32 win in the previous year's shootout, but the 1988 game was to be played in Tishomingo. Though both teams had put up big offensive numbers, they were a contrast in styles. Smithville favored an aerial attack versus Tishomingo's misdirection-based ground game. Both coaches claimed they were perplexed by the offensive schemes of the other, so an offensive shootout was almost guaranteed.[1]

* * *

Tishomingo's playoff hopes always seemed to boil down to the Smithville game. There was no love lost between the two programs; a pair of incidents in one game—allegedly precipitated by racist comments directed toward Powell by the Seminole head coach—had landed both teams on probation with the MHSAA a few years earlier. Kenneth McClain recalled, "One of the coaches for the other team reached up and grabbed Eric. That was a mistake. Eric knocked him to the ground. He never did grab Eric again."[2] The 1984 team had beaten Smithville in the last game of the season to secure the team's first playoff game. The Seminoles had "scalped" Tishomingo in 1985, a rebuilding year for the Bulldogs in which they finished 2-7, a year whose highlight was a come-from-behind win over Middleton (TN) on Tish's homecoming. The 1986 team, the second Tish team to make the playoffs, secured the berth in the season's first game. With the district split into small North and South divisions that year, the Bulldogs' 39-0 shellacking of county rival Burnsville in the season opener spoiled any drama about advancing to the postseason.[3] Smithville, playing on the other side of the division, came into the Tishomingo game as the North division champions with a record of 5-2. The Seminoles were favored over Tish, who had clinched the South side with the Burnsville win but had played to an overall record of 3-4.[4]

The first half of the 1986 Tishomingo-Smithville game—played on a Monday night at Tishomingo after heavy rains had postponed the Friday start—was the usual slugfest between the two teams but with more defense. Smithville scored early, but Tishomingo tied the game 6-6 when Brad Howie connected on a fifteen-yard touchdown pass to Bryant Southward. Big rushing performances from Bobby Brock, his brother Danny Brock, and Gary Walls powered a dominant second half for the Bulldogs in the surprisingly easy 27-6 win over the Seminoles.[5]

The win set up Tishomingo to play Vardaman in the first round of the playoffs. Vardaman, with a record of 3-7 coming into the game, hosted what was billed as an even match. Howie threw a seventeen-yard touchdown to Lee Hollingsworth for the first score of the game in the first quarter, but Vardaman bounced back with a touchdown run and extra point kick for a 7-6 second-quarter lead. Bobby Brock's two-yard run, followed by Howie's conversion pass to Sidney Bennett, put the Bulldogs up 14-7 at halftime. Vardaman came back to tie the game in the fourth quarter with a short run to complete a ninety-yard drive. The extra point kick was good, and the game headed to overtime with the Bulldogs still in search of their first playoff win.[6]

Tishomingo's defense barely averted defeat in the first overtime by blocking a twenty-three-yard field goal attempt to keep the game tied. In the second overtime, Vardaman faced fourth and goal from the one yard line and appeared to get into the end zone, but the referees judged that Bulldog defenders had stopped the Vardaman ball carrier's forward progress before he crossed the goal line, sending the game into a third overtime. In that extra period, Walls' three-yard touchdown run gave Tishomingo a 20-14 win. With what little energy that had left, the Bulldogs celebrated the first—and, ultimately, the only—playoff win in school history.[7] Tishomingo was paired with Falkner the following week in the state quarterfinals. The Bulldogs could not get any offense going against their future division mates in a 21-0 defeat that brought their 1986 season to a close. Falkner—a regular opponent on the Bulldog schedule until 1982—would become prominent in Tishomingo High School football history as a district opponent for the next two seasons.

* * *

Another significant part of the next two football seasons was the arrival of assistant coach Vince Jordan. Hired in 1986 as the school's head baseball coach, Jordan was a young coach from Ripley, Mississippi, who would serve as David Lee Herbert's assistant in football, as well. The Tish job was his first. Like Herbert, he was a disciplinarian with a passion for the game. He was impressed by Herbert's knowledge of his offense and was accustomed to the iron-man variety of football that small schools play from his background as a two-way player at Ripley.

A high school quarterback in a more traditional offense, Jordan picked up the Wing T quickly, but his penchant was defense. Multiple broken bones as a player had nurtured in him the idea that contact on the gridiron was better given than received. With just the two football coaches on staff, Jordan took charge of the varsity defense and, as the head junior high coach, became familiar with calling most of the same offensive plays that the varsity was running.[8]

Jeff Holt played junior high football and served as manager for the high school team. He remembered playing for Jordan as a young lineman looking to rise through the ranks to play high school football one day:

> Coach Jordan was serious about coaching. He had a passion and a drive to coach kids to get the very best out of them, not to be lollygaggers. I slacked playing one night at a junior high game, and the next practice,

I paid for it. After I finally got over all that running, he come to me and told me, "I didn't punish you just to be punishing you. I'm trying to make you a better athlete." In life I realize, looking back, what it was...to make me better and to help my team. I had the size to play, but he had a way to get that ability out of you, and at a small school, you had to be in shape enough to play multiple positions.[9]

Just like Falkner High School's arrival on the Tish football landscape, Jordan's presence in 1986 set the stage for a November night two seasons later to which the world would pay attention.

* * *

Tishomingo was close to returning to the playoffs during the 1987 season, but the shootout loss to Smithville had doomed them to third place in the district. However, when the Dixie Bowl in Sturgis came calling, it gave the Bulldogs another taste of postseason action. Scott Central provided a sturdy opponent. As it turned out, though, Tishomingo faced a more formidable opponent hours before the game. The pre-game meal served in the Sturgis cafeteria did a number on quite a few of the Tishomingo players.

Brad Howie was in the bathroom when he heard someone enter and rush toward the toilet to throw up. He didn't make it, heaving all over the floor. Howie walked out of his stall to find Coach Herbert doubled over in the middle of the floor. Coaching and playing at less than full strength, Herbert and his players suffered a 41-6 defeat at the hands of the Rebels.[10]

* * *

The week of the Smithville game in 1988 must have brought back recent memories from the series for Coach Herbert; he had only to go back to the 1987 game film to relive a scare. Chris Burrows covered that game for the *Daily Journal*. He recalled David Lee Herbert coaching from the sidelines with the use of a cane. "They had a play where a kid from Smithville picked off the ball and he was running down the Tish sideline. They tackled him and Coach Herbert was a few feet away, and it was like a snowball. He had no chance to get out of the way."[11]

As players recall the play so many years later, they still cringe. Assistant coach Vince Jordan doesn't remember how the play developed, but he still had a vision of the result:

> He got plastered. The play was coming to the sidelines, and I hit the road, but he couldn't get out of the way. I thought he was going to be able to get out of the way, but he just couldn't. He jumped up and said he was okay. As far as I remember, he went right back at it. After that it became, in my opinion, very dangerous for him to be on the sideline. His reaction time—his body just wouldn't let him."[12]

A few weeks later, expert neurologists would confirm what David Lee Herbert had first been told in August as the reason his mobility had declined so rapidly and why nothing he did to try to rehabilitate it was working.

* * *

Herbert's players and colleagues had noticed something had gone awry with his left leg before his family knew. Jordan remembers a practice shortly after his arrival in Tish in which he noticed the first hint of something amiss in Herbert's physical abilities. The Bulldog players were running forty-yard sprints, the standard for football speed, and the coaches were timing them. Jordan, still young and "full of pee and vinegar" stepped to the line to be timed in the forty. "I ran mine to see what mine would be, and Coach Herbert said, 'All right, let me go.' He ran and noticed something in his leg wasn't right. He nursed it several days and it just wasn't getting better. Then I think it even got worse driving a bus."[13]

Principal Danny McClung knew when Herbert first experienced then-undiagnosed symptoms of ALS. He remembered the progression:

> During football season, the football coach drove in the morning, and during basketball and baseball, he would drive in the afternoon. The other coach would work with him. I remember he started complaining. He started walking with Brother Gene, our pastor at the time. He started complaining about his calves and ankle. He started using the hot stuff that basketball players get. He thought it was from working the clutch. It just didn't get any better.
>
> Later, I noticed it at church. When he was walking down the aisle a couple of times, his foot was dragging. He began to get medical attention to determine what the problem was.[14]

* * *

Coach Herbert had wondered about the persistent issue with his foot. Every time he came to Carrollton, he had Anne look at it to see if she could figure out what might be causing the pain in the bottom of his foot. "If I looked at that foot one time, I looked at it a million times," she said.[15]

Anne had not seen her brother in several months when he came to their Uncle Alton's funeral. Earlier in the year, he had served as a pallbearer at his cousin Bernard Taylor's mother's funeral. Over the few months separating the funerals, the pain in his leg had worsened to the point that he had to use a cane.[16] Anne remembered seeing her brother's condition: "He was to be a pallbearer. When he walked in there dragging that leg, he was so pitiful that we were all appalled. He couldn't even stand up, and he had not told us."[17] Anne called Joyce in Michigan, and Joyce began to talk with David Lee about his condition. Joyce remembered, "He had an idea what was wrong."[18]

Not too long after he began to lose feeling in his leg, David Lee had read an article in *Sports Illustrated* about a coach in North Carolina who had ALS[19]. Even as he kept his suspicions from his family, he began to do his own research and come to his own conclusions. After getting the call from Anne, Joyce urged David Lee to come to Detroit to undergo a battery of tests at Henry Ford Hospital not too far from where she lived in order to catch whatever was troubling him as early as possible. At forty-five years old, her brother began to prepare for a diagnosis of Lou Gehrig's disease. When the doctor confirmed David Lee's suspicions and a Tupelo doctor's initial diagnosis of ALS, he sat quietly in his chair for a few moments, tears welling up in his eyes. Then, he looked at Linda and said, "I am not going to give up."

Linda responded, "We will fight this together."[20]

Stacie was in her father's American history class as an eighth grader when the pain in his foot moved rapidly toward limiting his mobility and led to his diagnosis. "His walking was very jerky. He was very unsteady. He fell a good bit. Through that year he went from being able to walk to being on his Rascal a lot."[21] The personal mobility scooter would transport David Lee through spring practice, summer workouts, and his final season as a football coach a year later.

* * *

Looking forward to preparation for the 1988 football season that was to begin with spring practice, David Lee paid a visit to his principal. McClung related the progression from David Lee's diagnosis in the fall of 1987 to the school's plan for the 1988 football season:

> So he wants to talk to me one day and tells me the diagnosis. What do you say back to a person who has told you something like that? We talked for a few minutes, and I told him, "I don't know of anything that I can say other than this: I'm going to treat you like I've always treated you. I'll be here to help, whatever I can do." His condition had gotten worse over the summer. Toward the end of the 1987 school year, his teaching situation was a concern.[22]

Coach McClung urged him to retire early because if Herbert died while still actively teaching, his family's payout would be less than it would be if he had just retired. "He sure wanted to coach one more year because his son would be a senior," McClung said. The two worked out a situation where Coach Herbert would retire but then come back as a type of adjunct coach. "We paid him a dollar to be an adjunct, and he got his little Rascal and was able to move around pretty good with that. His assistant, Vince Jordan, had to do most of the running for everything. They worked well and had been successful."[23]

For Coach Herbert, his 1987 diagnosis started the clock that would allow one last season with his Tishomingo Bulldogs, one last season to coach his son. A head football coach and his offensive coordinator, by necessity, form a special kind of bond with their starting quarterback. David Lee Herbert was both head coach and offensive coordinator, and the bond that he had with his senior quarterback in 1988 would carry over to the dinner table.

If any animosity had ever existed from Dave Herbert toward his father and head coach, the son could not have escaped it. David Lee taught him social studies every year through ninth grade and coached him through his six years at Tishomingo. Not only that, Linda Herbert taught him math each year from seventh grade through graduation. Asked if he felt like he had little room for error, Dave responded that he thought nothing of what others might have seen as suffocating; it was all he knew and all that several other players on the team with parents in the school system knew. Furthermore, he considered the familial relationships he had with all his teachers and coaches an advantage. "They want the kids to do as well as they can do, and you've got that personal relationship, so you might get a little more attention in the classroom and with your classwork. I wouldn't change a thing; I'd go back and do it all over again."[24]

FOURTH QUARTER

* * *

Coach David Lee Herbert's focus in mid-October of 1988 was how to outscore Smithville's potent offense. While the city of Los Angeles celebrated the Dodgers' World Series win behind the iconic pinch-hitting heroics of Kirk Gibson, two tiny Mississippi teams known for their offensive prowess were looking for a little bit of defense to move a big step closer toward a playoff berth. The fireworks did not take long. Tishomingo's Shane Hill returned the opening kickoff eighty-eight yards for a touchdown, and the slugfest began in earnest. Both teams scored three times in the first half, and the Bulldogs took a 22-21 lead into the locker room. Hill scored a second touchdown on a short run, and Danny Brock added a four-yard TD run. Herbert and Hill each ran for a two-point conversion.

Smithville's versatile quarterback Eric Spann, who led his team to 426 yards of total offense in the game, ran two yards for his second touchdown of the night to give the Seminoles the lead in the second half. Jimmy McClanahan booted a thirty-seven-yard field goal to increase his team's lead to eight heading into the fourth quarter. Tishomingo responded by driving sixty-five yards and scoring on Herbert's sneak. Brock broke several tackles to get into the end zone on the conversion to tie the game 30-30. With time winding down, Tishomingo's defense gave the offense one more try to win the game in regulation. With thirty-two seconds remaining, Dave Herbert heaved a deep ball, but Joseph Freeman of Smithville intercepted his pass at his team's thirty-one-yard line and returned it to the Tishomingo twenty-nine. Spann completed a screen pass for fourteen yards to set up a thirty-two-yard field goal try with four seconds remaining. McClanahan's kick flew just inside the right upright for the game winner. The interception that led to the field goal was Tishomingo's only turnover of the night.

Smithville's 33-30 win kept the Seminoles' playoff hopes alive. Tishomingo, on the other hand, had a much more complicated route to the postseason, but one part of their path was sure: they had to beat division-leading Falkner. Smithville, meanwhile, had played the toughest part of their division schedule. After the game Coach Dwight Boling said, "It was a great football game, especially for the fans. Now, we've got to beat Burnsville and see what happens with Tish and Falkner. But this division race is a long way from being over yet." Coach Herbert knew his team could have all but clinched a playoff berth with a win and called the long pass late in the game with that in mind. "We had to try the deep pass. It was just a great return to set up the field goal. Our kids played their hearts out." Far from giving up hope, he said, "We're still in it, and I think our kids will bounce back from this."[25]

* * *

A couple of close calls notwithstanding, the upper and lower tiers of the division were remarkably defined. With two weeks to go, Falkner was undefeated in division play, and Tishomingo and Smithville had one loss each. The other four teams had a collective overall record of 1-29. That lone win belonged to Thrasher over winless Burnsville. Thrasher held the last opportunity to be the fly in the ointment of the Division 1-1A standings if the Rebels could pull off an upset of Falkner. They had come close to knocking off Tishomingo when the Bulldogs returned to the field after consecutive open dates earlier in the season. As expected, though, Falkner continued its divisional dominance to set up the Eagles' showdown with Tishomingo that would decide the fate of three teams. The Smithville game would not be Tishomingo's last to come down to the final play of the game.

16

Spring practice in 1988 brought the beginning of new roles for the Tishomingo football team. With Coach Herbert not able to physically take part in practice like he had in the past, Vince Jordan—fresh off his baseball team's playoff appearance—took on a greater on-field role. He remembered Herbert's honesty with himself and with Jordan about the limitations that his disease had already imposed on him and how they would only become more constricting over the following summer and fall. "We had a very good, trusting relationship. He allowed me flexibility because he knew that he couldn't do everything he needed to do. That was the thing about him—he was honest about it." The two began to work on practice strategies together, with Jordan drawing them up with Herbert's input.[1]

Jordan, married by his second season at the school, considered leaving Tishomingo after the 1987-88 school year but changed his mind after a conversation with Herbert. "I wanted to be there to help him through it because I knew how important it was. I wanted to stay for Dave's senior year." The bond forged between the coach and assistant coach was a special one based on mutual loss. Herbert took Jordan into his confidence about his struggles with Lauriann's death, which had happened two football seasons before Jordan arrived in Tish. In February of 1987, Jordan's father passed away from cancer at the age of forty-nine. Jordan will never forget how Herbert's understanding helped him fill the void of a father who was never able to watch him coach a game.[2] With Herbert's diagnosis, he would be able to offer his head coach something in return.

* * *

The United States Department of Health and Human Services defines amyotrophic lateral sclerosis as "a rare neurological disease that affects nerve cells (neurons) in the brain and spinal cord that control voluntary muscle movement." The gut punch for those diagnosed with ALS and their families and loved ones is at the end of the first paragraph of the department's informational pamphlet on the disease: "The disease is progressive, meaning the symptoms get worse over time. Currently, there is no cure for ALS and no effective treatment to halt, or reverse, the progression of the disease."[3]

A number of notable people have died from complications from ALS. On June 4, 2018, former San Francisco 49ers wide receiver Dwight Clark succumbed to the disease at age sixty-one. Most famous for his game-winning touchdown—dubbed simply "The Catch"—against the Dallas Cowboys in the 1981 NFC Championship game, Clark remains an iconic figure for a San Francisco franchise that won five Super Bowls between 1981 and 1994.[4] The cruel irony of the two-time All-Pro receiver's battle with ALS was that the disease began to manifest itself in his hands. One day, they refused to tear open a sugar packet, and he was diagnosed shortly afterward, leading to his very public battle with the disease that ended in the summer of 2018.[5]

Unlike Clark, actor and playwright Sam Shepard kept his plight with ALS out of the public eye. An actor in over fifty films and a playwright with more than fifty-five works to his credit, Shepard continued to write between his diagnosis in 2015 and his death in the summer of 2017. In his early days with ALS, Shepard was able to type his own words, but he turned to dictation in his latter days. Though he crafted characters to reflect his struggle, at the time of his death at age seventy-three, only his closest professional relations, family, and friends even knew of his diagnosis.[6]

British actor David Niven was diagnosed with motor neuron disorder (MND)—as ALS is called in the United Kingdom—in 1981 after he had problems falling while working on a movie set. Niven is best remembered for his portrayal of Phileas Fogg in the Michael Todd film adaptation of the Jules Verne classic novel *Around the World in Eighty Days*, as well as his work in the *Pink Panther* movies. Niven's public slurred speech as a result of the disease led to rumors of drunkenness and stroke. He resisted hospitalization and passed away just two years later at his home in Switzerland. Similar to how ALS in known as Lou Gehrig's disease in the United States, it is known as David Niven's disease in Europe.[7]

Of course, professional baseball player Lou Gehrig is most famously associated with amyotrophic lateral sclerosis. Gehrig was the great New York Yankee first baseman who in 1925 stepped in for starter Wally Pipp, who had a headache. Pipp would later comment that he took the two most expensive aspirins in history. Gehrig went on to play every game at the position until his retirement in 1939, an incredible 2,130 consecutive games. The "Iron Horse's" record stood for over half a century until Cal Ripken, Jr., of the Baltimore Orioles surpassed it on September 6, 1995. Gehrig's capsule on the Baseball Hall of Fame website reads like a made-up player on a video game:

- ◆ Scored at least 100 runs and drove in over 100 runs for thirteen straight seasons.

- ◆ Eight seasons of at least 200 hits (and this in the 154-game season era as opposed to today's 162-game schedule)

- ◆ Won baseball's Triple Crown in 1934 by batting .363 with forty-nine home runs and 166 runs batted in.

- ◆ Selected to the All-Star team every year from its creation in 1933 until his retirement.

- ◆ Along with fellow superstar Babe Ruth, led the Yankees to seven American League pennants and six World Series championships during his seventeen-year career. [8]

Gehrig is generally considered by baseball writers and fans alike to be the greatest first baseman to ever play the game. After a start to the 1939 season that was well below his lofty standards because of unexplained neurological issues, Gehrig announced his retirement in a speech that became the stuff of legend. Yankee Stadium echoed his famous words: "Today (today), I consider myself (myself) the luckiest man (man) on the face of the earth (earth)." Soon after, amyotrophic lateral sclerosis became known more commonly in America as Lou Gehrig's disease. [9]

For decades after Gehrig's retirement and his death in 1941, the public knew little of ALS except that it was a mysterious and fatal neuromuscular disease that carried a Yankee All-Star's name. The Ice Bucket Challenge of the summer of 2014 purposed to educate the masses about the disease. Spawned by the ALS Society, the Ice Bucket Challenge prodded individuals to post videos on social media of being doused by a bucket of ice cold water to raise awareness of ALS and to raise funding for research. The challenge went viral, with ALS Society statistics through 2017 claiming over seventeen million uploaded Facebook videos with ten billion views by over 440 million people.[10] In addition to raising over $115 million for ALS research in the summer of 2014—tripling the annual amount spent on research before 2014—ALS awareness has expanded exponentially. Though no longer the viral sensation that it was during that first summer, the Ice Bucket Challenge has become an annual event, taking place in August each year.[11]

The usual life expectancy from an ALS diagnosis is three to five years after initial diagnosis. British physicist Stephen Hawking died on March 14, 2018, at the age of seventy-six, fifty-five years after being diagnosed with ALS. Hawking's extremely rare longevity included over thirty years as a mathematics professor at the University of Cambridge and a position as director of research at the school past the age of seventy. Hawking, who communicated through a computer by the use of his cheek, is not, however, a case study for all ALS patients. A tiny percentage of ALS patients like Hawking progress very slowly through the typical neuromuscular symptoms of the disease. It is likely, too, that Hawking's age at diagnosis played a significant role in his longevity. Though Hawking was able to afford the best medical care available and the round-the-clock care that he required for decades, his care is also not believed to be a significant factor in his endurance.[12] Even with outlying cases like Hawkings', the life expectancy for persons diagnosed with ALS has remained about the same.

Amyotrophic lateral sclerosis is a cruel, unrelenting disease. It usually alerts its victims through symptoms that might be dismissed as clumsiness. Slurred speech often follows, possibly giving the appearance of drunkenness, like with Niven. ALS is a disease of the nervous system that gradually destroys the motor neurons that allow the body to move. It is progressive in nature, shutting down one muscular function after another but, surprising to many, leaving its victim with the ability to use some of his or her senses.

One of the major steps that most ALS patients take is some type of breathing assistance, similar to a device that might help someone with sleep apnea. As ALS progresses, its patients often face a decision of whether or not to have a tracheostomy, which creates a hole in the front of the neck so that a respirator can inflate and deflate the lungs through the windpipe. A feeding tube helps ALS patients avoid problems related to malnutrition and dehydration during advanced-stage ALS, at which point an ALS patient requires full-time assistance. Death most often comes when the disease eventually reaches the muscles that control breathing.[13] According to the Mayo Clinic, between 5 and 10 percent of ALS cases are hereditary, while potential sources of the remainder are unknown. Among the possibilities that researchers are pursuing are gene mutations, chemical imbalances, disorganized immune responses, and protein mishandling. Researchers are also looking into environmental factors like smoking and exposure to various chemicals, though nothing has yet yielded a promising connection to ALS.[14]

* * *

David Lee had coached Dave since he started playing football in seventh grade. Those years included a pair of losing seasons. The Weirs and Pucketts and Stringers of small-school Mississippi football lore notwithstanding, single-A schools rarely build dynasties. The nature of football in the smallest classification was waiting on the next class with a few athletes around which to build and often suffering through a losing season or two in the process. At the end of football season at a tiny school, the coach rarely has the luxury of looking at empty positions and moving underclassmen up the depth chart. Instead, as Coach Herbert did at Tishomingo after each group of seniors graduated, he looked at the players he would have the following season and moved them around to the positions that he thought would give his team their best opportunity to win games.

David Lee had twice moved Dave from his natural tight end position to quarterback when he was the best option for the team. Though the younger Herbert and left tackle Grant Horn were the only players on the 1988 team to weigh in at over two hundred pounds, Dave Herbert knew the offense backward and forward and from any position on the field. In addition, he must have been one of very few quarterbacks in the state to turn around and play defensive end on defense. About the position change, Dave said, "Back then, you did what the coaches told you. Nowadays, you show up and tell the coach what you want to do."[15]

Brad Howie, a year ahead of Dave Herbert, had been the quarterback throughout his career at Tishomingo. Howie was the better passer of the two, and his presence as the team's signal caller allowed Dave to play his more natural tight end position. Dave's only other stint as a signal caller came during his freshman year, when ninth graders still played on the junior high team. When Howie moved up to the varsity squad, Dave quarterbacked the junior high team that marked the first step into competitive football for a number of seventh graders who grew into the sophomores who would bolster the 1988 roster. Dave Herbert never desired to play quarterback, knowing that his skills of the offensive side of the ball were better served as a run blocker from the edge and as a big pass target near the end zone. However, his knowledge of the Wing T and his ability to get his teammates in the right places to make the most of their talents necessitated the move, which he never resisted.

Dave was not the only Bulldog player getting comfortable with a new position for the 1988 season. Sophomores Terry Enlow and Shane Hill had played tackle and guard, respectively, on the undefeated and unscored-upon junior high team from the year before. Both were moved to the backfield for their tenth grade seasons. Hill called his switch from left guard to his new wingback position was a relatively easy one because of the simplicity of the offense that he had already run for three years—albeit from another position. The transition from the junior high to the varsity team was also a smooth one since the players had been on the same field as one another.[16] Furthermore, most of the older players had played with the younger players at some point in their short football careers.

For four years Coach Herbert had been able to instill his system with the 1988 seniors without the effects of ALS. The 1987 season had brought about some changes, like his needing a cane for assistance. In preparation for the 1988 season—which would be the last for them all at Tishomingo and the first in which he would not coach the junior high team—David Lee relied heavily on his seniors to be his hands and feet in teaching the younger players. They would run little, if anything, on offense that they had not already been running since seventh grade. The roster numbers of the 1988 team dictated half-line scrimmages as the most effective means for the Bulldog offense to run its plays against some of the Bulldog defensive starters. Even then, the backside action of the Wing T is an important aspect of its success, so the Tishomingo offense had to depend upon the game experience of its upperclassmen to propel them toward their goal of the state playoffs.

* * *

The games of the 1988 season required a number of further accommodations for Coach Herbert. The football boosters and others in the community rallied to build a ramp and a landing on the side of the press box onto which he could drive his Rascal. From there, he had a safe vantage point from which to see the game and to communicate with Coach Jordan on the sidelines. Road games were a bit more complicated until someone offered a flatbed truck. At each road game, the truck was backed up as close to the field as possible, and a team of men would lift Coach Herbert and his Rascal atop the flatbed. Linda also adjusted her routine of prior years. Where she had once sat in the stands and cheered, she now sat with David Lee and became his hands and feet. The men who had hoisted him up to his coaching perch were never far away, either.

* * *

Through her assisting her husband, Linda came to know football in a way she had never known before. She knew that football, at its core, was "all these little circles and X's." When David Lee was at Itta Bena early in his career, he began to put together his playbook and had Linda draw up the plays for him. Occasionally in her math class, when her football players were talking about a recent game, she would turn to the chalkboard and draw up a play, though she couldn't have told them exactly what it meant. "They thought I knew everything about football. I probably would have enjoyed it more if I had studied it." One thing she knew for sure about those X's and O's: If those football players in her class could learn all those football plays and who to block and so forth, there was no reason they couldn't pass school, particularly her math class.[17]

Along with his wife's help and that of his group of men and his seniors, Coach Herbert leaned heavily on Vince Jordan as the only coach on the sidelines in 1988. Jordan was tasked with calling most of the plays, handling substitutions on both sides of the ball, tending to injuries, and maintaining order. Dave Herbert remembers Jordan's effectively managing the increased chaos of a Friday night on the Tishomingo sidelines:

Everybody knew what to do, so there weren't any issues on the sideline like people goofing off or anything like that. When you're a small school with twenty-something players and everybody's playing, you pay attention to the game and stay ready when it's time for you to go in, so you don't have the extracurriculars on the sideline. Coach Jordan pretty much had control of the sidelines.[18]

Jordan communicated with Coach Herbert through the back-up quarterback, who wore a headset and listened for any instructions from Herbert. Those were the days when players ran the plays from the sideline to the huddle, so Jordan called most of the plays himself and sent them to his quarterback on the field.

From a strictly football standpoint, the shifting of roles of the coaches did nothing to dampen the team's expectations for the 1988 season. The year began with the same goal as in previous seasons: win the district and go to the playoffs. Vince Jordan remembered thinking Tish's chances were as good as anyone else's:

We were still thinking we were going to be pretty good. For 1A, we had a good little run of athletes. Anytime you run the Wing T, you give yourself a chance. We had a bunch of gritty kids. They really worked hard. We got them in the weight room, and they started seeing some results from the weights. It started making a difference, and they started believing in themselves.[19]

* * *

The effects of Coach Herbert's ALS intensified as the season progressed. He tried his best to deal with his disease and still give as much as he could to the football team, Dave Herbert was a starting quarterback seeing the physical capacities of his father and coach diminish by the week. Phillip Whitehead, two quarterbacks ahead of the younger Herbert in the Tishomingo football legacy, spent time with Dave as he came up through the ranks. He remembered Dave's shouldering the stress of his father's condition with a quiet strength.

> Dave didn't wear anything like a pity party. I think, if anything, it made him have a stronger constitution and a stronger identity at a younger age about who he was, where he was going, what he was going to do— just a good-spirited guy. I don't know if I ever met anybody that didn't like Dave Herbert. He reminds me of his dad, same spirit and personality.[20]

Dave Herbert's leadership on and off the field and his ability to move forward despite his father's difficulties was a catalyst for the 1988 squad that had much more for which to play than the typical senior class.

17

The break at the end of the third quarter seemed to be just what the Tishomingo defense needed to counter the Falkner running game that had dominated the second half. Always known more for their offense than their defense, Tishomingo High School's 1988 roster listed only the players' offensive positions with their height, weight, and class. Dave Herbert played defensive end and outside linebacker. Running backs Danny Brock, Shane Hill, and Terry Enlow played linebacker. Bryant Southward was the team's leading receiver and one of its key defensive backs. Hill and Brock returned kicks, and Hill was the team's punter. Herbert kicked the team's handful of extra points before his coach cast aside that part of his team's arsenal in favor of the two-point conversion.

On the first play of the fourth quarter, the Bulldogs stuffed the Falkner fullback in the middle of the line for no gain. On second and ten, the Eagle running back could only gain two on an option pitch around left end. Facing third and long, Falkner quarterback Tyrone Gaillard took to the air for only the second time in the game, and like his first attempt, the pass across the middle was incomplete. Facing fourth and eight from the Tishomingo twenty-six, Eagle coach Joe Horton decided to punt. Perhaps he felt that the game's momentum had swung enough to his side's favor that his defense would stop Tish again, and they could get the ball back in great field position. Perhaps he considered his own team's conservative approach in the first half with poor field position and wanted to give Tishomingo a taste of playing in the shadow of its own end zone. Whatever the case, the high, wobbly punt toward the right sideline covered seventeen yards and went out of bounds at the Tishomingo nine yard line.

The Bulldog ground game roared back to life in the fourth quarter as senior Danny Brock carried behind left tackle John Moore for gains of eight and five for a Bulldog first down and a little breathing room. Vince Jordan recalled how "smash mouth" the game was, a good physical football game.[1] He continued to send in plays that challenged the Tishomingo line to push back the bigger, quicker Falkner defensive front. Horn called the Falkner team—a team that his Bulldogs hated in a high school football version of *hate*—one that commanded their respect.[2]

Terry Enlow and Mark Blunt stayed behind the left side of the Tish line for pickups of five and six and another first down. Shane Hill rushed over right guard for five yards on first down, but Brock was stopped on a trap play over left tackle for just one to bring up the first third down of the drive. Quarterback Dave Herbert continued to feed Brock over the left side, first for seven yards and a first down and—after a four-yard pickup by Enlow—for gains of four, four, and one. Facing fourth and one from the Falkner forty-four yard line, Brock dove over right guard for two yards to keep the drive alive.

On first and ten, Herbert dropped back and heaved a deep pass that went right between the arms of a Falkner defender, who flailed his arms in frustration. A flag in the backfield would have penalized Tishomingo for holding, but Coach Horton elected to decline the penalty and bring up second down with ten yards still to go. On the next play, Herbert set up a screen pass to the speedy Hill. The pass fell incomplete, but the Falkner defense was flagged for a late hit on Hill behind the line of scrimmage. It was the only accepted penalty of the game to that point, a monumental one that Horton would argue after the game was unnecessary. Nevertheless, the penalty gave Tishomingo a first down at the Eagle thirty-one. Brock gained four over the left side. Running behind Moore on the next play, Brock broke into the clear and scored the go-ahead touchdown from twenty-seven yards out. The senior running back carried around left end one more time for a successful two-point conversion. With just 3:27 remaining in the game, Tishomingo led 16-8. That seemingly left a highly run-dependent Falkner offense one more chance to try to cut the deficit to within the necessary four points for the Eagles to win the division.

Disaster struck for the Eagles on the kickoff when their kick returner struggled to pick up the ball that bounced crazily deep in his team's territory. He eventually tucked it away but not before retreating to the ten yard line, where he was tackled by several Bulldog defenders. After a fullback dive up the middle netted only a yard, Gaillard breathed life into his team by escaping for a forty-four-yard quarterback keeper around the left side. Enlow made a touchdown-saving tackle for the Bulldogs, but just like that, Falkner had moved into Tishomingo territory. On the next play, Gaillard tried to break around the left end again, but this time Horn met him just across the line with a jarring hit that knocked the ball free. Senior Bulldog outside linebacker Antony Oaks pounced on the loose ball. Tishomingo took over on their own forty-four yard line and needed a single first down to run out the clock and claim the district championship.

Hill ran behind the right side of the Bulldog line for no gain on first down. Brock was stopped after a pickup of two behind left guard. Hill ran again on a counter play to the right side of the line on third down and lost four yards. Still, as Hill dropped back to punt, the Bulldogs carried all the game's momentum as the seconds continued to tick off the clock. However, just as a bad snap had benefitted Tishomingo early in the second quarter, one of their own changed the course of the game yet again. The errant snap flew over Hill's head, and both teams raced for the ball. Hill reached it first and fervently booted it away. The punt netted just eleven yards, and the Eagles had a spark of hope.

On the first play of what he hoped would be his team's pivotal drive, Falkner quarterback Gaillard went back to the left side where he had been so successful until the fumble on the previous drive, picking up five yards. On second down Coach Horton called the same pass play on which his quarterback had misfired to an open receiver late in the first half. This time, Gaillard launched a perfect pass into the waiting arms of wide-open Stacey Edgeston, who caught the aerial in stride and covered the rest of the fifty-eight yards to the end zone to cut the Tishomingo lead to two.

With the necessary point spread safely covered for his team's playoff tiebreaker, Coach Horton elected to kick for the extra point instead of going for two and the tie, a maneuver that went largely unrecognized in the press coverage of the game. No doubt the tiebreaker factored into his decision. No doubt many Falkner fans were befuddled by their coach's choice to go for one and still trail by a point if the kick was successful. The kick sailed wide, though, leaving Falkner behind 16-14 and setting up a last-gasp effort by Tishomingo to score a miracle touchdown to make the playoffs. In an odd twist to the usual angst of a close football game in its waning moments, the desperation was squarely on the team *with* the lead.

* * *

Reporter Chris Burrows recalled the excitement of the game's playoff implications. "Tiebreakers in football were kind of a new thing. People forget that they weren't playing high school playoff games in Mississippi until 1981, and this was 1988. We were learning on the fly." The playoff-caliber teams in most districts were apparent but not in 1A football in north Mississippi. Burrows remembers, "District 1-1A teams were in a spot. Quite frankly, there wasn't much difference between all the teams in that division—just who played well on a given night."[3] Unlike many divisions in contemporary Mississippi high school football that have only four teams, Division 1-1A boasted six schools and a far greater likelihood that ties of this nature would occur at season's end.

Joe Horton was taking no chances on a long return by the Bulldogs on the ensuing kickoff, so the Falkner kicker booted the ball hard along the ground. A Tishomingo player fell on the ball at the Bulldog forty-eight yard line. Herbert's pass on first down fell incomplete. Brock took a quick pitch for a gain of sixteen and a first down at the Falkner thirty-six. Herbert's screen pass to Brock netted only a yard, bringing up second down and nine yards to go. The bigger issue for the Bulldogs, however, was that the clock had ticked down to seven seconds, leaving time for one last play. Of the option that some teams might have had the luxury of considering at that point in the game, Dave Herbert said, "Nobody in Tishomingo County could kick a fifty-two yard field goal."[4]

* * *

After the Falkner touchdown and missed extra point a few real-time minutes earlier in the game, a message from a group of the "Tishomingo think tank" in the stands made its way to Coach Herbert's spot on the flatbed truck and eventually to the sideline: "What would a safety do here?" A safety on the last play of the game—for certain a bizarre call from the opponent's thirty-five yard line—would tie the score and send the game into overtime, giving the Bulldogs a chance to win by the necessary points to secure a playoff berth... and an equal chance of losing the game outright. It was up to Dave Herbert to communicate the wrong-way play call in the Tishomingo huddle.

The Bulldog signal caller remembered getting the play from the sideline:

> When the play came in—I can't remember who brought it in—they said, "All right, here's what your daddy said to do." My big ol' tackle was like, "Yo' damn daddy's done gone crazy." Originally, the play called for me to take the ball and turn and run it back to the end zone. I changed it just a little bit because they were faster than I was. In the huddle I told Danny Brock that I was going to turn and pitch it to him, and he would turn around and run. Well, he

didn't want to do it. I don't guess he understood or just didn't want to do it. You can see on the film, right there before the play, I was turning around telling him, "I'm throwing it to you," and he was saying, "I'm not doing it. "[5]

During the disagreement between the younger Herbert and his running back and the ensuing chaos as the Tishomingo signal caller tried to rally his team around the play, the Bulldogs were assessed two delay of game penalties to move the ball back to the Falkner forty-five. Looking back, Brock admitted that he was paralyzed by the thought, *what if it doesn't work*?[6]

Thirty years after the fact, John Moore, the left tackle who had paved the way for the go-ahead touchdown, voiced the thoughts of several in the huddle that night after they had fought hard for four quarters to gain a two-point advantage over a team they had never beaten: "Coach Herbert had so much confidence in us as a team, he threw away a win. I'll be honest, I would have just taken the win."[7] Grant Horn, the big tackle who questioned his coach's sanity in the huddle that night, remembered the game being a dogfight from the beginning whistle to the end, just as it was every year against Falkner. "They had those Prathers at running back, and they would flat run over you. Falkner was our nemesis." Horn realized the necessity to win by four, but after doing battle in the trenches for the better part of two hours, he was not thinking about point spreads. "We knew it, but to beat 'em, that was our ultimate goal, regardless if by one point. Coach Herbert, he was doing all the figuring in his head, but we wanted to win."[8]

Indeed, though Tishomingo led the overall series 11-7 going into the 1988 matchup, this group of seniors had never beaten the Eagles and viewed them as a next-level team. The two schools were located about sixty miles apart but had nevertheless developed a rivalry that dated back to 1966. In Tishomingo's first football season that year, Falkner took a 28-0 victory. Though the record of wins and losses in the series was close, the games rarely were, with just four contests decided by less than a touchdown. In 1972, Tishomingo's 8-0 win was part of an undefeated season for the Bulldogs. The 1974 game had been a highlight of the series, with Tish claiming a 44-42 win over Falkner in a shootout. In between those two Bulldog wins, Falkner had trounced Tish, 69-0, and the year after, they won by three touchdowns. After Tishomingo's 12-6 win in 1982—the last before David Lee Herbert arrived at Tish—the rivalry took a hiatus, though the teams met in the playoffs in 1986. The extent of the 1988 seniors' participation in the rivalry amounted to that 21-0 defeat and a 19-13 loss in 1987 when the teams first played in the same district. Now, Dave Herbert could have kneeled and won the game. Instead, David Lee Herbert and Vince Jordan led their team to play for a division crown and a spot in the MHSAA 1A playoffs.[9]

* * *

At last, the Bulldogs stepped to the line to run what would need to be a miracle play. By that time Vince Jordan made sure the Bulldog ball carrier knew not to take a knee until he heard the buzzer sound. Dave Herbert barked out the signals, finally taking the snap. Shane Hill had already turned his hips toward his own end zone when Herbert turned to toss him the ball. Hill kept his shoulders square with his quarterback long enough to secure the ball before taking off on a lonely fifty-five yard dash that caused all the cheering on both sides to cease. Tony Dawson, the ball boy for Tishomingo, tried to match strides with the Bulldog sophomore, hollering, "Hey, Shane, you're going the wrong way!"[10]

As Hill raced for his own end zone, Falkner Coach Joe Horton recognized what was happening. Joe Tucker, the senior tight end who alternated running plays to the huddle, was on the Tish sideline during the wrong-way play. "I was watching the other coach during that play; I just happened to see him over there. Shane got about ten yards back, and that's when the coach knew; he took his hat and flung it."[11] Jordan watched his counterpart across the field put his hands on his head and let loose an expletive.[12] Hill did not notice the opposing coach, but as he raced down the field, he did see several of the Falkner players with their helmets off and befuddled looks on their faces as they tried to figure out just what was unfolding before them.[13]

Other than the faces of a few of his opponents, Hill was focused on nothing but the end zone. As he sprinted for his own end zone, he was unaware of whether or not he was being chased. He did not look over his shoulder as he ran, not about to slow down until he reached a different kind of pay dirt than he had ever experienced in a football game. Asked what he expected to see when he turned around, Hill said, "I was expecting to see somebody close to me. The closest one to me was one of my teammates." When Hill crossed his own goal line, finishing the play with a pop-up slide that should have made baseball coach Jordan proud, both sides of the stadium were left in disbelief. Even the ebullient female Falkner fan sitting near the Tishomingo camera stood silent, shocked, unable to let out another of her countless shouts of "Let's go, Eagles!" It didn't occur to Hill at the time that he had just become part of a moment bigger than the game, one that would stand as the greatest play in his school's history.[14] The sophomore would finish the night with ten carries for negative twenty-six yards, his final carry of the game broadcast nationally by the weekend and written about for decades afterward.

Freshman Stacie Herbert was in the visitors' stands with much of the rest of the town of Tishomingo that night in Falkner when both sides were stunned by "the play":

> We always went to the football games; that was just what you did in a small town, even when your dad wasn't the coach. We were there in the bleachers cheering; we all pretty much lost our voices from screaming. When the play was called, nobody knew what was going on. Everybody was cheering and then they stopped cheering, like we couldn't figure it out. When he went the wrong way, we were like, what in the world? It was quite exciting.
>
> Whoever it was that was around Dad—some of the older gentlemen—knew and kind of told everybody that is was on purpose. By the time it went into overtime, everybody had figured out it wouldn't have done any good if we had just won; we had to win by a certain amount. As students we didn't exactly understand that part... for us a win was a win. It was a big deal, but I don't think anybody would have ever thought that it would have gone as crazy as it did.[15]

Horton was gracious about the ingenuity of the play after the game, giving credit to the Tishomingo side for finding a way to push their way into the playoffs. In pre-game interviews with Mike Talbert from the *Daily Journal*, both coaches came ominously close in their coach speak to predicting the way the game would play out. Herbert predicted that Tish would be in trouble if they allowed Falkner more than two touchdowns. Horton said, "Tishomingo is a good team. This game may come down to that one play again."[16]

As David Lee Herbert and Joe Horton prepared their squads for overtime, the playoff scenario was still muddled. In most high school overtimes, the goal is as simple as outscoring the opponent. Under high school overtime rules, both teams have an opportunity to possess the ball from the opponents' ten-yard line—that is, unless the team on defense scores first or unless the offensive team gives up a safety. The idea that Falkner might try to copy his strategy crossed Coach Herbert's mind as he prepared for overtime. He had to prepare for a Falkner touchdown and missed conversion, in which case he would want his offense to score but miss the conversion to send the game into another overtime period. With playoff berths still very much on the line, the strategy going into the extra time was anything but simple.

* * *

Overtime. Brice Durbin thought there had to be a better way to break ties after regulation than the mathematical formula he had used to send a team forward in the playoffs in 1969. The director of the Kansas High School Athletic Association, Durbin was charged with determining what to do in the event of a tie during his state's new state playoff system. Ties had long been a part of football's history. The saying that "a tie is like kissing your sister" became so popular in college football that it is attributed to no fewer than four coaches. Regardless of the feeling of players and coaches toward the dreaded tie, no one bothered to provide a solution until playoff systems like the one in Kansas demanded that a team advance to the next round.[17]

A few months after the mathematically induced tiebreaker in the Kansas playoffs, Durbin determined a better route to deciding a winner of a game that was tied at the end of four quarters. Each team would have one possession on its opponent's ten yard line and four downs to score. If the game were still tied at the end of one overtime, the game would continue in similar fashion until a winner was determined. Durbin's plan allowed for a quick resolution to a tie in most cases, not causing as great a danger to player safety than any other on-field solution to that point. College football soon adopted what came to be known as the "Kansas plan," with two additional stipulations: the teams would start at the twenty-five yard line and two-point conversion tries would become mandatory after two overtime periods.[18]

The Kansas plan has worked as designed in most overtime situations through the past four-plus decades with a few notable exceptions. Through the 2018 season, five college games have taken seven overtimes to decide a winner: Arkansas-Ole Miss (2001), Arkansas-Kentucky (2003), North Texas-Florida International (2006), Western Michigan-Buffalo (2017), and Texas A&M-LSU (2018).[19] Those games, however, don't hold a candle to a high school game played in Texas in 2010 between Jacksonville High and Nacogdoches High. In a similar situation to the one Tishomingo faced in the Falkner game, Nacogdoches needed to win by eight points to remain in playoff contention while Jacksonville simply needed to win. As a result, during several of the overtime periods, the Nacogdoches quarterback intentionally sailed several two-point conversion passes through the end zone in order to keep the game tied and force another overtime. An amazing *twelve* overtimes after ending regulation tied 28-28, Jacksonville won 84-81 to earn a berth in the playoffs.[20]

The Tishomingo brain trust hoped for a much simpler solution to their own playoff dilemma in 1988. The best they could hope for was to win the coin toss, choose to play defense first, hold Falkner scoreless, and then score a touchdown themselves for their necessary margin of victory. That was a simple enough plan. However, if the game went into a second overtime, the advantage to playing defense first—and, thus, knowing exactly what the offense must do to tie or to win the game—would revert to the Eagles. Furthermore, the element of surprise was immediate; the longer Joe Horton had on that Falkner sideline to figure out a counter move to the Bulldog strategy, the greater the chance he would be able to foil their scheme.

Overtime

18

Tishomingo won the coin toss to start the overtime session and elected to go on defense first. The psychological advantage of knowing exactly what they would need to do on offense to win would only be to the Bulldogs' advantage during the first overtime; if the game went to a second overtime, Falkner would play defense first. The Eagle option game had riddled the Tishomingo defense throughout the second half and was a more versatile offense than the Wing T in the tight space of the ten yards of real estate that both teams would be trying to cover. On the other hand, Falkner had been largely unable to stop Danny Brock when Tishomingo ran the same trap play again and again to the left side of the Bulldog line.

After four quarters of doing battle with their counterparts across the line, big Grant Horn and his fellow seniors knew that the time had come for the Tishomingo defense to call on every ounce of reserve they had left. "It had sunk in that this was why Coach Herbert had (called for the safety), so this was do or die. If you're going to get to play another game football game at Tishomingo, this is where you've got to do it, right here. I think everybody sucked it up right there and got tough."[1]

Falkner quarterback Tyrone Gaillard took the first snap of overtime and tried the right side but, finding his option keeper well defended, cut back to the middle where he was only able to make the line of scrimmage before he was collared by Tishomingo lineman John Moore. Gaillard forced the ball to the left side on second down but was taken down behind the line by Jeff Daniel for a loss of two. On third and twelve, Gaillard's pass into the end zone spiraled toward a teammate who had a step on his defender; before the pass reached him, though, the long arm of Bulldog defensive back Bryant Southward swatted it away. On fourth down the Eagle quarterback sprinted around the left end on another option keeper, but several Bulldog defenders turned him back to the inside. There, Bulldog sophomore Vince Stanley stood Gaillard up until Antony Oaks arrived to finish the tackle.

Like most coaches of small schools of the late 1980s, Coach Joe Horton did not have enough confidence in his kicking game to attempt a field goal—one that would be a chip shot by the standards of most high schools today—on fourth down. Had the Eagles been able to kick a field goal, Tishomingo's only legitimate chance to make the playoffs would have been to score a touchdown *and* convert a two-point conversion for a five-point win. The Tishomingo defense made the math easy with a fourth down stop. The Bulldogs simply needed to score a touchdown to make it to the playoffs.

Tishomingo lined up for their overtime possession with little doubt as to how they would attack the Eagle defense. During the season Tish had had frequent success lining Brock up to quarterback Dave Herbert's left and running the ball to the right. In the Falkner game, however, the Bulldog coaches felt like they had a decided advantage against the right side of the Eagle defensive front, so they had Brock and Shane Hill switch places. Brock had piled up yardage in the fourth quarter running behind the left side of the Bulldog line, evidence of the strategy's success. Unlike the typical positioning of a wingback, a yard back from other running formations—usually a yard wide of the tight end and a yard behind the line of scrimmage—in Coach Herbert's version of the Wing T offense, the wingback was the running back to the quarterback's right. Running from the wingback spot was nothing new for Brock; he had played wingback during his sophomore and junior seasons.

Just as Joe Horton had done during his team's possession, the Bulldog coaches returned to what had worked best for their offense in the second half. Brock took the handoff from Dave Herbert on first down and followed Oaks, who pulled from his left guard position and took out the Falkner defensive end, opening a gaping hole. Brock plowed ahead for seven yards to set up the Bulldogs with three opportunities to score from the three-yard line. An old adage in the South advises *if it ain't broke, don't fix it*. The Tish offense adhered to this principle, calling the same play again. This time, Brock turned the corner, where he was hit up by the Eagle cornerback, but he was able to fall forward to set up third and goal from a yard out. One more time the Bulldogs counted on their senior running back and the left side of the line. As Oaks pulled, left tackle Moore opened a hole that allowed Brock to plunge into the end zone for a touchdown, setting off a wild celebration on the Bulldog side.

The Tishomingo cameraman who was trained to remain quiet throughout the game as he recorded, yelled,

"Yeahhhh! All right!" By the weekend that sentiment was shared by people across America as the story was told and the video shown again and again. Tishomingo won the game 22-16 and claimed a share of the district championship and the number one seed for the playoffs that would begin the following week.

Brock was so exhausted after the winning score that he just lay in the end zone for several moments after the game was over.[2] The mood of the team was pure elation, not so much because of the wrong-way play but because every ounce of their energy and passion for high school football had paid off with another opportunity to play the game. The Tish players who played the game shrugged off the wrong-way play as just doing what they needed to do to win the game and get to the playoffs. Horn said, "We knew it was awesome, but we didn't think as much about the play, the backwards run being as big as it actually was. It was just awesome. I don't think any of us could hardly stand it coming back from Falkner on the bus. Everybody was happy, ecstatic."[3]

Smithville would join the Bulldogs in the playoffs as the number two seed with a 47-0 demolition of hapless Burnsville two days later. The defending North Half 1A champion Falkner Eagles became the odd team out in the tiebreaker mathematics, gaining little consolation by claiming a part of the three-way tie for the division championship. Coach Joe Horton was left to answer questions from around the nation about his perspective on the wrong-way play.

* * *

WTVA sport director Will Kollmeyer explained why the grainy Tishomingo game film with the Courtesy of Tishomingo High School tag became the default video television stations across the nation used to air the story:

> It's unfortunate. Where they're located, you can't stay four quarters and get back and put together the highlights for the news that night. A lot of times, highlights are of the first quarter, second quarter, or maybe if it's like your second or third game you hit that Friday night, you might get a little of the second half on your way back to the station. I would spend hours trying to coordinate where these people would go to these different spots and still get back in time to get highlights on the air. That's why they had to use that "Courtesy of Tishomingo High School" because I'm sure that was the only camera that was there at that stage.[4]

Even though the game at Falkner was played on a Thursday night, proof of the wrong-way play was limited to the Tishomingo footage (and most likely a similar video from Falkner High School). Even newspaper coverage of the game almost didn't make deadline on that Thursday night. Wayne Clements, covering the game for the *Daily Journal*, had about forty-five minutes after the game's conclusion to find a phone, type his story, and send it back to the newspaper office. He could not find a Falkner official who had earlier promised access to a phone and was relegated to typing his story while sitting in an aisle of a convenience store on Highway 15. The store was set to close five minutes after Clements walked in the door, so he hammered out his story in record time surrounded by vanilla wafers and bemused customers. He finished just as the store's owner began to turn off the lights.[5] The story ran the following morning, and Clements' account of the game spawned articles and editorials for weeks, months, and years to come.

News of Coach Herbert's call and his team's execution and ultimate victory slowly made its way around the state on Friday. By the weekend, however, news outlets from across the world were picking up the story. *USA Today* ran the story in its High School Notes section. Papers from Cincinnati to Detroit to the Philippines to Hong Kong picked up the Associated Press version of the game story. Several weeks after the game, columnist Russ Conway of Lawrence, Massachusetts *Eagle-Tribune* wrote that Joe Horton still had not recovered from what Conway called "the football play heard around the world." Fascinated by the accents of the Mississippi coaches he interviewed, Conway quoted Horton as saying, "We all just never thought of it happening quite like this. There's nothing you can do 'bout something like that. The boy already had a 10-yard head start. They gave us the two points, so I wasn't complainin' 'bout hoping to win the game."[6]

Coach Herbert told Conway that he figured out what he wanted to do with forty-seven seconds left in the game (unless, of course, his team had managed to score a touchdown before then). Herbert added that he waited until the last play so that Falkner would not have the chance to see through his strategy and do the same thing to his team, taking a loss on the field to assure themselves a spot in the playoffs. His fears carried over to Falkner's overtime possession. "Ya know, I was only worried 'bout one thing in the tie-breaker. They could have done the same thing. We play four downs from the ten-yard line in overtime. I was worrying Falkner would take the safety, lose 18-16, and beat us out for the playoff. "[7]

Northeast Mississippi Daily Journal reporter Chris Burrows talked with Joe Horton about the play weeks after it happened, as well. Horton told Burrows, "I've got to admit that obviously everybody was stunned; it caught everybody by surprise. I'm sitting there thinking boy, how smart this is; what a great move." Horton later considered how gutsy the call was with all of the possible outcomes. "What if we'd have scored in overtime? If we would have scored and missed the conversion, they would have been forced to score and fall on the ball. They were in a spot where they had to constantly figure out ways to keep it tied until they win by six."[8]

Kollmeyer ran a follow-up story on WTVA about the game after the Tishomingo brain trust had a few days to reflect on the risky play. Coach Vince Jordan said, "The kids knew the situation going into the ball game. We could have won the ball game by two points and stayed at home. So what? We end up with a record of six and two; we were still at home. Our goal was set at the first of the year: to make the playoffs, to win our district." Herbert, sitting on his Rascal and wearing his trademark thick glasses, answered the reporter's question matter-of-factly in his Southern drawl that was beginning to show the effects of his disease: "You've heard of intentional safeties but not fifty-five yards. I hadn't, and we were just lucky it paid off. If it had been the other way around—if he had gotten tackled or if we hadn't a won the ball game, we'd have been . . . a goat."[9] In the days and weeks to follow, Herbert got a kick out of the rest of the world's interest in what he thought was just another football play, one that fit the situation at that particular moment.

* * *

Though Coach Herbert received credit for calling the wrong-way play, there was much more going on behind the scenes. Burrows described the dynamic of coaching 1A football in North Mississippi in the 1980s and at Tishomingo in particular, where a strong athletic history included a "cup of coffee" major league baseball player in Dolan Nichols,[10] the Southward brothers—Billy, who played linebacker and defensive back for three years at Mississippi State, and Jim, the current director of athletics for the Mississippi Association of Community and Junior Colleges and longtime head football coach at Mississippi Delta Community College prior to that—and the McClung brothers, Benny and Danny. Of the McClungs, Burrows said, "Those guys had played, they had coached, so you're talking about a high school where David Herbert was—he was working with guys who got it. Basically, they had the whole administration as supplemental coaches. Those guys were tight."[11]

Dave Herbert was in the center of the confusion of the wrong-way play, orchestrating the play and calling for the changes that made it work. He pieced together the behind-the-scenes aspects after the game:

> The principal was Danny McClung. He was the basketball and baseball coach. He was a real good coach too. He was the baseball coach that took two teams to the state championship. He became the principal, but he was a big sports guy. He said, "What would a safety do? What about a safety?" I think Dad said something like, "I don't know, but we're going to do it." That's when he sent in the play to do it. Daddy

and Coach McClung had a good relationship, so it wasn't like he was trying to tell Daddy what to do.[12]

Burrows was initially reluctant to share what he knew about the play from talking to others who attended the game that night.

> The school was really gracious about making sure that David got the credit for it, and I don't mean like arrogantly got the credit. Even though I think McClung had a lot to do with the call and even though it still took kids doing what they were told to make it work, you never heard anybody go, *well, I thought of it first*. It was always just, *David did a great job*. And I thought, what a classy thing."[13]

Indeed, the Tishomingo community, including McClung and Jordan, are still quick to deflect any involvement in the play to Herbert's memory. As for the Tishomingo football players themselves, they shrug and say that the play did not define their coach anyway; it just helped the rest of the world discover what they already knew about the coach to whom they had handed the gift of one more game.

* * *

David Lee Herbert was never one to draw attention to himself, but attention for the play came fast and furious from newspapers, TV stations, and radio shows all over the country. Letters poured in from former colleagues, high school and college coaches, and family friends. Linda kept them all in a scrapbook. They even received letters from total strangers from all over the world. Elizabeth Beard, who had family in Iuka, wrote that they would be pulling for the

Bulldogs from east Tennessee, where they had read the story in the *Knoxville News-Sentinel*.[14] Larry Heffner sent well wishes from Covington, Louisiana, after reading about Coach Herbert's decision in "the heat of the battle" in *USA Today*.[15] Martha Patterson from Red Oak, Iowa, sent a clipping from the *Des Moines Register*.[16] Others sent clippings from Cincinnati, Detroit, and Richmond, among others, not to mention papers all over Mississippi. One clipping came from the Philippines, another, from Taipei. Larry Green, the superintendent of education in Tishomingo County at the time, wrote to commend Coach Herbert on how he was an inspiration. Mississippi governor Ray Mabus wrote, "You are a great ambassador for our state. Sports enthusiasts around the nation are learning that all the great coaches in the South do not coach in Alabama."[17]

19

Carrollton, Mississippi, took pride in its native son's moment of fame. Clint Littleton and Delbert Edwards still beam about how their childhood friend's fame due to such a unique play. Asked when they heard about it, Littleton said he thought it was at church.

> Out back used to be the smoking (and spittin') area. All of us smoked back then. In between Sunday school and church, that was the gossip place. I think that's where I heard it. We were all interested in David Lee. Anybody that we grew up with that was still in sports, we always kept up with them. I said he didn't get the wrong-way play from the courthouse yard. We used to run some crazy stuff when we were playing in the courthouse yard too—hide the football and stuff like that—but nothing like that."[1]

After graduating from Tishomingo High School, Herbert's former player Eric Powell took a meandering route toward a college degree. From a scholarship football player at Ole Miss to playing a year for Northeast Mississippi Community College in Booneville to Western Kentucky University, Powell eventually earned his degree from Wingate College in North Carolina. It was when Powell was at Western Kentucky in Bowling Green when he heard about the wrong-way play. He walked into the dorm lobby a couple of days after the Tishomingo-Falkner game. His teammates were gathered around the television watching a fledgling network called ESPN. They called, "Hey, Eric, hey,

Eric, they were talking about your school." His teammates told him about the play and the coach who called it, and Powell recognized that it was indeed his alma mater.[2]

Letters continued to pour in throughout the week—from church members at Carrollton Baptist Church to former students to Mississippi State's head football coach Rockey Felker. People who had no connection to Tishomingo or Mississippi were inspired by the story and wrote to Coach Herbert. A doctor in Ohio even requested a team photo.[3] In the days following the game, the story of the wrong-way play was re-told on Paul Harvey's *The Rest of the Story* radio program.

Long-time football broadcaster Brent Musburger was the host of CBS's *NFL Today* pregame show. Part of his weekly commentary included a Top Ten recap from the college football action during the previous week, with number ten often serving as a segue to a human interest story to follow. On the Sunday after the wrong-way play, Musburger listed Tishomingo High School in his number ten slot after the likes of Auburn, Oklahoma, and UCLA. Using the same grainy "Courtesy of Tishomingo High School" game film— right down to the final "Yeahh, all right!" from the cameraman—Musburger saluted Coach Herbert and the Bulldogs:

> Number ten today, we honor a small school in Mississippi, Tishomingo. Look at this story: On Thursday night, they were in the high school playoffs. Tiebreaking format—they had to win by four points. They led the game by two points. Seven seconds to go. Forty yards away from the end zone. (Actually, forty-five after the second penalty. The yard lines were not readily apparent in the video.) Coach Herbert, who

suffers from Lou Gehrig's disease, coaches his team from the back of a pickup truck. He had three options: go for the long field goal and try to make five and cover that four-point number, go for the touchdown...or option number three: His son, the quarterback, tosses the ball to the fastest player on the team, and the tailback sets sail for the end zone before a stunned crowd. He slides in and takes the safety. They go into overtime tied. Falkner High, with four plays from the ten, can't get it in. Now, it's third down, and Tishomingo gets it in for six points to advance to the next round. Let's hear it for Coach Herbert and the Bulldogs! Good luck on Friday night.[4]

* * *

Lost in the whirlwind of local and national media wanting to talk about "the play," Coach Herbert's squad still had a playoff game to host on Friday night. During the week that the nation was electing George Bush its forty-first President and Mississippi was sending Trent Lott to the Senate for his first term, the Tishomingo Bulldogs were balancing publicity and preparation for the playoff game that Friday night. The response of members of the 1988 team to the media attention varied. Some were in awe of the unparalleled television coverage of their little school. Others were annoyed at the disruptions at practice that week. Some remembered it as just another week of practice. Since the Falkner game had been on Thursday night, the media parade began on Friday, a day Shane Hill remembered spending on the phone with reporters.[5]

Television stations from at least three states made their way to Tishomingo the following week for coverage of the small school with a big idea. Shannon Edmondson remembered the excitement of getting out of class to watch Coach Herbert's interview on the *Today* show.[6] Dave Herbert admitted that the attention probably bumped the team off of its normal routine at least a little bit.[7] Lance Hollingsworth viewed the attention as more of a distraction. The sophomore receiver for the 1988 team said, "It was exciting, but looking back, it always came during practice. I wish they would have just stayed away."[8]

* * *

Anguilla traveled from Sharkey County in the Mississippi Delta for the opening round of the Mississippi High School Activities Association 1A playoffs. The Wildcats, the runner-up in Division 3-1A, carried a 9-1 mark and had steamrolled their last four opponents with an average of over fifty points a game. Their wishbone attack featured a bigger line and faster backs than Tishomingo had seen. The lone loss of the Anguilla season was a 34-22 setback to East Flora, one of the favorites in 1A in 1988. An 8-6 win over O'Bannon early in the season and a 62-0 dismantling of St. Aloysius completed the Wildcats' district slate, clinching the runner-up slot and earning a trip to northeast Mississippi for a November playoff matchup.[9]

Anguilla started the scoring against Tishomingo with a one-yard run and a two-point conversion early in the second quarter. Danny Brock answered for the Bulldogs with a five-yard scoring run. Dave Herbert's conversion pass to Bryant Southward knotted the game 8-8. Anguilla took another lead on the opening drive of the third quarter on another short run and two-point conversion. The Wildcats added another

TD late in the third quarter to extend their lead to 22-8. Brock scored a late touchdown to cut into the lead, but there was no magic for the Bulldogs this time as Anguilla defeated Tishomingo 22-14 in Coach Herbert's last game as a high school coach.[10]

The road to the state championship from the Tishomingo-Anguilla game is an interesting study in the direction of football programs in Mississippi's smallest division. Like Tishomingo, which consolidated with other small county high schools into Tishomingo County High School in 1991, Anguilla High School ceased to exist as a high school in 1994, becoming part of the new South Delta School District.[11] Anguilla's next opponent, Weir, merged with Ackerman in 2013 to form Choctaw County High School. East Flora, who defeated Anguilla for the north half championship, joined forces with Madison-Ridgeland in 1991 to form Madison Central High School.[12] Only East Flora's championship game opponent, Mize High School, still exists as of the 2019 football season, but as a 2A school. Unlike many small football programs that have seen consolidation looming on the horizon, East Flora finished with a flourish that included five straight playoff appearances and two close losses in the 1A state championship game in 1988 (27-26 to Mize) and in its last season in 1990 (24-20 to Stringer).[13]

* * *

Smithville went on the road to East Flora in the first round of the playoffs in 1988 and lost, 26-3. Both the tiny town and its coach would make national headlines over two decades later. After winning state football championships in

1993 and 1998 and coaching at Smithville for a total of twenty-eight years,[14] Coach Dwight Bowling retired from the Mississippi public school system after the 2004-05 school year and took a job at Sulligent High School in Alabama. On September 18, 2010, on his way home to Mississippi from a football game, Bowling was arrested and charged with a number of sexual misconduct and trafficking charges. He pled guilty in federal court in April of 2011 and was sentenced to twenty-five years in prison.[15]

During the same month that Bowling was sentenced—on April 27, 2011—Smithville was dealt a much more direct and devastating blow when a category EF5 tornado tore through the town. Over two hundred homes, two churches, and all but two of the town's businesses were either completely destroyed or severely damaged. Just an hour after high school students had been dismissed because of the impending bad weather, their school building was leveled. Sixteen people died that day in Smithville. The Super Outbreak of 2011 saw 350 tornadoes across the South take the lives of 348 people and leave such damage that many of the places where the worst of the storms touched down still have not fully recovered.[16]

A year after the tornado devastated Smithville, its part-time mayor Gregg Kennedy was recognized nationally for his leadership in Smithville's recovery efforts. His town— without building codes or a comprehensive plan in place— faced an uphill battle getting back on its feet. Though the town still features a number of slabs onto which houses were never rebuilt and though the Piggly Wiggly—the only grocery store in town at the time of the tornado—did not return, Smithville now features a new city hall and a new high school.[17] In the weeks after the tornado, one rebuilding effort became prominent: rebuilding the high school's football field in time for its August home opener against rival Hatley. Kennedy said, "We rebuilt that field first thing. Our superintendent and I knew that that first football game would be the best healing process because around here everybody goes to high school football."[18]

* * *

The Tishomingo playoff loss didn't stop the platitudes for the ingenuity of the wrong-way play from continuing to pour in. One congratulated Coach Herbert for receiving a local Spirit of Mississippi award. Another, dated December 9, 1988, was a letter from Bernard Blackwell, president of the Mississippi Association of Coaches, informing Coach Herbert that he has been selected for induction into the Mississippi Association of Coaches Hall of Fame as an honorary member[19], just the ninth individual bestowed with the honor at that time.[20] About all of the acclaim, Chris Burrows of the *Journal* wrote, "I'm glad to see Tishomingo Coach David Herbert get the national attention he deserves. He should be credited for his accomplishments, not his illness."[21]

On July 28, 1989, Coach David Lee Herbert was inducted into the Mississippi Association of Coaches Hall of Fame during ceremonies at the Holiday Inn Downtown in Jackson. He joined Lafayette "Strib" Stribling, Lum Wright, Jack Carlisle, Robert Hooker, and Steve Clark in that year's class. A large contingent of Coach Herbert's extended family was present at the ceremony. Dave was unable to attend as he was preparing the state all-star game, returning to his more comfortable position of tight end and playing for someone other than his dad for the first time in his life. Herbert's hall of fame recognition brought on another onslaught of congratulatory letters, among them from Southern Mississippi head football coach Curley Hallman and Mississippi State assistant athletic director Wesley Reed. Hallman wrote, "I have always felt that it's not how many years an individual coaches but what his contribution to the young men and women was during all those years."[22]

* * *

Two months before Coach Herbert's Hall of Fame ceremony, the *Daily Journal* reported that Jim Drewry had been hired as Tishomingo High School's new football coach. The fifty-eight-year-old Drewry had been retired for two-and-a-half years after a stellar career at Booneville and Kossuth but would be taking the reins of the Bulldog program that had known nothing but Coach Herbert's Wing T for the previous six years. *Journal* sportswriter Make Talbert wrote that "Drewry, with some of the biggest shoes around, has managed to find a job with tough shoes to fill."[23] He would also be replacing assistant Vince Jordan, who was leaving the program for a job in the private sector after leading the baseball Bulldogs to the 1989 north half finals. He would return to coaching after a year's absence at Ripley High School, his alma mater, eventually retiring from a career in school administration.[24]

Drewry took over a team full of players who had been successful through their junior high and high school careers. The juniors of 1989 were the same ones who had gone 7-0 and had not allowed a point as ninth graders. Though Jim Drewry was, according to Dave Herbert, a nice guy and very capable, he was not able to find success at Tishomingo.[25] The 1989 Bulldogs finished 2-7. Perhaps appropriately, Drewry's last game as the Tish head man was a two-point loss to Falkner.[26]

After carrying the ball on the famous wrong-way play, Shane Hill's final two years of Tishomingo High School football were "miserable" because "I had lost the best coach I ever had." Hill felt like the changes on the field—especially the move away from the Wing T—just didn't fit the Bulldogs. As to why David Lee Herbert was the best coach he ever had, he said, "It was like you were family to him. He treated you like you were one of his. He would get on you if you messed up, but he was there to praise you if you did good, too." Hill dropped by to visit his former coach occasionally the following season on his way to the field house if Herbert was outside on his front porch. Still able to speak in the fall of 1989, Herbert always asked about the progress of the team and about Hill's performance.[27]

John Moore's sentiments paralleled Hill's:

> The year after our district win, our first game was against Burnsville. We won by fourteen, and our new coach screamed and cussed us. I saw Coach Herbert and he said, "It's okay, John, y'all played a good game." The last time I saw Coach, he could only blink his answers. It hurt to see a strong man that had such a strong influence on my life in that condition. He was still Coach, though.[28]

Two years after the wrong-way run, the Bulldogs of Tishomingo High School played their last football game and finished 2-8. With new coaches all around, two of the team's blowout losses came at the hands of Smithville and Falkner.

Following the 1990-1991 school year, Tishomingo High School was no more, merging with Burnsville and Iuka to form Tishomingo County High School. Belmont High School was a holdout to consolidation and absorbed some of the students from other schools; nevertheless, the era of 1A sports in Tishomingo County was over.

20

Almost as quickly as consolidation marked the end of an era in extreme northeast Mississippi, David Lee Herbert's plight against a relentless disease fell off the public's radar. Aside from a few "best of the decade" type articles in the *Journal*, his story faded into Tishomingo High School folklore. The Herbert family, though, continued to live in the house on the Tishomingo campus even as its days as a high school dwindled.

Bruce Heath grew up with David Lee and graduated high school with him. The two had taken a drive around Carrollton, reminiscing about old times, when the Herberts had come back for summer break in 1987. They spent about two hours together that day, and David Lee talked about the trouble he was having with his leg. When the trouble with his leg turned into an ALS diagnosis and eventually confined him to his bed in Tishomingo, Heath came to visit on several occasions. He began to pay attention to the aspect of the Herbert home that would define their next decade and a half: "Linda inspired me, how she was just so attentive to David Lee. She acted like it was a joy for her to wait on him."[1] Others began to notice Linda's care for him as well and come alongside to help.

During the remainder of the 1988-1989 school year, Linda Herbert continued to teach but moved to a classroom right across from their house. If David Lee needed anything during the day, she would notify her students and a next-door teacher that she was going home for a few minutes to tend to his needs. She sped up those errands by using the Rascal that her husband could no longer operate.[2] Sometimes, when she was unable to leave his side, her classes walked across the parking lot to have class in her home.[3]

Tishomingo High School remained open as a K-12 school for another two football seasons after Coach Herbert's last season in 1988 before giving in to consolidation. Linda made sure he sat up some each evening, so when he felt up to it on home game nights, she would wheel him out to the deck on the back of their house where he could watch his team play. She could tell that he did not trust her tiny frame to lift him back into the bed, even with the aid of a hydraulic lift, so one of the Herbert children had be home by around 10:00 to help Linda move him back to his bed. Dave had gone away to college, so Linda relied mainly on Stacie and Hollie for help. One of the girls often stayed up to sit with their father to give Linda some rest since their insurance paid for only a certain number of nights of home care. David Lee's journey from his first symptoms to being confined to a hospital bed in his own house took about four years. After that, he experienced little physical change for more than a decade.

In the fall of 1989 reporters Chris Burrows and Gene Phelps were heading to an assignment near Tishomingo County. Burrows had an idea.

I said, "Geno, why don't we stop in and see Coach Herbert?" We stopped in and we saw him, and at that point, he couldn't speak anymore. He could still move his hand, and he could still wink, and he could squeeze Linda's hand yes or no if you asked him a question. He wasn't totally without communication. That was the last time I saw him. I was just shocked. I could see such a difference in him then than where he had been a season ago and two seasons before that.[4]

* * *

After two decades of impacting the young men and women he coached, David Lee's influence grew to include the community around him—first with his family's dealing with the hardship of the wreck in 1984 and then during his fight against ALS. Kathy Haynes first met David Lee when she was a nurse and he was a patient at North Mississippi Medical Center in Tupelo after he had been diagnosed with Lou Gehrig's. His sweet brown eyes reminded her of a deer and endeared him to her. She walked with the Herberts through a choice that is trying for many ALS patients, whether or not to go on a ventilator once they begin to have trouble breathing. "A lot of people who have Lou Gehrig's— when they get to the point where they can't breathe anymore, they choose not to go on a ventilator. He was still talking to us at that time. When we knew he had made that choice, it was pretty profound."[5]

Before David Lee underwent a tracheostomy that would limit his communication to eye blinks, he and Linda worked out a system of communication that would transform their next decade and a half from mere survival to the best life for which David Lee could hope. Their system called for Linda to call for *one*, which indicated the first word began with A-M, or *two*, N-Z. If David Lee blinked *one*, Linda started through the alphabet until he blinked again. Once she had a letter or two, witnesses watched with astonishment while Linda usually determined what her husband was trying to say—similar to the way predictive text works. Later, Bernard Taylor would sit and visit with his cousin, always with Linda serving as translator. "She would say, 'Well, David Lee told me the other day…' It was absolutely amazing how they communicated. She was not talking for him but saying what he wanted her to say. He could talk to you about any subject, whether it was sports or politics or whatever."[6]

* * *

The Herbert family accepted the changes as they came with the grace that people in both Tishomingo and Carrollton apply to the entire family. Stacie compared how she viewed the changes in her father to the way an outsider who didn't see David Lee very often might view the rapid changes brought about by ALS:

> I think it made a lot of people uncomfortable, or they didn't quite grasp it because they talked to him sometimes like he didn't understand. You'd have to tell them he understands everything you're saying; he just can't respond. But it was just the norm for us. When you're thirteen, fourteen—more of your life was like that than normal life, so you just really didn't think that much.[7]

In the fall of 1990, the Tishomingo community came together for a fund-raiser for the Herberts to help with their medical expenses and to purchase a computerized communication device they hoped would help David Lee to spell words on a screen. Sensors would pick up minute movements and help him communicate via the computer. By that time Linda Herbert, a three-time STAR teacher at Tishomingo and Carroll Academy, had taken a leave of absence from her teaching job to care for David Lee full time. The *Journal* pointed people in northeast Mississippi toward the fund-raiser, as did the Herberts' hometown *Conservative* and nearby *Greenwood Commonwealth*. The financial goal of the benefit was seven thousand dollars, but after donations from individuals and merchants arrived in the days that followed, neighbors and friends had come together to raise over fourteen thousand dollars.

Unfortunately, the first-generation technology of the device rendered it more frustrating than useful. Stacie remembered it being difficult to manipulate and that the mouse movement was not very accurate. "He'd have to redo it, and it was frustrating and mental exhausting; it just wasn't worth it. We could talk to him and figure out what he was trying to tell you a lot easier than for him to use the computer was because we were just so used to it."[8] The family kept cassette tapes of David Lee's singing in church, but over time, Stacie began to lose the memory of her father's voice. "After the first few years, you kind of forgot what his voice sounded like."[9]

Former New Orleans Saints special teams star Steve Gleason, who continues to fight a very public battle with ALS at the publication of this book, video journaled his battle against the cruel onslaught of Lou Gehrig's disease for the benefit of his son. When he faced the impending loss of his ability to speak, he spoke directly to his son through the camera:

> Rivers, I'm having a bad day. I can't talk. I think the last of my talking days are here. The drugs I take don't work. I have no faith that I can heal. I have no hope. None. I want to punch something but I can't. The only thing I can do is scream.[10]

David Lee's I-can't-take-this-anymore moment came not from his loss of communication but in his diet after his tracheostomy. After just a few days of subsisting on liquid protein drinks, he indicated that he wanted no more. Linda thought through her options and found a solution that many believe is a primary reason he far outlived his diagnosis:

> Whenever he first got the feeding peg, the health care professionals said to feed him liquid protein drinks, like six cans a day, and that was all. Finally, he said—well, he didn't say, but he told me—he couldn't tolerate any more of that, even though I was giving it to him through his feeding peg. For some reason I just thought, well, why can't I just blend his food up, get it thin enough, and put it through that feeding peg.[11]

Hollie noticed that her daddy had lost considerable weight on the doctor-prescribed diet. "He was really skinny. When Mama started feeding him food, he started gaining weight."

Linda never consulted the doctor about her idea for blending household food for David Lee to eat. "The next time we went back, I told the doctor that I was blending up his food, and he said, 'Looks like it's doing okay, so just keep at it.'" The dietician at the Tupelo hospital sent her some information on what she could blend, but she just blended what her family was eating. Tomato seeds stopped up his initial peg, but a different type of feeding peg allowed even the tomato seeds to pass through. Even though the food never entered his mouth, he had some type of sensation of satisfaction, even to the point of having a "taste" for certain foods. With the help of her blender and chicken broth, Linda fed David Lee hamburgers, spaghetti—whatever she was eating. To determine portion sizes, she "fixed his plate" and then dumped it in the blender.

David Lee could indicate through his eyes if Linda was feeding him too fast or if he had eaten enough. A little while after supper, he enjoyed dessert or a snack, also blended. Oatmeal sufficed for breakfast every morning, but he liked a variety of foods for supper. Linda said, "If he'd have stayed on those protein drinks like they said, he wouldn't have been here very long."[12] David Lee rarely ran a fever and was never seriously ill. He never suffered from bedsores, and he was able to keep a healthy weight. Linda may not have been a doctor or nutritionist, but what she did worked.

Linda Herbert never lost her optimism throughout a decade that brought one blow after another to her family: Lauriann's accident in 1984, her own injuries sustained in the same wreck, David Lee's ALS diagnosis in 1987, and her retirement from teaching to become his full-time caregiver. Asked for the source of her perseverance, she turned her attention to her faith and to others: "It always seems that it was worse on somebody else than it was on you. I know now that when somebody gets some bad health news, I feel bad, but I didn't feel that way when it was us." She recalled one of the caregivers sent to help with David Lee one day while the family was still in Tishomingo:

One day when I was still teaching, there was a lady from Oxford who worked with rehab or something, and she had come to Tishomingo before I had gotten out of school. She was in the den on my daybed, and she didn't have any arms. I looked around, and I didn't see another soul around. Then I happened to pay attention—she was writing something on a tablet. She had the pen in her toes. She was writing with her foot. I thought, goodness gracious, I can't imagine anybody being able to do that. Then, she was wanting to make a call for something. Back then, all we had was the phone on the wall. I asked her can I help you with that, and she said, "No, I can get it." She used her foot and dialed the number. After a little bit, she said there was something out in the car that she needed to go get; I asked her if I could get it for her, and she said, "I'll get it." I thought, how are you going to open the door. She went out there and got whatever she needed.

She had driven herself to Tishomingo from Oxford by herself. I didn't see how that worked. I wish I had now. I guess she did it with her feet; she did everything with her feet. Two weeks after they had David Lee on the "Spirit of Mississippi" on the Tupelo TV station, they showed her pinning a diaper on her baby with her feet and cooking with her feet. I thought then, never again will I complain about anything. I just couldn't get over it. She was born like that. Boy, her feet … there wasn't anything she couldn't do with her feet.[13]

One aspect of David Lee and Linda Herbert's life together that remained steadfast was their faith in God. Just as their faith was not about coming into money to avoid a pending bankruptcy or that their daughter would survive the automobile accident, their faith was also not that David Lee would defy the odds and beat amyotrophic lateral sclerosis. Neither was their faith a fatalistic, whatever-is-going-to-happen-is-going-to-happen type of faith, which is not really faith at all but an acquiescence to an ethereal higher power. It was a faith that deferred to their Maker's sovereignty. They took up the mantle of suffering that was appointed to them without complaint. They chose not just to *say* they were okay but to actually *be* okay, without complaint and without losing hope in God. Former colleague Kenneth McClain thought back: "I still don't see how he survived nearly twenty years. His heart had to be unbelievably strong for him to exist that long."[14] From all accounts, his heart was indeed strong but in more than just a physical aspect.

To the Tishomingo community, the amount of suffering that the Herberts had endured must have seemed unfair, except that David Lee and Linda never allowed their lives to be defined by their suffering. They continued to love God, to put others before themselves, and to move ahead with the very different lives they had been allotted. The *for worse* and *in sickness* parts of their marriage vows had been put to the test time and time again and found sufficient. However, their intimate acquaintance with life's difficulties had only just begun.

Linda's optimism and resolve were tested again in 1991 when she was diagnosed with breast cancer. By then she had tirelessly attended to David Lee on a daily basis for three years. She responded to the cancer diagnosis with typical frankness, never considering that she might not be a breast cancer survivor because she had to take care of David Lee. Many of the nurses at the hospital remembered the Herbert family when both husband and wife were admitted and placed in rooms next door to one another. This was arranged by a doctor who used the opportunity to replace his peg line to keep the couple close together.

David Lee's cousin Jo Leta Carpenter said that Linda would not agree to have the surgery unless David Lee was also admitted to the hospital and had a room next door to hers. She stayed in Linda's room while Minnie Herbert attended to her son in his room.

> Aunt Minnie said he kept looking at the clock wondering how much longer it would be before (Linda) returned to her room. Whenever the nurse would call Linda's room to give an update, I would go next door to let David Lee and Aunt Minnie know. Linda had not been back in the room very long before she wanted to go see if David Lee was okay and let him know that she was okay. I commented about her having the drain tube, and she didn't hesitate. I helped her out of bed and walked with her while she held the little drain bag in her hand. Because of his ALS, he could no longer turn his head, so she walked to the foot of his bed. I wish everyone could have seen the look of love between them. Their eyes locked and it was as if no one else was in the room. They both were satisfied after knowing each was okay.[15]

Sure enough, as soon as Linda began to recover from her surgery, she moved back and forth between rooms, helping to care for David Lee as she recouped her own strength. She needed only low-grade chemotherapy over the next few months. A recurrence of the cancer in 2008 required only surgery.[16]

21

In 1994, David Lee and Linda decided to move back to the Carroll County home they had kept through the years. There, Linda could have easier access to family who could help with David Lee. After Stacie and Hollie graduated from Tishomingo County High School, the Herberts said goodbye to a community that had been so good to their family. The Rascal found a new home too, with the son of one of Coach Herbert's former players from back at Carroll Academy; the fifth grader suffered from spina bifida and required a scooter as he began to change classes at school that fall.[1]

Gracious help from the Herberts' extended community continued even as David Lee's battle changed venues. After Coach Herbert's tracheostomy that had placed him on a ventilator full time, Kathy Haynes, the nurse from North Mississippi Medical Center in Tupelo, had helped the Herberts set up the ventilator in their Tishomingo home in her part-time role with a home health services company. Tishomingo County was in her company's service area, so she visited their Tishomingo home for the remainder of their time there, changing out his tracheostomy tube every three months. However, when the Herberts moved back to Carroll County, they also moved outside of her service area. She wouldn't see the family again until they showed up at the emergency room in Tupelo several months later to have David Lee's tube changed. The trip took a toll on the family.

> The tracheostomy tube needed to be traded out periodically. He had come back to our hospital and had it changed out in the ER, and it was tough making that trip. It was just so uncomfortable, and we had been doing it at home in Tishomingo. At that time I told him, "I won't make you go through that again. I will come to your house in Carrollton and change it out off-duty, as a layperson." Otherwise, they would have had to go to Jackson or Tupelo to have it changed out. They were just so excited that I was willing to do that. That ended up being many, many years.[2]

Linda fondly remembered coming to know Haynes through her regular care. Linda recalled, "She was coming from Houlka (a two-hour drive away). Sometimes her husband or somebody else would come with her, so I'd try to have a good supper for them. David Lee didn't want anybody else doing his trach except Kathy."[3]

For her part, Haynes became an honorary member of the Herbert family. Over the next decade that she continued to drive from Houlka to Carrollton several times annually, she shared her life with the Herberts, introducing them to whichever friend or family member she brought along for the ride each time. However, Linda and David Lee were more interested in her life.

> My husband was a basketball coach and assistant football coach, and my kids were playing football. They would follow all that. Linda would have a meal

made for me. And let me tell you, the lady's a good cook. We would go through the process, and I would change out his breathing tube for him; that was our routine.

I worked full time. By the time I drove down there and spent about an hour, hour and a half with them, it took about five or six hours. Sometimes, I was thinking how that was a chore, but I would walk into that house and they would make me forget all of my troubles. I always came away from there feeling so blessed. They had so much on them over the years and just kept on going.[4]

* * *

The days turned into months and the months turned into years for the Herbert family. Dave graduated college and moved away. Stacie and Hollie left home after graduation, too. Family, friends, and neighbors stepped in to equip the the old family home for David Lee's needs. Linda cared for him eighteen hours a day, sleeping when overnight help arrived, which it often did not. For his part David Lee was not relegated to a back room. Though he spent his days and nights in a hospital bed hooked to a ventilator, he was at the center of family life. From his bed in the den, he kept abreast of the world outside his walls by reading the newspaper that Linda hung from a clip in front of him every day. His children and eventually grandchildren visited with him there. His sister Anne stopped most days after teaching at J. Z. George, helping to suction his tube and sitting and talking. Joyce moved from Michigan to nearby Grenada and visited her brother regularly: "I never quit talking to him."[5]

Delbert Edwards stopped by once or twice a week so that David Lee could listen to the previous week's sermon from Carrollton Baptist Church on tape and talk football. An avid Mississippi State fan, Edwards's visits often included his bringing the Herberts' mail inside to them. If David Lee—the lone Ole Miss fan in the Herbert household even after years of the rest of the family's trying to convert him—had received a copy of the *Ole Miss Spirit* magazine, Edwards would toss it on David Lee's bed and say, "Well, here's your Ole Miss pornography." Thinking back on their mostly one-sided running joke, he wisecracked, "Somebody ought to have sued the United States Postal Service for allowing that kind of pornography to come through the mail like that. We had a lot of fun."[6] Unfazed, David Lee watched Ole Miss games on television whenever they were available, and Edwards continued to aggravate him about it. Hollie called her father an aggravating, picking type, shaking her head and comparing her brother to him. Edwards's weekly back and forth, she said, brought a smile to her daddy.[7]

Not all of David Lee's friends—either in Tishomingo or in Carrollton—felt comfortable dropping by as his disease progressed. It was difficult for them, knowing that he could understand everything they said but could not answer them. Linda, always by his side, would communicate with David Lee the best she could or just answer for him if she knew how he might answer. Hollie remembered,

> For some people, it was hard to see him in that shape. They knew him before and knew his personality and then to see him in that shape, it was just hard for them. They didn't want to show their emotions or anything in front of him and didn't know how to communicate with him.[8]

For the most part, though, David Lee's eyes could say what they needed to say, whether it was the testimony that his pastor asked him to "write" to be read at church or something more pressing, like the day Anne sat down on his bed to visit with her brother and sat on his leg. "I kept noticing him doing his eyes toward Linda, and I told Linda something was wrong. I asked him everything—is your vent okay?" Linda began going through the alphabet and eventually arrived at: "Anne is on my leg."[9]

Kathy Haynes remembered another time when David Lee struggled to communicate what was on his mind:

> A lot of times Linda would auto figure out what he was saying. One time it took him a really long time. She just kept on and kept on, and it was just so challenging trying to figure out what he was trying to tell her. Well, he was trying to ask if my husband wanted his football playbook.

Though the plays in Coach Herbert's playbook had been successful throughout his career, the one that he was most famous for could not be found in the book. Haynes remembered hearing about the wrong-way play on Paul Harvey's show but didn't realize until well into her care for David Lee that her special patient was the one who had gained international fame for it.[10]

* * *

Every Friday night during the fall, a visitor to the Herbert home—and visitors were always welcome—would find Coach Herbert watching *Friday Night Fever*. Will Kollmeyer did not know until recently that the little football show he had once fought for so vigorously was part of Coach Herbert's weekly routine.

> Isn't that something? That just means the world to me, because producing the show is stress like I've never had before, but it's a rush. Those stories like Coach Herbert's were the kind of stories that were the reason you did that. When you're talking about that large of a viewing area—keep in mind that back then the technology wasn't always there—people were really having to push themselves to get those highlights on… all those scores. It was quite a team concept that we had to crank that out every week. It's cool to hear stories like that because—4:30, 5:00 in the morning—I'm still staring at the ceiling fan. Ambient noise—nothing could touch it because you couldn't wind down; it was so stressful, so last second. But hearing those stories like with Coach David, it made it all worthwhile.[11]

Kollmeyer wasn't the only northeast Mississippi football reporter who had lost track of Coach Herbert. D. E. Wheeler had begun covering high school sports for the *Journal* long after Herbert's tenure. In 2000, after Joe Horton passed away from a heart attack, Wheeler wrote a story about the wrong-way play game and Horton's remark after the game to Tishomingo assistant Vince Jordan: "Didn't think of that one." He didn't mention David Lee Herbert in the article, but a voice mail during the week from a nurse alerted him that thirteen years after his diagnosis, Coach Herbert was still alive and residing in his hometown. Wheeler wrote in a subsequent article, "I think my assumption would be the same as most of you that while Herbert's efforts to continue coaching despite his illness were heroic, he eventually died after a gallant fight." He wrote of what some would consider a sad sight of the coach hooked up to a ventilator for eleven years, only able to move his eyelids. However, Wheeler continued, "But it is also a brave picture to think that one's spirit can still survive despite an illness robbing him of the physical freedom that you and I take for granted. His mind is still quite sharp, too, I'm told, still keeping up with many of the area's sports teams."[12]

Despite the pretty sedate daily life around the Herbert house, there were some wild adventures and scary moments, like the time Carrollton lost electricity and the Herberts' generator stopped working. After surviving that situation, Carrollton Baptist Church saw to it that they received a new, dependable generator for future power outages.[13] Other close scrapes brought occasional interruptions to what had become a life of routine.

David Lee's ventilator setup included water from his trach that drained through a hose. On a trip to Jackson once, the alarm from his main ventilator sounded. Hollie swapped it out with the spare while Linda gave him air through a ventilation bag. The spare worked fine, but when they reached the medical supply store in Jackson to get another ventilator, the store didn't have one. Store employees rigged one that was good enough to work, and the Herberts started home. Then the van would not pick up speed like it should have. Followed by a family friend who joined them in Goodman where she was working at Holmes Junior College near Interstate 55, the van sputtered all the way home, badly in need of a new fuel pump.[14]

Another time, David Lee wanted to watch his nephews Shane and Matthew play football in Winona, about a twenty-minute drive away for any other spectator driving from Carrollton. However, with all the equipment that David Lee required, it was a much longer process than his sister Anne might have expected. She drove her non-wheelchair accessible van to her brother's house. In retrospect, she can't imagine what she was thinking not bringing her husband along to assist her, Linda, and her mother—then in her seventies—to move David Lee from his bed to his wheelchair and into the van.

When the three ladies finally situated David Lee in a seat in the van, he quit breathing and started turning red. The line feeding him oxygen had come unplugged, and Anne had to administer resuscitation until Linda could run in the house and replace the necessary part. Though David Lee enjoyed watching his nephews play, Anne said, "By the time I got over to Winona, I was ready to go to the hospital myself." To make matters worse, Shane suffered a concussion during the game, necessitating someone else's driving the Herberts back home while Anne and her husband took Shane to the hospital. After that episode and one more trip to Winona for Christmas, Anne declared that she was ready to give up the risks of transporting her brother and do all of their visiting at his house.[15]

Those situations were not the scariest the Herberts encountered. Linda left nurse Joyce in charge of David Lee another time while she and Hollie drove to Jackson. Linda recalled that

> Hollie was about to get married. She was going to take me to Jackson to get a dress because I didn't have too many clothes to wear out because I didn't go anywhere. David Lee's sister was a nurse. They were real close, so he didn't mind her coming and staying with him. We were just fixing to leave Jackson to come

home, and she called and said that the ventilator wasn't putting out any air; he wasn't getting any air. I called a friend, a Farm Bureau man here. I had another ventilator; it was under his wheelchair, but it was in another room, and Joyce couldn't leave David Lee long enough to go in there and get it. I called Russell and told him to go down to the house and help them get things situated. Joyce used a manual resuscitator until Russell got down here. I was telling him over the phone how to hook it up and all, but when he did, the air wouldn't come through it. I told Hollie, you just go as fast as you can go, and if a highway patrolman comes up behind you, just keep on going and whatever fine he wants to give us, we'll pay it.[16]

Meanwhile, Joyce was back at her brother's home using her training to care for her brother until help in the way of the spare ventilator could be connected properly. She picked up the story there:

I was sitting there; I think that's why David Lee trusted me because I wouldn't leave him. All of a sudden I heard that vent go, and I said *this is not right*. David's eyes got big, but I said, "Dave, don't worry about this. Your sister's got a lot of hot air, you know that." I just popped that thing off and started doing CPR through the trach, and he just pinked up and he was fine. I said I've got to get some help up here because we gotta get this vent started. I had a cell phone—praise God for cell phones—and I said I can do air and do cell phones; you'll be fine. It's just a matter of me getting somebody down here so we can get the other vent in here. I knew people, but I didn't have any numbers.

I called Linda, and she said they were just leaving Jackson. She said I'll call somebody and have them come down there, and that's when she called Russell Wilson, the Farm Bureau agent, and he came down. Well, we put that other vent on there—I was still doing CPR—and it didn't work. I said call 911 and have them come out.

They had no idea what to do with a vent, none whatsoever. Well, Linda and Hollie—they were breaking every kind of law to get there because Linda was panicking. I said, "Linda, he's fine; I can do CPR forever. It's not that much trouble to do for me; I know it sounds bad... we're fine." They got there and I said, "You know more about the vent than any respiratory therapist." She got to checking the lines, and one of the lines had a hole in it. She fixed it and we popped it back on there, and he was fine. But it took about two hours.[17]

Even with his sister firmly in control that time, situations like that were scary for Linda but not just for her. "David Lee couldn't express how that might have worried him. I know it did."[18]

* * *

For those who knew the family throughout their various trials, several themes emerged over the years. During the extensive interviews conducted for this book, every single person who knew the family said about David Lee and Linda in some shape, form, or fashion, "They never complained, not one time." Another theme that presented itself during Linda's long recovery from the wreck and

David Lee's long battle with ALS was their deep and abiding love for one another and for their children. For most of their lives as teachers at the smallest of schools, their family barely scraped by financially but made up for it with love and companionship with one another. As the trials began to come, they continued to lean on one another and the faith that they had in their Creator to sustain them. One of the Herberts' neighbors who knew them through the long haul of David Lee's disease revealed a recurring theme. Janis Herbert Clatyton said it like this: "Everything focuses on David, but Linda is the real hero."[19]

Many who were interviewed for this book felt like they were falling short by calling Linda an angel on earth. All three of her sisters-in-law shook their heads and, often through tears, expressed great admiration for Linda. Those who knew her used words such as *angel* and *saint* to describe her, and the newspaper *Greenwood Commonwealth* named her an "unsung hero" in 2004.[20] Daughter Stacie, a nurse herself, claims, "If we'd have put him in a nursing home, he probably would have lived maybe a couple of years after he got his trach."[21] Indeed, though everyone in the Herbert family took part in his care, they agree that Linda was the primary reason David Lee survived for so many years.

22

On July 16, 2005, at the age of sixty-three—eighteen years after he was diagnosed with amyotrophic lateral sclerosis and seventeen years after his moment of fame—the last of David Lee Herbert's muscles that had been shutting down one by one through the years stopped working. Joyce Bowman, who was living in Grenada and taking care of their mother in her home, remembered the phone call:

> Dave had spent the night at his mom's that night. He called me early that morning; I had my mother here— I had fixed a hospital room. Dave called and said, "Aunt Joyce, Mama needs you." I said what's wrong, and he said, "Dad's gone." Okay, I'll be there in just a few minutes. My husband was here, and I said, "Bill, would you watch Mama. Dave's gone."[1]

Anne had seen her brother just the previous day. Though she had noticed that his body was getting tired and that he had been sleeping more, she hadn't noticed any other changes and couldn't believe he was gone. "Linda was totally shocked. When we got there, she was apologizing because he had died, and she had fallen off to sleep. She had just gotten up and given him some meds not long before."[2]

Stacie was living in Jackson when she received her brother's call. With two very young children, she packed and hurried north up Interstate 55. "It's probably the quickest I've ever gotten there."[3] Hollie was on a camping trip that weekend and soon joined the rest of her family in Carrollton.

* * *

The church was packed for David Lee's funeral, so many that they could not all fit into Carrollton Baptist Church for the weekday service. A significant number in the crowd were from Tishomingo, but the representation from northeast Mississippi would have been much larger had they all heard about Coach's passing in time for his funeral. Some of his ball players came to the service. Before he lost the ability to speak, David Lee had told Anne that he didn't want much fuss over his funeral services for Linda's sake. She remembered the brevity and depth of emotion of her brother's funeral: "It was short and sweet. Delbert Edwards sang at his funeral, and he almost didn't make it through. Delbert has a beautiful voice, but that day I prayed for him to get it over. He was heartbroken."[4] He was not alone.

* * *

David Lee Herbert's memory still lives on in the communities he touched but none more significantly than Tishomingo. They have the wrong-way play to call their own, if not a high school football team these days. When county supervisor Jeff Holt runs into older Falkner natives at one of his son's baseball tournaments, he always asks if they remember the play. They do. Holt noted, "They ain't as fired up about it as people over here, though."[5] The play always comes up when Tish graduates get together and start swapping stories, but, to a one, they will tell you that the play falls far short of defining who Coach Herbert was nor does his family's response to Lauriann's death nor does his coaching with Lou Gehrig's disease. Instead, the character that David Lee and Linda poured out to a school and a town through tragedies that might have individually undone most people is the legacy that Tish residents of the mid- to late-1980s treasure. Former lineman John Moore said, "Coach Herbert had a big impact on me. He taught me confidence in myself. He was a father, a friend, and a teacher. The 'play' didn't make Coach Herbert a great man or a smart man. He was already a great man before that game."[6] To many from Tishomingo, Mississippi, in the 1980s, the influence of Coach and Linda Herbert not only impacted their lives but defined them.

Few people knew David Lee as long as his cousin Bernard Taylor. Asked about his friend's legacy, he thought a moment and replied, "There was no fake in David Lee. What you saw in David Lee was a strong·family man. He loved Linda, he loved his children, and he loved his church. He was just a person that everybody admired, enjoyed being around. He enjoyed children and that was very evident in his coaching."[7]

After years as a high school principal and administrative consultant, Danny McClung considers the key to success in a small school whether or not that school has good teachers. Coach Herbert came to a school with good teachers and good parental support and was poised for lasting success there. McClung shook his head when he thought about what the Herbert family faced in Coach Herbert's six years coaching at Tish: "A man outlines the story of his life when he's young, but then he writes another one. It may not match what he originally planned, but how you write those chapters when things don't end like you think they should, and how you write those last chapters sums up a lot about you." He remembered David Lee Herbert's life as one of grace. "He took what happened and dealt with it as best he could with the help of his friends and his faith."[8]

Ronny McKee sat in Coach Herbert's old classroom with teammates Derrick Brock and Brad Howie in the summer of 2018. He recalled the respect he had for his high school coach and one principle that Coach Herbert hammered home to his players before the car wreck and before his ALS diagnosis: "Life is hard. I won't ever forget that. That means so much to me because I got out early and started my own family. And through my life struggles, I remember him saying that, and that man told the truth because life is hard." With over thirty years of marriage now under his belt, McKee kept going back to one word to describe the man he called his second dad: *respect*. "There will never be another Coach Herbert."[9]

* * *

Dave Herbert remembered how his parents persevered through one tragedy after another. A strong family and strong church families were the building blocks that made coping easier. There was something more, however. Something that is part of his family's fabric like the small communities and schools where his father coached, something in short supply in today's world: "Just never feeling sorry for yourself. In a small town, everybody kind of rallies around each other, whether it's us or somebody else. You tend to be close like family, so they take care of you like family."[10]

Mike Reans calls his former colleague and friend the truest of Southern gentlemen. On the way to his own Hall of Fame career—he was inducted into the Mississippi Association of Independent Schools shrine in 2012 honoring a stellar basketball coaching career—he has never forgotten the friendship and camaraderie that he and his wife built with the Herberts around their mobile homes and shared garden in Marvell, Arkansas.[11] As their careers took them to different schools, but never too far away from one another, he and Beverly visited the Herberts through the years. They were saddened by the road that their friends traveled. He has often told his Sunday school class that he knew a modern-day Job. Even during their visits after David Lee's ALS diagnosis, Reans never recalled a bitter tone to their story. Instead, the Herberts always looked for ways to serve those who came to serve them.[12]

Reans has not been the only one through the years to use Coach Herbert as an example of a modern-day Job. Royce Howie has, as well.

> I've used it in classes that I teach and other speaking that I've done. Coach Herbert—when he got down, when he couldn't function anywhere near what he formerly could—he never, ever said one negative word about that. He just kept going down, but he never complained, and when you'd walk in and he'd recognize you, a smile would come on his face when he could still smile. You knew Coach Herbert was not

gonna be all right; he *was* all right. He was flat on his
back, but he knew where he was going.[13]

Linda Herbert came across a sermon from a pastor in
Texas who used her husband's famous play call as an
illustration for the death and Resurrection of Jesus Christ:
The Lord sending in the play to His Son—one that the world
never would have expected—and the Son executing the play
to perfection. The pastor reflected on the wrong-way play
call as he called the cross "a game plan that looked to the
entire world like craziness."[14]

Vince Jordan remembered David Lee Herbert as the right
man at the right time in his life as a young coach who was
about to suffer close personal loss himself within months of
coming to Tish:

> David and I kind of fed off each other. He imparted
> wisdom and knowledge to me, and I brought youth
> and vigor to him. He trained me. The Lord worked
> everything out for us. He was a battler. He was
> courageous, and you know, he never complained
> about it. He never wavered in his faith. So many
> times, people whine and cry and blame God, and I
> never heard him do it, even to me—or anyone, that
> I'm aware of. He was a godly man who lived a good
> life that made an impact on a lot of people, and it has
> been my honor and pleasure of being able to know
> him and being affiliated with him, and I hope in some
> small way, I made a contribution to his life and to
> those around him and his family because they are
> dear people.

Jordan did not hear of his old colleague's death until
about a month after he had passed away. In the busyness of

his career and family life, he has never been back to Tishomingo. Like so many, though, he feels a deep sense of wishing that he had spent more time with David Lee.[15]

* * *

Some might wonder for a family that depended so much on its faith—with a business failure, Lauriann's accident, Linda's devastating injuries, David Lee's Lou Gehrig's disease, Linda's nearly around-the-clock care for him for so long, and her own cancer—didn't it seem like maybe God should draw a yellow penalty flag for piling on? Joyce Bowman knew David Lee his entire life. She watched him grow up as a carefree young man, marry, have a healthy and happy family, and enjoy a career that he loved. She watched it all seemingly crumble as one tragedy after another bombarded her brother's family. Yet she saw something else at work at the same time—something both simple and extremely profound:

> Linda's faith and David's faith were so strong. To the outsider, it looked like God was giving them more than they could handle. Your heart breaks for them. At the same time, you admire and you're so grateful that they have that strength and that they have what they have that's brought them through it and made them what they are. I have watched Linda's and Dave's family walk through a lot besides this.
>
> I've heard Linda say to me and to her children, "God is in control. I know it looks impossible to you right now but wait on Him. He will get you through this, and it will be okay. You're going through the storm right now. I've seen a lot of things in their family that

look very difficult that they had to walk through. Just knowing—and it took a long time—this is what I witnessed: them being able to sit back and not man-make trying to resolve it and let God resolve it. And that's hard to do. That takes a lot of restraint. It takes a lot of faith.[16]

To those on the outside looking in, Linda Herbert appeared to have sacrificed many of the best years of her life caring for her invalid husband. Looking back over more than a decade of visiting the Herbert home to change out David Lee's tracheostomy tube, Kathy Haynes begged to differ:

You could walk in that house and any troubles you had, you laid those down in a hurry, and you walked out of there grateful and blessed. It wasn't that you felt sorry for them because they didn't give you anything to feel sorry for. They were so joyful; they just gave you a blessing. David Lee was more of a man of the house than many, many able-bodied men. The whole time he was sick and on that ventilator, Linda did not make family decisions without conferring with him and talking with him about it. And he was still the man of that house.[17]

The old saying goes that behind every good man is a good woman. Perhaps then, the key to being a great man is having a great woman *beside* him. David Lee Herbert certainly did. All of the sports teamwork metaphors fall short of what this husband and wife team was able to accomplish in the lives of those they touched. Linda's daughter Stacie called her mother the glue that held the family together and attributed her fortitude to a vow she took so many years earlier: "in sickness and in health...that was her husband."[18] Anne Whitfield could not adequately describe her brother without first starting with her thoughts about her sister-in-law:

> Words can't describe what she's done in her life for people, especially my brother—the love she had for him and her family. Family always came first, just like with David Lee. She's such an inspiration for the life she's led, just like the life he led. What you see is what you get from them, inside and out, always a smile and always wanting to help and do what's right, regardless of the circumstances. I've never heard her say a derogatory word about anybody or feel sorry for herself. She was small in stature but overwhelming how she prevailed through all this with a smile on her face.[19]

* * *

Two of Coach Herbert's hawgs from his early days at Tishomingo High School—lifelong friends of different races—reminisced in the summer of 2018 about how their coach instructed them over and over again that life is hard. Before the accident that took his daughter and before his battle with ALS, their coach was preparing them for life, just like he was his own family. Both men look back at a coach who told the truth as they recalled the struggles of their own. They recalled watching their coach live out what he taught his team during the succeeding years. One said, "The fortitude that he showed, even toward the end of his coaching days, that speaks volumes. What he went through in his time here—he was forged in a way that he was able to deal with it. It shows in Dave; it shows in his daughters; it shows in Mrs. Herbert. It still shows to this day."[20]

Outside of his immediate family, perhaps no one in Tishomingo County could understand the depth of David Lee Herbert's high cost of leading through his own agony like his friend Paul Whitlock. Retired from public life after careers with the railroad and in public service, Whitlock said that David Lee and Linda are still the topic of conversation for many in Tishomingo County today.

> There was no way to ever know David—adult or kid—without being affected by a very quiet, humble, unassuming individual who never had to say much to impress how sincere and God-fearing and loving of a human being he was. I cannot imagine the number of young men and women—not only through football but through classrooms—whose lives in some way have been touched by just knowing him, by just being around him a while, not only with David but with Linda. That's the legacy I see that he's left, and it's one that's hard to duplicate. It's hard to explain in a lot of ways because the wrong-way play didn't make David. What made David was in everyday life—adversity, turmoil, trouble, problems—it's who he was through all that.
>
> Brother Gene Tennyson, who was the pastor of Tishomingo Baptist Church, said to Phyllis and me in the midst of our daughter's death and funeral to always remember one thing: God cannot use an individual until He breaks him. And we were all broken.[21]

Forever linked through the passing of their daughters from that fateful wreck in 1984, two men opened their own stories of adversity for others in their community to experience in real time. Because of that, the families that walked through that period of time with them have never been the same. The town of Tishomingo, Mississippi, has never been the same.

* * *

More than two decades ago, not too many years after Coach Herbert coached his final game, this author heard Dave Dravecky speak at a school event. Dravecky was a Major League Baseball pitcher for the San Francisco Giants who lost much of his throwing shoulder to cancer in 1988 before he miraculously came back to pitch again a year later. Cancer would take his left arm not too long after that return to the game. On the day he spoke, empty sleeve and all, he made a profound statement that this writer has never forgotten: "When God wants to do an extraordinary work, he takes an ordinary man and crushes him." Coach David Lee Herbert was such a man. The proof lies in the lives that this ordinary man and his family touched and his extraordinary legacy of "playing for overtime" that lives on in them.

Epilogue

One might expect that a drive through Tishomingo, Mississippi, today would be a trip through a ghost town. Not so. Though the high school closed after the 1990-91 school year, the school grounds remain active. Shannon Edmondson is the principal of Tishomingo Middle School that now occupies the buildings that formerly housed an entire twelve grades, though neither the sign above the driveway nor the one on the school building itself include the word *middle*. The Tishomingo School campus has seen few changes since David Lee and Linda Herbert filled spaces bigger than any would have ever imagined when they brought their family of outsiders to Tish in 1983.

Jerry Hollingsworth's Sunflower grocery store still provides a vital service to the small town, as does the Dollar General up Highway 25 a piece. The NAPA auto parts store has new stonework across the front, and Main Street Cycle across the street buzzes with patrons checking out the latest off-road vehicles. Tishomingo State Park is just south of town on the way to Belmont. A number of the Tish players from Coach Herbert's day have married girls from Belmont, but aside from a mention of Chris Moss's chiropractic office there, you won't hear them making too many positive comments about a rival that they never could beat. You still have to drive a few miles to find a fast food restaurant, but mama 'n 'ems is still open for dinner for many of these guys.

Typical of most small towns, many of Coach Herbert's players moved away when they went to college, and they stayed away to find better employment opportunities. Quite a few stayed, though, and proved that a small town guy can become a doctor or lawyer or engineer or salesman and still call Tishomingo home. Brad Howie still hangs out every week or two with a half-dozen former teammates from Tish. He lives just around a bend in the road from his dad and next door to his uncle just outside of town. Hardly a day goes by that he doesn't see deer in the hollow below his house. He has traveled around the state and across the country with his sales job but has never been anywhere quite like home.

Stacy McClain Craig moved with her family to Munford, Tennessee, after her sophomore year when her father, Coach Herbert's first assistant coach, took a job teaching math at the University of Memphis. Though she lived near her mother's side of the family, graduated from Munford High School, and remains active in that community today, she still considers Tishomingo home.

> The things that I think of fondly about Tishomingo is not just going to school there. It was the fun times, the innocence of life from what you're going through growing up as kids. You went down to Mr. Green's house to get a soda pop and a Hershey bar when you're watching a baseball game there at the field or if you're hanging out at the field house while Daddy was coaching or practicing with the boys. Those are just memories of living in a small town. We had one road you could really drive up and down on Friday

and Saturday night; otherwise, you had to go up to Iuka or to Corinth. Those are fond memories that you build on.

It was built on because a lot of kids in our classes were teacher's kids; we all had the same kind of connection because our parents were teachers, so we would all be at the same place and doing the same things. We lived near the Melvins and the McClungs, and when it snowed, we all went sliding down the hills. We had good fun, and we all had great memories growing up. I was born in Iuka, have connections in Mathiston, have served and lived in Munford, but Tishomingo is my hometown.[1]

* * *

Linda Herbert walked into her old classroom in the summer of 2018, the first time she had been back to the school since moving back to Carroll County in the early years of David Lee's battle with ALS. She saw shelves that held memories of her time teaching principles of mathematics. She walked across the hall to her last classroom, the one with the view of their on-campus sandstone home that had been the home of their friends the Melvins when they had first moved to Tishomingo. She stood on her tiptoes to stare out new windows—the other ones reached a foot or two lower—while a former advanced math student told her about a class that scrambled to finish its homework while the appointed lookout waited for her to finish whatever Coach needed before scooting on the Rascal across the parking lot to class.

Like the school building, the campus has not changed much, including the towering oaks just outside the corner of the football field that once shaded the Herbert family's mobile home and the house in the center of campus where David Lee fought his first few rounds against ALS. The addition to the tiny press box that gave him a bird's-eye view during the 1988 season came down the following year, but the press box is still there, wrapped in several more coats of bright gold paint. The old flatbed equipment truck that doubled as Coach Herbert's away-game perch sits in waist-high weeds out in the county.

* * *

One of the biggest fears of the community is further consolidation. The loss of the middle school would likely do what consolidation has already accomplished in so many other parts of Mississippi, to hollow out another small town and usurp another chunk of its identity. Tishomingo Middle School is one of the smallest schools in the county and a likely target should consolidation talks again commence in the county. Much of the town's legacy is already derived from a high school that graduated its last class in 1991, but the buildings are still there, the physical reminders of the centerpiece of society in a small town like Tishomingo.

Thirty-five years ago, David Lee Herbert was a no-frills football coach just trying to teach a bunch of undersized kids a quirky offense. He prepared them for life's difficulties through their mutual love for a game. Then, the worst parts of life happened to his family, and he practiced what he preached. As life inevitably became hard for each of his players through the years, they continued to learn from their high school coach. Far from forgetting him, they know him better than they ever have as they realize they are now about the same age Coach Herbert was when they played for him. They wonder how he kept going in the face of the adversity that would have felled a normal man and consider what they might do if they found themselves in his shoes. Around these parts, those are shoes that will never be filled.

When word began to circulate that an author was doing research to write a book about Coach David Lee Herbert, the response from Tish graduates was overwhelming. Coaches have come to small towns and rallied towns around teams because they won big. Coach Herbert had some winning seasons, and a few of his teams played in the postseason, but he never won big here. His determined faith through overwhelming tragedy, though, galvanized a town. They say small towns never change much, and that may be true for parts of Tish; heck, if you know where to go, you can even find the Herberts' old trailer out in the county, still in use. But once upon a time, a simple man with his faithful wife and their family moved to Tishomingo to help a friend at his school. Thirty-five years later, his influence is more present than it ever was.

* * *

Linda Herbert told me many tremendous stories over the first two and a half years I worked on her husband's biography. Funny stories. Sad stories. Hopeful stories. Down home good country people stories. But not one story of regret. Not one story of lament. One of her daughters wrote of her: "She was one of the greatest people who ever lived." No one—*not a single one*—of the scores of people that I have talked to while researching *Playing for Overtime* would argue that.

I would tell her bits and pieces about the interviews I was doing and how fondly people spoke of her. She would wave it off with that "aw, shucks" manner of hers. I wish she could have seen the stories all in one volume, physical evidence of David Lee Herbert's legacy that is as much hers as it is his. But Mrs. Linda Herbert passed away in January 2019, a few months short of the completed manuscript. She won't be able to read the book and hear from others what an impact she had on their lives.

I wish she could have heard the stories others told about her. I wish she could have heard *every single person* that I interviewed say, in some fashion, "And I never heard her complain." For the better part of two decades, she survived on just a few hours' sleep per night as she cared for her husband with Lou Gehrig's disease. Without complaint. I wish she could have heard them say that he was able to *live*—not just exist—because of her.

I wish she could have heard her students from three decades ago praising her. Some of them talked about her math classroom, but *all* of her former students talked about the life lessons they learned from her. I wish she could have heard how Coach Herbert's former players talked about her. Some of them were able to see her last summer for the first time since the Herberts moved back to Carrollton in 1994. Thirty years ago, David Lee entreated her to "get these boys some sweet tea" when they would drop by to visit. Those boys are all grown up now and forever shaped by their coach and his wife who loved them like their own.

I *really* wish she could have heard how each of her sisters-in-law described her with words and phrases such as *angel* and *sent from God* and how she was much more of a sister than a sister-in-law. I wish she could have seen them shaking their heads trying in vain to come up with better words to express their high regard for their brother's wife.

Don't get me wrong. Ms. Linda knew she was loved, no doubt. I just wish she could have heard what I heard, too. As much as I wish she could have read this book and as much as I wish she could have heard how her children and grandchildren and former students and in-laws and others spoke of her, I know that Linda Herbert had some other voices that she longed to hear on that January day. She heard the voice of a daughter for whom she had ached for almost thirty-five years. About five years after she last heard Lauriann's voice on earth, she became the voice of her husband, who had lost his. On that Tuesday in January, she heard his strong, clear Southern drawl again. And on that day, she heard another voice, One that welcomed her into eternity and told her all she needed to know: *Well done, good and faithful servant.*

In Their Own Words

Behind Every Cloud There Is a Silver Lining

Paper presented to the Tishomingo County High School

Hollie Herbert

November 24, 1992

I am the youngest in my family and until I was nine years old, life was quite normal. My dad coached football and my mom taught science and math in Carrollton, Mississippi. My two sisters, brother, and I enjoyed playing together and with our friends. When I was five my family moved to Marvell, Arkansas, where my dad and mom had new coaching and teaching jobs. Because I was young and had not started to school, I did not have a big adjustment to make. Then when I was eight, we moved to Tishomingo, Mississippi, where we still live. The adjustment was a little harder that time since I had to leave my friends in Arkansas, but it was only a few days until we had met several new friends there.

The next year, 1984, however, I began to face many changes. I lost my older sister, Lauriann, who was a senior in high school, and a best friend because of a tragic automobile accident caused by two guys racing on the highway. My mom, sisters, and I had gone to a football game near Corinth, Mississippi, where my dad was coaching and my older sister was a cheerleader. When the game was over, the football team and many of the fans were going to Corinth to get something to eat. My friend Kimberly Whitlock and her four-year-old sister Amy wanted to ride with us. Near Corinth one of the boys that was racing lost control of his car and swerved into our lane and hit us head-on. He was also killed. My mom, sister Stacie, and Amy were seriously injured, but I was not injured as badly as they were. I didn't realize Lauriann had been killed because my dad told me she was in the next room to me, so I didn't think anything else about it. My dad waited until my mom was out of her coma and Stacie was out of intensive care to tell us. When he told us it was like he pulled the carpet out from under our feet. I couldn't sleep for days. I was in the hospital for four days and Stacie went home after two weeks. Mom had to stay over two weeks because one leg was crushed and the other was broken badly, and she had to have surgery on both.

My dad stayed with mom and wasn't there for me, but my family was there. Their support helped tremendously. I miss my sister still, and it gets me down sometimes when I think about Lauriann and Kimberly being taken away so suddenly, but I haven't lost them completely. I still have them in my heart. Losing my sister makes me aware of how quickly someone can be taken from us. My family and I have gotten closer because of this. We don't take each other for granted, and we bless each day that we spend together. This has made me a stronger person, and I have a better understanding of how other people feel when they must face a similar situation.

Three years later my dad began to have trouble with his left leg. In the summer of 1987, he was diagnosed with Amyotrophic Lateral Sclerosis (ALS) also known as Lou Gehrig's Disease. This was another drastic blow to my family and me, but my dad was determined not to give up. He continued to coach and teach that year but had to use a cane, and by spring practice of 1988 he was unable to walk. He used an electric mobility chair called a Rascal. As the disease continued to affect my dad's muscular system, he was unable to teach and coach both. He was given special permission to continue coaching. Since he was unable to coach from the sidelines, several of his friends built a special platform at the football field that he could drive upon with his Rascal and be able to see over the field. My mom became his hands and sat with him and helped him send plays to the sidelines, using walkie-talkies. At the end of his final regular season game, he sent in what became known as the Wrong-Way Play. In order to advance to the state playoffs our team had to defeat the opponent by four or more points; with seven seconds to go in the game and only two points ahead. My dad sent in a play to my brother Dave, who was quarterback, to give the ball to the running back and for him to run the wrong way into his own end zone, which produced a safety and gave the opponent two points. This tied the game which then went into overtime. The opponent was unable to score during the first series of downs, and then when Tishomingo had the ball, they were able to score a touchdown and win by six points. The media picked up the story and my dad received national recognition and was also inducted into the Mississippi Coaches Hall of Fame.

This, I think, is an example my dad himself. He was going to fight until he won, and he did win. Today he is still fighting.

After that year he had to quit coaching and in May 1989 had to have a tracheostomy done and now breathes with the use of a ventilator. The following year he had to begin to eat with a feeding tube. My mom had to quit her job of teaching to stay home to take care of my dad.

Because my dad is disabled, I have had more responsibilities at home. Since he must have constant care, my sister and I must help my mom with the cooking and housework. We do all of the shopping for her. On weekends we take turns on who gets to go out earlier because one of us must help my mom get my dad into his wheelchair. I get frustrated often because I don't get to do what I would like, but I get mad at myself and realize that I have my family who loves me.

In February 1991, we were stunned again when my mom was told she had breast cancer and would have to have a mastectomy. Her main concern was how my dad would be cared for while she was in the hospital. He is unable to talk now, and my mom is able to communicate with him better than the rest of us. After talking to the doctors, my dad was admitted into the hospital room next to my mom. She was able to help with my dad which made him feel more secure. My mom had chemotherapy and is now doing fine. I have become stronger as a result of this because my mom always says that even though things seem to be bad, the Lord has something good in mind and we should always be thankful for what we have.

I sometimes get upset by what I've been through, but then I look at it in a positive way. I've become a Christian since my older sister was killed, and I want to be with her and my family when I die. Since my dad has been sick, I have learned to be thankful for what I have: a happy, loving family and thoughtful, caring friends. Also I no longer take for granted things such as eating, breathing, and talking. My mom and dad and the problems we have had to face have taught me to have a positive attitude, never give up, and above all, let God guide you and give you the strength needed to face what life may bring. As my mom says, "Behind every cloud there is a silver lining."[1]

Hollie added the following to her essay that was published on the ALS Association's website after her father's death:

> Despite the fact that he was only expected to live a short time after being diagnosed with Lou Gehrig's disease, and although his condition progressively worsened and he needed the full-time care of his wife, Linda, he lived 17 more years before finally succumbing on July 16, 2005. Hope symbolizes courage, determination, and faith. Hope gave us a reason to move forward and to eventually become my dad's arms, legs, and voice. My mom who is a two-time breast cancer survivor cared for my dad for 18 years, 24 hours a day. She is our rock. God is the only one that knows what tomorrow will bring. We had hope and faith in God's plan. We did whatever it took to make the best of the worst circumstances. "Rejoice in hope, be patient in tribulation, be constant in prayer" (Romans 12:12, ESV).[2]

On Faith in God

Linda Herbert's Testimony

Martin R. Dehaan, Bible teacher and founder of Our Daily Bread Ministries, said, "Nothing happens by chance. God is in control. Obediently trust God in your circumstance—even when you can't understand what He is doing." Reflecting on my own life, I know now that God has always been in control. He has always watched over and taken care of my family from the beginning.

As a teenager I would ask God to direct the right person to me when it was time for me to marry and He did. I married David Lee Herbert on May 26, 1965. I knew David Lee was the person God had directed into my life on our first date. I just didn't tell David Lee. After we started dating our love for each other began to grow, and we knew that we were meant to be together. We were for forty years until he died on July 16, 2005.

For the first nineteen years of our marriage our life together was that of a typical family. I taught school, David Lee coached and taught, and the Lord blessed us with four beautiful children: Lauriann, Dave, Stacie, and Hollie. As David Lee changed coaching jobs, our family moved four times. With every move I know the Lord guided us in our decision.

As our children grew, I often thought about how I would be able to cope if some bad tragedy were to happen to my family. While we were living in Tishomingo, Mississippi, our Friday night tradition during the fall was to attend the football game David Lee was coaching and to watch Lauriann, our oldest daughter, cheer on the sideline. On Friday night November 2, 1984, my three daughters and I were going to McDonald's after the ballgame. Hollie, our nine-year-old daughter, invited her friend and her friend's four-year-old sister to ride with us. As Lauriann drove we were hit head-on by a car that was drag racing. The accident took the lives of Lauriann, who was seventeen, Hollie's nine-year-old friend, and the fifteen-year-old boy that was driving the other car. Stacie, our ten-year-old daughter, had severe facial injuries, Hollie had a severe cut on her head, and the friend's little sister had severe brain damage. I had several facial cuts, my left leg was badly broken below the knee, and my right femur was crushed. I had to use a wheelchair for about five months and then crutches for about a year and a half. During this time I had to have five surgeries on my legs. My prognosis was the possibility of never walking again. That, however, was not the Lord's will. I do require a one inch buildup on my right shoe because as my femur healed it became shorter.

After this tragedy I often asked the Lord why He couldn't have taken me and let Lauriann live. A fellow teacher eased our heartache by sharing with David Lee and me that even though we loved Lauriann and she loved us, she would definitely choose heaven. I finally realized that we cried because of our loss of not having Lauriann, but that she had reached the ultimate happiness.

Three years passed and August of 1987 David Lee, age forty-five, was diagnosed with ALS or Lou Gehrig's disease. I knew that God had answered my question "Why not me?" after the accident. He intended for me to be David Lee's caregiver.

Then in March 1991, I was diagnosed with breast cancer. I was immediately scheduled for a mastectomy. My only concern was how I would care for David Lee. He was on a ventilator and had a feeding peg, and I had stopped teaching the year before to become his caregiver. My concern was relieved when the doctors at Northeast MS Medical Center in Tupelo admitted him into a hospital room next to mine. My children, who were teenagers then, and a woman who helped me at night at home helped me care for David Lee while we were in the hospital. Again God was handling everything.

I had six months of chemo for precautionary reasons, but it never occurred to me that I would not be cured. I knew the Lord was caring for me. Now I realize that the Lord knew that David Lee would live many more years beyond the three to five years for most ALS patients and that I would be needed to care for him.

During the eighteen years David Lee had ALS, seven were spent in Tishomingo and eleven in Carrollton. We moved back to Carrollton in August 1994. Our youngest daughter, Hollie, who lives in Carrollton, has always lived near us. She took care of my grocery shopping or any other outside help I needed. She said one time that she was a mistake since she and her sister Stacie are only sixteen months apart. I told her she was not a mistake, just a surprise. God knew what He was doing when He gave Hollie to us as well as our other children. Dave, Stacie, and Hollie have always been ready to help us whenever we needed them, and without a single complaint.

My faith and communication with God grew tremendously during those tragic times. There were times when I felt as if I were being deprived of being able to live a normal life since I seldom left home. Whenever I wanted to feel sorry for myself, though, I would think of David Lee who could only move his eyes and how much I loved him. I thank the Lord every day that I am a cancer survivor and was able to be here to care for him.

The blessings we gained through these happenings have been enormous. The Lord blessed David Lee in his coaching career with several championships and allowed him to work with so many young people, which he thoroughly enjoyed. The Lord made it possible for David Lee to coach his final season in 1988 when Dave, our son, was a senior even though his ALS was rapidly progressing, and he had to use a motorized wheelchair.

During his final regular season game he had to win by four or more points to win the district and be able to go to the state playoffs. With seven seconds to go in the game, our team was ahead by two points. David Lee sent in a play that became nationally known as "the wrong-way play." Dave, who was the quarterback, handed the ball to our running back, who carried the ball the wrong way and cross the wrong goal line, giving the other team two points. This tied the game, which in turn went into overtime. The other team was unable to score but our team did, enabling us to go on to the state playoffs.

Even though David Lee sent in the play, God was directing. The chance of our team being two points ahead so that a wrong-way safety would tie the game had to be God's handiwork. David Lee's career ended with his most cherished accomplishment. In 1989 he was inducted into Mississippi Coaches Hall of Fame.

During all this time I have learned to be more patient and to turn all my problems and concerns over to the Lord and let Him guide me. I stop and talk to the Lord many times each day if only for a minute to thank Him for always being there and listening to whatever I have to say or ask.

The tremendous amount of love I had for David Lee and have for my children is small, though, compared to how much the Lord loves us and wants to do for us. I know that I am a much stronger Christian today and that everything that happens is in God's plan.[1]

This is my favorite devotional from *Streams in the Desert* that I would like to share with you.

> Do not look forward to the changes and chances of this life in fear. Rather look at them with full hope that, as they arise, God, whose you are, will deliver you out of them. He has kept you hitherto; do you but hold fast to His dear hand, and He will lead you safely through all things; and, when you cannot stand, He will bear you in His arms.
>
> Do not look forward to what may happen tomorrow. The same everlasting Father who cares for you today will take care of you tomorrow, and every day. Either He will shield you from suffering, or He will give you unfailing strength to bear it. Be at peace, then, put aside all anxious thoughts and imaginations. (Frances de Sales)[2]

A Legacy of Love

Joyce H. Bowman

Overuse of the word *love* seems to have watered down the real meaning. We love McDonald's, our clothes, our house. These are inanimate things. They do not require giving of ourselves. Therefore, it is inspirational when we see lives expressing the real love—love like David and Linda Herbert have shared since saying I do, love with depth, with caring, with commitment which weathers the storms of life.

College sweethearts, David and Linda began their lives together without much notice. It was a private wedding—just the two of them and the Justice of the Peace. David, a very private man, hadn't wanted all the trimmings. Linda, a very understanding and giving lady, honored his wishes.

From that day forward, they began a very "together life" caring what the other wanted or needed. Shortly after the wedding, they began their teaching careers. David began coaching while Linda listened, supported, and cheered him on.

When the family began growing, they shared responsibilities together. It was not unusual for David to handle the household chores while Linda sewed for all of them. Together, they gave love to all four children—Lauriann, David, Stacie, and Hollie.

Actually, the family was able to grow, pray, and play together, privately. However, the events of November 2, 1984, changed their life from private to public, when tragedy hit the Herbert family after a Friday night football victory. David, driving the football team bus, came upon the horrifying sight of an automobile accident to find it had just taken the life of their precious daughter, Lauriann. But that was just the beginning of the horror. Stacie was in Intensive care with a concussion, Hollie was hospitalized for observations, another child in their car was killed, and another one injured. David's beloved Linda had a crushed leg and was in a coma from head injuries. Her prognosis was poor. If she survived, she probably would not walk again.

The love which poured out from the community was overwhelming. The power of prayer was a constant reality. But the depth of David's love as he prayed, stayed, and cared for Linda was life-changing. Linda faced multiple surgeries and physical therapy, but never alone. The whole way, it was David, Linda, and their family pulling together.

Today, the rules have changed somewhat. It is now David who needs his team pulling for him. Three years after the automobile accident David was diagnosed with Amyotrophic Lateral Sclerosis (ALS), also known as Lou Gehrig's Disease. David and Linda were searching for help and hope when they made the trip from Mississippi to Henry Ford Hospital in Detroit.

When David's doctor, Dr. Glassenburg, told David the final diagnosis, he became very quiet for a short time. Then, with tears in his eyes, he looked at Linda and said, "I am not going to give up!" Her reply was, "We will fight this together!"

And, fight they have. David continued to teach and coach until it became impossible to do both. When David could not do both, he gave up teaching, but they continued to coach. I say they, because it was a team effort. As always, Linda was listening and supporting, however, this time, not just emotionally but physically.

As the disease began to effect David's muscular system, Linda became his hands. When talking was no longer possible, Linda became his lips. But, even now, David never stops thinking. In fact, he thinks quite well. David demonstrated how well during the deciding game for the state championship playoff. David made a coaching decision that became heard around the world. Realizing his team, who was winning, would not go to the state championship without a decisive win, David sent in a call to run a safety for the other team. This meant the game would end in a tie and force an overtime situation. Even though some of the players questioned his decision, his son, the team quarterback, showed his faith by running the play.

David made his decision because he believed his team could win in overtime. His confidence was justified. They did! They went to the playoff and the call went to the media. Television, radio, and publications picked up on the unique call and the courage of the man and his family.

What a family! They have pulled together when others would have pulled apart. Why? Love. The love and commitment of David and Linda has grown, giving them comfort through the trials of life. Even more, they have given to their children a legacy of love—love that stands through the storms showing their faith in God.

Beyond their own family, these two special people have touched the lives of their extended families, their friends, their community. The bottom line—their example is a legacy of love for all of us.[1]

On God's Presence in the Time of Trouble

David Lee Herbert

Carrollton Baptist Church

Before anything drastic happened—such as the death of a loved one or a serious illness—I thought, like many people, that I would not be able to cope if something like this should happen to me. But when it does happen, however, God is always there to hold you up and to enable us not only to be able to cope but to gain blessings from it.

I taught elementary physical education at Tishomingo Elementary School. In the spring of 1986, we were playing softball and I was pitching. I noticed I was falling when trying to stop a routine ground ball. By the spring of 1987, my whole left leg began to give way; I would be walking and all of a sudden fall. In *Sports Illustrated* I had read about Bob Watters, a coach at a North Carolina college, who had ALS, amyotrophic lateral sclerosis, also known as Lou Gehrig's Disease. The article told how he had been afflicted and was forced to use a wheelchair as he continued to coach. I remember his symptoms as my condition got worse, and I began to think that my problem might also be ALS. In

August of 1987, Dr. Coats, a neurologist in Tupelo, ran tests and found that I had nerve damage. He diagnosed that I did have ALS.

When our daughter Lauriann was killed, and Linda and Stacie and Hollie were severely injured in an automobile accident in 1984, it seemed as though the world had come to an end. The Lord, though, was with me and helped me care for Linda and the children. When I was diagnosed with ALS, the Lord again lifted us up, and with the help of our family and our many friends here and in Tishomingo, and spending serious times in prayer, the Lord has allowed me to continue to live many years beyond the average ALS victim. By 1989, my breathing had worsened, and I had to decide if I wanted to have a tracheostomy done and use a ventilator to breathe. Many people do not want to become dependent on a ventilator. I asked God to guide us, and he led me to have a tracheostomy done. I am so thankful for His guidance because I have been able to see my children become adults and to see and hold my grandchildren. Even though I had to retire from coaching in 1988, I am still able to enjoy watching sports, especially football on television.

In 1990, I had to get a feeding peg since I was no longer able to swallow. Linda blended food in an electric blender, so I eat what everybody else eats. The Lord has made is possible for me to have a sensation of what I am eating. I would not be living now without the Lord working through Linda to love and care for me. I am so thankful he led us thirty-three years ago to make the vow "till death do us part." The most assuring promise the Lord had given us— and I pray that each of you believe it as I do—is John 3:16 (KJV): "For God so loved the world that He gave his only begotten Son, that whosoever believeth in him should not perish but have everlasting life."

Lou Gehrig's Farewell Speech

Yankee Stadium, New York

July 4, 1939

Fans, for the past two weeks you have been reading about the bad break I got. Yet today I consider myself the luckiest man on the face of the earth. I have been in ballparks for seventeen years and have never received anything but kindness and encouragement from you fans.

Look at these grand men. Which of you wouldn't consider it the highlight of his career just to associate with them for even one day? Sure, I'm lucky. Who wouldn't consider it an honor to have known Jacob Ruppert? Also, the builder of baseball's greatest empire, Ed Barrow? To have spent six years with that wonderful little fellow, Miller Huggins? Then to have spent the next nine years with that outstanding leader, that smart student of psychology, the best manager in baseball today, Joe McCarthy? Sure, I'm lucky.

When the New York Giants, a team you would give your right arm to beat, and vice versa, sends you a gift—that's something. When everybody down to the groundskeepers and those boys in white coats remember you with trophies—that's something. When you have a wonderful mother-in-law who takes sides with you in squabbles with her own daughter—that's something. When you have a father and a mother who work all their lives so you can have an education and build your body—it's a blessing. When you have a wife who has been a tower of strength and shown more courage than you dreamed existed—that's the finest I know.

So I close in saying that I may have had a tough break, but I have an awful lot to live for.[1]

Acknowledgments

Thank you to my sister and brother-in-law, Wilagene and Stan McElhenney, whose generosity in sponsoring this book went a long way toward making it possible.

To my extended family and friends who have served as benefactors to my writing career, I hope that this book inspires you like your belief in me continues to inspire me to write great stories that you can be proud of.

Writing a book involves many read-throughs, and as well as I know the English language, I am not my best editor. Because of my editor, Geoff Stone—who believed in this project from his first look at it and worked tirelessly in tightening up the content and correcting my style errors—this book is infinitely easier to read.

Thanks to my beta readers, who found little things that may have otherwise slipped through the cracks.

Thanks to my advance reader team, who helped the rest of the world find this book.

My Kickstarter backers' partnership made it possible to send a copy of this book to every Class 1A coach in Mississippi as an encouragement to an underappreciated group of professionals. Thank you to every one of you who made those gifts possible.

The newspaper and television reporters who covered the games, who freely shared their parts of Coach Herbert's story, and who always pointed me toward others who might add something to my research are kindred spirits. Will Kollmeyer and Chris Burrows, your willingness to give of your time to swap stories related and unrelated to this book were some of the most fun conversations I had in writing the book.

I will never be able to adequately express my gratitude to the members of the Herbert family, whose hours of conversations with me through laughter and tears was the heart and soul of my research.

I discovered the deepest meaning of this story through interviews with Coach Herbert's former players and managers, where I found the lasting impact of a coach's life well lived.

When I felt like I had enough background to begin interviewing Coach Herbert's former players, Dave Herbert put me in touch with Brad Howie, who set me up with many of the interviews that took his coach's story to other levels that I could have only hoped for. What a great ambassador you are for Tishomingo, my friend.

To my wife Loretta, I cannot emphasize enough how much I appreciate your understanding of this project that has consumed so much of my extra time through the three years I have worked on it. I love you.

The Lord wrote this story into the Herbert family's lives and into my heart. Without His work in each of our lives, you would not be holding this book in your hands today. To God be the glory for the great things that He has done and will continue to do through the Herbert family's remarkable story.

Bibliography

Online Sources

"2016 Visitor's Guide." Tishomingo County Tourism Council. Accessed June 17, 2018. http://www.tishomingofunhere.org/pdfs/2016%20Visitors%20Guide.pdf.

"2017-19 Football Regions." Mississippi High School Activities Association. Last modified June 14, 2018. https://www.misshsaa.com/2017/02/02/2017-19-football-regions/.

"2019-21 MHSAA Classifications." Mississippi High School Activities Association. Last modified October 23, 2018. https://www.misshsaa.com/2018/10/23/2019-21-mhsaa-classifications/.

"About." Carroll Academy. Accessed June 13, 2018. http://www.carrollacademy.org/about/.

"Ackerman Football Team History." Mississippi High School Football History. Accessed April 14, 2019. http://www.ahsfhs.org/MISSISSIPPI/teams/gamesbyyear.asp?year=1997&Team=Ackerman.

"ALS Ice Bucket Challenge – FAQ." ALS Association. Accessed June 11, 2018. http://www.alsa.org/about-us/ice-bucket-challenge-faq.html.

"Amyotrophic Lateral Sclerosis (Lou Gehrig's Disease)." *LifeExtension*. Accessed June 24, 2018. https://www.lifeextension.com/Protocols/Neurological/Als/Page-01.

"Amyotrophic Lateral Sclerosis." Mayo Foundation for Medical Education and Research. Last modified May 12, 2017. https://www.mayoclinic.org/diseases- conditions/amyotrophic-lateral-sclerosis/symptoms-causes/syc-20354022.

"Amyotrophic Lateral Sclerosis." National Institutes of Health. Last modified January 2017. https://www.ninds.nih.gov/Disorders/Patient-Caregiver-Education/Fact-Sheets/Amyotrophic-Lateral-Sclerosis-ALS-Fact-Sheet.

"Area Attractions." Welcome to Tishomingo. Accessed August 4, 2018. http://tishomingo.ms/attractions.html.

BIBLIOGRAPHY

"Big Eight Records." Mississippi High School Football History. Accessed July 9, 2018. http://www.ahsfhs.org/mississippi/districts/big8.asp.

"Carrollton." Carroll County Development Association. Accessed August 4, 2018. https://carrollcountyms.org/carrollton/.

"Carrollton, MS." Data USA. Accessed August 4, 2018. http://datausa.io/profile/geo/carrollton-ms/.

Cleveland, Don. "Research Home Page." ALS Association. Accessed June 11, 2018. www.alsa.org/research/.

"Community House - Carrollton MS." Living New Deal. Accessed August 4, 2018. https://livingnewdeal.org/projects/community-house-carrollton-ms-2/.

"East Flora Playoff Results." Mississippi High School Football History. Accessed July 10, 2018. http://www.ahsfhs.org/MISSISSIPPI/teams/playoffs.asp?Team=East%20Flora.

"Falkner Coaches." Mississippi High School Football History. Accessed August 4, 2018. http://www.ahsfhs.org/mississippi/teams/Coaches.asp?Team=Falkner.

"Football Champions." Mississippi High School Activities Association. Last modified May 20, 2016. https://www.misshsaa.com/2016/05/20/football-champions/.

"Football Team History: Anguilla Wildcats." Accessed June 1, 2018. http://www.ahsfhs.org/MISSISSIPPI/teams/gamesbyyear.asp?year=1988&Team=Anguilla.

"God's Wonderful Game Plan—The Resurrection of Jesus." *Bible Center*. Accessed April 18, 2019. https://www.biblecenter.com/sermons/godswonderfulgameplan.htm.

"Historical Events in 1942." On This Day. Accessed August 4, 2018. http://www.onthisday.com/events/date/1942.

"The History of High School Football in Mississippi." Mississippi High School Football History. Accessed July 9, 2018. http://www.ahsfhs.org/mississippi/.

"Induction Certificates." Rockabilly Hall of Fame. Accessed March 11, 2019. http://www.rockabillyhall.com/Certificates.html.

"Jimmie Moore." Mississippi High School Football History. Accessed June 18, 2018. http://www.ahsfhs.org/coaches/coachestop.asp?Coach=Jimmie%2BMoore.

BIBLIOGRAPHY

"Lou Gehrig," National Baseball Hall of Fame. Accessed June 11, 2018. https://baseballhall.org/hall-of-famers/gehrig-lou.

"Luckiest Man." Baseball Hall of Fame. Accessed June 11, 2018. https://baseballhall.org/discover-more/stories/baseball-history/lou-gehrig-luckiest-man.

"Mississippi High School Activities Association Class 1A North and South State Football Champions." Mississippi High School Football. Accessed August 4, 2018. http://misshsfootball.com/Champions/Northsouth1A.htm.

"Mississippi High School Football Head Coaches: Dwight Bowling." Mississippi High School Football History. Accessed July 11, 2018. http://www.ahsfhs.org/MISSISSIPPI/coaches/coachestop.asp?Coach=Dwight%2BBowling.

Simmons Football Team History." Mississippi High School Football History. Accessed June 30, 2018. http://www.ahsfhs.org/MISSISSIPPI/teams/gamesbyyear.asp?year=2000&Team=Simmons.

"Smithville Football Team History." Mississippi High School Football History. Accessed March 13, 2019. http://www.ahsfhs.org/mississippi/Teams/gamesbyyear.asp?year=1988&Team=Smithville.

"Thomastown Football Team History." Mississippi High School Football History. Accessed July 8, 2018. http://www.ahsfhs.org/mississippi/Teams/teampage.asp?Team=Thomastown.

"Tishomingo Bulldogs Football Team History." Mississippi High School Football History. Accessed June 18, 2018. http://www.ahsfhs.org/mississippi/Teams/gamesbyyear.asp?year=1982&Team=Tishomingo.

"Tishomingo Bulldogs: Tishomingo vs. Falkner." Mississippi High School Football History. Accessed July 27, 2018. http://www.ahsfhs.org/MISSISSIPPI/teams/opponentseach2015.asp?Opponent1=Falkner&Team=Tishomingo.

"Tishomingo County Football Team History." Mississippi High School Football History. Accessed July 28, 2018. http://www.ahsfhs.org/MISSISSIPPI/teams/gamesbyyear.asp?year=2017&Team=Tishomingo%20County.

"Tishomingo Football Team History." Mississippi High School Football History. Accessed June 18, 2018. http://www.ahsfhs.org/mississippi/Teams/gamesbyyear.asp?year=1983&Team=Tishomingo.

"Town History." Welcome to Tishomingo. Accessed June 17, 2018. http://tishomingo.ms/history.html.

"Walking Tour of Carrollton, Mississippi." Tour Buddy Apps. Accessed August 4, 2018. http://www.tourappbuilder.com/portfolio-item/_walkingtourcarrolltonmississippi/.

"Weir Football Team History." Mississippi High School Football History. Accessed July 8, 2018. http://www.ahsfhs.org/mississippi/Teams/teampage.asp?Team=Weir.

"Works Progress Administration," *Encyclopædia Britannica*. Accessed February 28, 2018. http://www.britannica.com/topic/Works-Progress-Administration.

Film

Gleason, directed by Clay Tweel (2016: Amazon Studios), Amazon Prime, www.amazon.com/gp/video/detail/B01I2BH93Y/ref=atv_dl_rdr.

Newspapers

Chicago Tribune
Carroll County Conservative
Des Moines Register
Greenwood Commonwealth
Los Angeles Times
Madison County Journal
Neshoba Democrat
New York Times
Northeast Mississippi Daily Journal
Heber Springs (AR) *Sun-Times*
Tuscaloosa News
USA Today

NOTES

Chapter 2

1   "Mississippi High School Activities Association Class 1A North and South State Football Champions," Mississippi High School Football, accessed August 4, 2018, http://misshsfootball.com/Champions/Northsouth1A.htm.

2   "Falkner Coaches," Mississippi High School Football History, accessed August 4, 2018. http://www.ahsfhs.org/mississippi/teams/Coaches.asp?Team=Falkner.

3   D. E. Wheeler, "HED: Horton's Death Shocks Already Stunned Area," *Northeast Mississippi Daily Journal* (Tupelo, MS), September 2, 2000.

4   Will Kollmeyer (sports broadcaster), in discussion with the author, December 2017.

5   "Tishomingo Breezes to Division Win," *Northeast Mississippi Daily Journal* (Tupelo, MS), September 3, 1988.

6   "Tishomingo Rallies for Victory," *Northeast Mississippi Daily Journal* (Tupelo, MS), September 10, 1988.

7   Mike Talbert, "Tishomingo Counting Heavily on Sophomore Production," *Northeast Mississippi Daily Journal* (Tupelo, MS), August 19, 1988.

Chapter 3

1   "Walking Tour of Carrollton, Mississippi," Tour Buddy Apps, accessed August 4, 2018, http://www.tourappbuilder.com/portfolio-item/__walkingtourcarrolltonmississippi/.

2   "Carrollton, MS," Data USA, accessed August 4, 2018, http://datausa.io/profile/geo/carrollton-ms/.

3   Rick Ward, "The Carroll County Courthouse Massacre, 1886: A Cold Case File," Mississippi History Now, accessed July 1, 2018, http://www.mshistorynow.mdah.ms.gov/articles/381/the-carroll-county-courthouse-massacre-1886-a-cold-case-file.

4   "Carrollton Courthouse Massacre," MS Civil Rights Project, accessed July 1, 2018, http://mscivilrightsproject.org/carroll/event-carroll/carrollton-courthouse-massacre/.

5   Ward, "Carroll County Courthouse."

6   Ibid.

7   Sheila Weller, "How Author Timothy Tyson Found the Woman at the Center of the Emmett Till Case," The Hive, *Vanity Fair*, last modified January 27, 2017, https://www.vanityfair.com/news/2017/01/how-author-timothy-tyson-found-the-woman-at-the-center-of-the-emmett-till-case.

8   "Historical Events in 1942," On This Day, accessed August 4, 2018, http://www.onthisday.com/events/date/1942.

9   Ibid.

10   Ibid.

11   Phil Vettel, "The Cubs Get Lights at Wrigley Field," *Chicago Tribune*, last modified July 13, 2008, https://www.chicagotribune.com/news/nationworld/politics/chi-chicagodays-wrigleylights-story-story.html.

12   "Works Progress Administration," *Encyclopædia Britannica*, accessed February 28, 2018, http://www.britannica.com/topic/Works-Progress-Administration.

13   "Carrollton Community House Featured in Mississippi Preservation Blog, Carroll County Development Association, last modified January 19, 2016, https://carrollcountyms.org/carrollton-community-house-featured-in-mississippi-preservation-blog/.

14   "Community House - Carrollton MS," Living New Deal, accessed August 4, 2018, https://livingnewdeal.org/projects/community-house-carrollton-ms-2/.

15   "Carrollton," Carroll County Development Association, accessed August 4, 2018, https://carrollcountyms.org/carrollton/.

16 "Area Attractions," Welcome to Tishomingo, accessed August 4, 2018, http://tishomingo.ms/attractions.html.

17 Joyce Herbert Bowman (sister of David Lee Herbert), in discussion with the author, January 2018.

18 Linda Herbert (wife David Lee Herbert), in discussion with the author, June 2018.

19 Linda Herbert interview, July 2018.

20 Joyce Bowman interview.

21 Ibid.

22 Ibid.

23 Bernard Taylor (first cousin of David Lee Herbert), in discussion with the author, October 2018.

24 Joyce Herbert, personal email to author, July 29, 2018.

25 Clint Littleton (friend of David Lee Herbert), in discussion with the author, July 2018.

Chapter 4

1 *Induction* Certificates, Rockabilly Hall of Fame, accessed March 11, 2019, http://www.rockabillyhall.com/Certificates.html.

2 Littleton interview.

3 Bowman interview.

4 Ibid.

5 Bowman email.

6 Ibid.

7 Taylor interview.

8 Ibid.

9 Bowman interview.

10 Littleton interview.

11 Ibid.

12 Taylor interview.

13 Littleton interview.

14 Anne Herbert Whitfield (sister of David Lee Herbert), in discussion with the author, November 2018.

Chapter 5

1 Richard Edwards and Peter Longo, "Rural Communities and School Consolidation-- Introduction to Special Issue," *Great Plains Research: A Journal of Natural and Social Sciences*, last modified 2013, https://digitalcommons.unl.edu/cgi/viewcontent.cgi?referer=https://www.google.com/&httpsredir=1&article=2262&context=greatplainsresearch.

2 Ibid.

3 "School District Consolidation in Mississippi," Mississippi Professional Educators, accessed June 24, 2018, https://mpe.org/mpe/documents/Consolidation.Final.pdf.

4 "Ackerman Football Team History," Mississippi High School Football History, accessed April 14, 2019, http://www.ahsfhs.org/MISSISSIPPI/teams/gamesbyyear.asp?year=1997&Team=Ackerman.

5 Ricky Black (head football coach at Jackson Prep), interview with the author, June 2018. At the time of the 90-yard football field, the baseball field at Ackerman High School had a unique set of ground rules, as well. The school's gymnasium made up part of the left field "fence." If a batted ball bounced off the gym wall, it was played at as a live ball. A ball that went through a window was a ground-rule double, and one that hit the roof was a home run.

6 "Ackerman Football."

7 "Weir Football Team History," Mississippi High School Football History, accessed July 8, 2018. http://www.ahsfhs.org/mississippi/Teams/teampage.asp?Team=Weir.

8 Black interview.

9 "Thomastown Football Team History," Mississippi High School Football History, accessed July 8, 2018, http://www.ahsfhs.org/mississippi/Teams/teampage.asp?Team=Thomastown.

10 Weir resident Roy Oswalt was a major league pitcher from 2001-2013. He spent most of his career with the Houston Astros.

11 Black interview.

12 Ibid.

13 Dave Herbert (son of David Lee Herbert), in discussion with the author, July 2016.

14 Dave Herbert interview, July 2017.

15 Chris Moss (former football manager for David Lee Herbert), in discussion with the author, July 2018.

16 Derrick Brock (former football player for David Lee Herbert), in discussion with the author, July 2018.

17 Brad Howie (former football player for David Lee Herbert), in discussion with the author, July 2018.

18 Jeff Holt (former football manager for David Lee Herbert), phone conversation with the author, July 17, 2018.

19 Parker, Buford, "Exploits and Frank and Jesse James," Southern Accents Architectural Antiques Old Photos Publisher's Collection, accessed March 24, 2019, http://www.sa1969.com/FrankJames-article.pdf.

20 Dave Herbert interview, July 2016.

21 "Smithville Football Team History," Mississippi High School Football History, accessed March 13, 2019, http://www.ahsfhs.org/mississippi/Teams/gamesbyyear.asp?year=1988&Team=Smithville.

22 "No. 7 Okolona Rolls past Nettleton Tigers," *Northeast Mississippi Daily Journal* (Tupelo, MS), October 8, 1988.

23 Dave Herbert interview, July 2016.

24 Chris Burrows, "Falkner Takes1-1A win," *Northeast Mississippi Daily Journal* (Tupelo, MS), October 8, 1988.

25 Ibid.

Chapter 6

1 Bowman interview.

2   Whitfield interview.

3   Janis Herbert Clayton (sister of David Lee Herbert), in conversation with the author, October 2018.

4   Linda Herbert interview, June 2018.

5   Jimmy Herbert (cousin of David Lee Herbert), in conversation with the author), January 2019.

6   Bowman email.

7   Linda Herbert interview, June 2018.

8   Ibid.

9   "About" Carroll Academy, accessed June 13, 2018, http://www.carrollacademy.org/about/.

10 Taylor interview.

11 Delbert Edwards (friend of David Lee Herbert), in conversation with the author, July 2018.

12 Taylor interview.

13 Ibid.

14 Littleton interview.

15 Edwards interview.

16 Ibid.

17 Taylor interview.

Chapter 7

1   Bowman interview.

2   Whitfield interview.

3   Taylor interview

4   Beverly Taylor (wife of Bernard Taylor), in conversation with the author, October 2018. (Notes marked "Taylor interview" are the author's conversation with Bernard Taylor.)

5   Whitfield interview.

6   Linda Herbert interview, June 2018.

7   Littleton interview.

8   Linda Herbert interview, June 2018.

9   Ibid.

10 Edwards interview.

11 Linda Herbert interview, June 2018.

12 Wilton Neal, "It Took Two Months, but East Holmes Beat Carroll Academy," *Carroll County Conservative* (Carrollton, MS), 1977.

13 Dave Herbert interview, June 2016.

14 Dave Herbert interview, June 2016.

15 Stacie Herbert Rector (daughter of David Lee Herbert), in conversation with the author, December 2018.

16 Mike Reans (coaching colleague of David Lee Herbert), phone conversation with the author, July 2018.

17 Ibid.

18 Ibid.

19 Linda Herbert interview, July 2018.

20 Linda Herbert and Hollie Spellman (daughter of David Lee Herbert), in conversation with the author, July 2018.

Chapter 8

1   Linda Herbert interview, June 2018.

2   Danny McClung (coaching colleague of David Lee Herbert), in conversation with the author, July 2018.

3   Ibid.

4   Paul Whitlock (friend of David Lee Herbert), in conversation with the author, January 2019.

5   "Town History," Welcome to Tishomingo, accessed June 17, 2018, http://tishomingo.ms/history.html.

6   Ibid.

7   "2016 Visitor's Guide," *Tishomingo County Tourism Council*, accessed June 17, 2018,

http://www.tishomingofunhere.org/pdfs/2016%20Visitors%20Gui
de.pdf.

8   "Elmore Is Buried Today on His Birthday," Elmore Leonard,
    accessed June 18, 2018,
    http://elmoreleonard.com/index.php?%2Fweblog%2F.

9   "Town History."

10 "Tishomingo Bulldogs Football Team History," Mississippi High
    School Football History, accessed June 18, 2018,
    http://www.ahsfhs.org/mississippi/Teams/gamesbyyear.asp?year
    =1982&Team=Tishomingo.

11 "Jimmie Moore," Mississippi High School Football History, accessed
    June 18, 2018.
    http://www.ahsfhs.org/coaches/coachestop.asp?Coach=Jimmie%2
    BMoore.

12 Rick Cleveland, "Reed's Teams Ran the Notre Dame Box to
    Perfection," Mississippi Sports Hall of Fame and Museum, accessed
    January 2018, https://msfame.com/ricks-writings/reeds-teams-ran-
    the-notre-dame-box-to-perfection/.

13 Reans phone conversation.

14 Kenneth McClain (assistant coach for David Lee Herbert), in
    conversation with the author, March 2019.

Chapter 9

1   Derrick Brock interview.

2   Ronny McKee (former football player for David Lee Herbert), in
    conversation with the author, July 2018.

3   Danny Brock (former football player for David Lee Herbert), in
    conversation with the author, July 2018.

4   Derrick Brock interview.

5   Bill Ross, "Athletic Classification Changes Almost Certain for State
    Schools," *Northeast Mississippi Daily Journal* (Tupelo, MS), September
    9, 1983.

6   Greg Smith, "Class B Schools Meet Outsiders Tonight," *Northeast
    Mississippi Daily Journal* (Tupelo, MS), September 9, 1983.

7   Bill Ross, "Thrasher Gets First Win Ever with 8-0 Victory over Mooreville," *Northeast Mississippi Daily Journal* (Tupelo, MS), September 16, 1983.

8   "Hatley 38, Tishomingo 30," *Northeast Mississippi Daily Journal* (Tupelo, MS), October1-2, 1983.

9   "New Hope Ends Hamilton String," *Northeast Mississippi Daily Journal* (Tupelo, MS), October 8-9 1983.

10 Associated Press, "Marcus Dupree Dropped from Oklahoma Squad," *Northeast Mississippi Daily Journal* (Tupelo, MS), October 12, 1983.

11 Bill Ross, "Golden Bears Nip Bulldogs 14-13," *Northeast Mississippi Daily Journal* (Tupelo, MS), October 28, 1983.

12 Bill Ross, Smithville Makes the Most of I-B Face-Off 22-14," *Northeast Mississippi Daily Journal* (Tupelo, MS) Nov. 5-6, 1983.

13 Joe Tucker (former football player for David Lee Herbert), in conversation with the author, July 2018.

14 Shannon Edmondson (former football player for David Lee Herbert), in conversation with the author, July 2018.

15 Eddie Blunt (former student at Tishomingo High School), email conversation with the author, September 15, 2018. Blunt played in the band until his last year at Tishomingo, cheering for the team that included cousins Mark Blunt and Shane Hill and the coach that cared enough to not allow him to play.

16 John Moore (former football player for David Lee Herbert), email conversation with the author, July 21, 2018.

17 Horn interview.

18 Dave Herbert, Lance Hollingsworth, and Joe Tucker, in conversation with the author, July 2018.

19 Edmondson interview.

20 Eric Powell (former football player for David Lee Herbert), in conversation with the author, January 2018.

21 Ibid.

22 Ibid.

23 Jay McGee (former football player for David Lee Herbert), text conversation with the author, July 11, 2018.

24 Dave Herbert and Jeff Holt interview, July 2018.

25 Moss interview.

26 Ibid.

27 Ibid.

28 Derrick Brock interview.

29 Ibid.

Chapter 10

1 Mike Talbert, "Tishomingo Could Stretch Walnut Skid," *Northeast Mississippi Daily Journal* (Tupelo, MS), October 13, 1988.

2 "Tishomingo Downs Walnut in Division Game," *Northeast Mississippi Daily Journal* (Tupelo, MS), October 15, 1988.

3 "2019-21 MHSAA Classifications," Mississippi High School Activities Association, last modified October 23, 2018, https://www.misshsaa.com/2018/10/23/2019-21-mhsaa-classifications/.

4 "The History of High School Football in Mississippi," Mississippi High School Football History, accessed July 9, 2018, http://www.ahsfhs.org/mississippi/.

5 Princella W. Nowell, "The Flood of 1927 and Its Impact in Greenville, Mississippi," *Mississippi History Now*, accessed July 12, 2018, http://www.mshistorynow.mdah.ms.gov/articles/230/the-flood-of-1927-and-its-impact-in-greenville-mississippi.

6 Ibid.

7 Laura Coyle, "The Great Mississippi River Flood of 1927," *National Museum of African American History and Culture*, last modified January 11, 2019, https://nmaahc.si.edu/explore/stories/collection/great-mississippi-river-flood-1927.

8 "Big Eight Records," Mississippi High School Football History, accessed July 9, 2018, http://www.ahsfhs.org/mississippi/districts/big8.asp.

9   "Football Champions," Mississippi High School Activities
    Association, accessed May 20, 2016,
    https://www.misshsaa.com/2016/05/20/football-champions/.

10 Ibid. Simmons returned to the state championship game in 2018 but
    was defeated by Nanih Waiya High School for the 1A title.

11 "Simmons Football Team History," Mississippi High School Football
    History, accessed June 30, 2018,
    http://www.ahsfhs.org/MISSISSIPPI/teams/gamesbyyear.asp?year
    =2000&Team=Simmons.

12 "2019-21 Football Regions," Mississippi High School Activities
    Association, Last modified October 31, 2018,
    https://www.misshsaa.com/2018/10/31/2019-21-football-regions/.

13 "Mississippi Burning," Federal Bureau of Investigation, last
    modified May 18, 2016, https://www.fbi.gov/history/famous-
    cases/mississippi-burning.

14 Douglas O. Linder, "The Mississippi Burning Trial," *Famous Trials*,
    accessed April 14, 2019, famous-
    trials.com/legacyftrials/price&bowers/Account.html.

15 Linda Herbert and Hollie Spellman, interview, 2018.

Chapter 11

1   "Tishomingo Football Team History," Mississippi High School
    Football History, accessed June 18, 2018.
    http://www.ahsfhs.org/mississippi/Teams/gamesbyyear.asp?year
    =1983&Team=Tishomingo.

2   McClain interview.

3   Howie interview.

4   McKee interview.

5   Whitlock interview.

6   Phillip Whitehead (former football player for David Lee Herbert), in
    conversation with the author, July 2018.

7   Ibid.

8   Bobby Harrison, "Tishomingo Must Have More than Powell,"
    Northeast Mississippi Daily Journal (Tupelo, MS) August 24, 1984.

9   Bobby Harrison, "Smithville, Tishomingo Take Different Routes," *Northeast Mississippi Daily Journal* (Tupelo, MS), September 14, 1984.

10   "Tishomingo 24, Blue Mountain 7," *Northeast Mississippi Daily Journal* (Tupelo, MS), September 15-16, 1984.

11   Whitehead interview.

12   "Belmont 26, Tishomingo 6," *Northeast Mississippi Daily Journal* (Tupelo, MS), September 22-23 1984.

13   Howie interview.

14   Whitehead interview.

15   "Vardaman Rams Breeze past Caledonia, 30-6," *Northeast Mississippi Daily Journal* (Tupelo, MS), September 29-30, 1984.

16   "Hatley 35, Tishomingo 12," *Northeast Mississippi Daily Journal* (Tupelo, MS), October 6-7, 1984.

17   Bobby Harrison, "Mantachie vs. Tishomingo Rated Toss-Up," *Northeast Mississippi Daily Journal* (Tupelo, MS), October 12, 1984.

18   Greg Smith, "Football Fever Fails at 17 Area Schools," *Northeast Mississippi Daily Journal* (Tupelo, MS), August 24, 1984.

19   Kollmeyer interview.

20   Black interview.

21   Andy Clay, "New Strategy Pays Off in Win," *Northeast Mississippi Daily Journal* (Tupelo, MS), October 13-14, 1984.

22   "Iuka 21, Tishomingo 12," *Northeast Mississippi Daily Journal* (Tupelo, MS), October 20-21, 1984.

23   "Tishomingo 13, Thrasher 7," *Northeast Mississippi Daily Journal* (Tupelo, MS), October 27-28, 1984.

Chapter 12

1   Howie interview.

2   Powell interview.

3   "Tishomingo Football Team History," Mississippi High School Football History, accessed June 20, 2018, http://www.ahsfhs.org/mississippi/Teams/gamesbyyear.asp?year=1984&Team=Tishomingo.

4   Powell interview.

5   McGee text conversation.

6   McClain interview.

7   Kollmeyer interview.

8   Powell interview.

9   McClain interview.

10 Rector interview.

11 Ibid.

12 Howie interview.

13 Ibid.

14 McGee text conversation.

15 Linda Herbert, and Hollie Spellman interview, July 2017.

16 Bowman interview.

17 Powell interview.

18 Whitehead interview.

19 Royce Howie (father of Brad Howie and friend of David Lee Herbert), in conversation with the author, July 2018. Except when otherwise stated, notes marked "Howie interview" are from conversations with Brad Howie.

Chapter 13

1   Whitfield interview.

2   Rector interview.

3   Whitfield interview.

4   Bowman interview.

5   Ibid.

6   Whitfield interview.

7   Reans phone conversation.

8   Spellman interview, July 2017.

9   Rector interview.

10 Linda Herbert interview, July 2017.

11 Ibid.

12 Bowman interview.

13 Whitlock interview.

14 Bowman interview.

15 Rector interview.

16 Whitlock interview.

17 Ibid.

18 Ibid.

19 Ibid.

20 Ibid.

21 Ibid.

22 Ibid.

23 Ibid.

24 Ibid.

25 Ibid.

26 Ibid.

27 Ibid.

Chapter 14

1   Whitehead interview.

2   Bill Ross, "Tishomingo Rallies to Top Smithville," *Northeast Mississippi Daily Journal* (Tupelo, MS), Nov. 10-11, 1984.

3   Ibid.

4   Whitehead interview.

5   Bill Ross, "Tishomingo Rallies."

6   Linda Herbert interview, July 2018.

7   "Tishomingo Football Team History," Mississippi High School
Football History, accessed June 20, 2018,
http://www.ahsfhs.org/mississippi/Teams/gamesbyyear.asp?year
=1984&Team=Tishomingo.

8   McClung interview.

9   Taylor interview.

10 Linda Herbert interview, July 2017,

11 Bowman interview.

12 Linda Herbert interview, July 2017,

13 McClung interview.

14 Linda Herbert interview, July 2017,

15 Bowman interview.

Chapter 15

1   Mike Talbert, "Key 1-1A Game May Turn into Shootout," *Northeast Mississippi Daily Journal* (Tupelo, MS), October 20, 1988.

2   McClain interview.

3   Chris Burrows, "Tishomingo Rolls to Win," *Northeast Mississippi Daily Journal* (Tupelo, MS), September 6, 1986.

4   "Tishomingo Captures Battle of I-1A Champs," *Northeast Mississippi Daily Journal* (Tupelo, MS), October 7, 1986.

5   Ibid.

6   "Tishomingo Wins in Triple OT," *Northeast Mississippi Daily Journal* (Tupelo, MS), Nov. 15, 1986.

7   Ibid.

8   Vince Jordan (coaching colleague of David Lee Herbert), phone conversation with the author, July 21, 2018.

9   Holt interview.

10 Howie interview.

11 Burrows interview.

12 Jordan phone interview.

13 Ibid.

14 McClung interview.

15 Whitfield interview.

16 Taylor interview.

17 Whitfield interview.

18 Bowman interview.

19 Linda Herbert interview, July 2016,

20 Bowman interview.

21 Rector interview.

22 McClung interview.

23 Ibid.

24 Dave Herbert interview, June 2016.

25 Chris Burrows, "McClanahan Kicks Smithville to Victory," *Northeast Mississippi Daily Journal* (Tupelo, MS), October 22, 1988.

Chapter 16

1 Jordan phone interview.

2 Ibid.

3 "Amyotrophic Lateral Sclerosis," National Institutes of Health, last modified January 2017, https://www.ninds.nih.gov/sites/default/files/ALS_FactSheet-E_508C.pdf.

4 Michael Middlehurst-Schwartz, "49ers Great Dwight Clark, Known for 'The Catch,' Dies at 61 after Battle with ALS." *USA Today*, June 5, 2018, https://www.usatoday.com/story/sports/nfl/49ers/2018/06/04/dwight-clark-dies-niners-san-francisco-catch/671400002/. Accessed 10 June 2018.

5 Sam Farmer and Lance Pugmire, "There's a Catch to Former 49ers Great Dwight Clark and His Battle with ALS," *Los Angeles Times*, Jan. 9, 2018, https://www.latimes.com/sports/nfl/la-sp-dwight-clark-als-20180109-story.html.

6   Alexandra Alter, "A Final Work by Sam Shepard Reveals His Struggle With Lou Gehrig's Disease," *New York Times*, last modified Dec. 4, 2017, https://www.nytimes.com/2017/12/04/arts/sam-shepard-novel.html.

7   Bob Taylor, "Battling ALS: David Niven - Actor, Gentleman, Died from ALS," *Communities Digital News*, last modified Nov. 12, 2017, https://www.commdiginews.com/health-science/health/battling-als-disease-makes-no-distinctions-96026/.

8   Gehrig was chosen for the All-Star team in 1939 but did not participate in the game.

9   "Lou Gehrig," National Baseball Hall of Fame, accessed June 11, 2018. https://baseballhall.org/hall-of-famers/gehrig-lou.

10   "ALS Ice Bucket Challenge - FAQ," ALS Association, accessed June 11, 2018, http://www.alsa.org/about-us/ice-bucket-challenge-faq.html.

11   Don Cleveland, "Research Home Page, accessed June 11, 2018, www.alsa.org/research/.

12   Katherine Harmon, "How Has Stephen Hawking Lived Past 70 with ALS?" *Scientific American*, last modified Jan. 7, 2012, https://www.scientificamerican.com/article/stephen-hawking-als/.

13   "Amyotrophic Lateral Sclerosis (Lou Gehrig's Disease)," *LifeExtension*, accessed June 24, 2018, https://www.lifeextension.com/Protocols/Neurological/Als/Page-01.

14   "Amyotrophic Lateral Sclerosis," Mayo Foundation for Medical Education and Research, last modified May 12, 2017, https://www.mayoclinic.org/diseases-conditions/amyotrophic-lateral-sclerosis/symptoms-causes/syc-20354022.

15   Dave Herbert interview, June 2016.

16   Shane Hill (former football player for David Lee Herbert), phone conversation with the author, July 28, 2018.

17   Linda Herbert and Hollie Spellman interview, June 2018.

18   Dave Herbert interview, July 2016.

19   Jordan phone interview.

20   Whitehead interview.

Chapter 17

1 Jordan phone interview.

2 Horn interview.

3 Burrows interview.

4 Dave Herbert interview, June 2016.

5 Ibid.

6 Danny Brock interview, July 2018.

7 John Moore email.

8 Horn interview.

9 "Tishomingo Bulldogs: Tishomingo vs. Falkner," Mississippi High School Football History, accessed July 27, 2018, http://www.ahsfhs.org/MISSISSIPPI/teams/opponentseach2015.asp?Opponent1=Falkner&Team=Tishomingo.

10 Tony Dawson, online discussion with the author, Nov. 2018.

11 Tucker interview.

12 Jordan phone interview.

13 Hill phone interview.

14 Ibid.

15 Rector interview.

16 Mike Talbert, "Tishomingo, Falkner to Decide 1-1A Title," *Northeast Mississippi Daily Journal* (Tupelo, MS), Nov. 3, 1988.

17 Michael Weinreb, "Why College Football Gets Overtime Right, and the NFL Gets It Wrong," *Sports*, last modified Feb. 9, 2017, https://sports.vice.com/en_us/article/aeb7n8/why-college-football-gets-overtime-right-and-the-nfl-gets-it-wrong.

18 Ibid.

19 Daniel Wilco, "The Longest Overtime Games in FBS College Football History," NCAA.com, last modified Dec. 17, 2018, https://www.ncaa.com/news/football/article/2018-09-21/longest-overtime-games-fbs-college-football-history.

20 "H.S. Football Game Ends in 12th Overtime," FOX Sports, last modified October 29, 2010, https://www.foxsports.com/other/story/texas-high-school-football-game-sets-national-record-with-12-overtimes-102910.

Chapter 18

1   Horn interview.

2   Danny Brock interview.

3   Horn interview.

4   Kollmeyer interview.

5   Wayne Clements, "It's a Tough Job, but Somebody Has Got to Do It," *Northeast Mississippi Daily Journal*, Dec. 4, 1988.

6   Russ Conway, "They Play a Different Brand of Football Down South," Lawrence, Massachusetts Eagle-Tribune, Nov. 24, 1988.

7   Ibid.

8   Burrows interview.

9   Will Kollmeyer interview with Vince Jordan and David Lee Herbert, WTVA-TV, November 1988.

10 According to Baseball Reference, Dolan Nichols (born February 28, 1930, in Tishomingo, Mississippi) pitched in twenty-four games for the Chicago Cubs in 1958, dropping his only four decisions and picking up one save in pitching to a 5.01 earned run average. It was his only year in the big leagues. https://www.baseball-reference.com/players/n/nichodo02.shtml. Accessed June 1, 2018.

11 Burrows interview.

12 Dave Herbert interview, July 2016.

13 Burrows interview.

14 Elizabeth Beard, letter to David Lee Herbert, November 6, 1988.

15 Larry Heffner, letter to David Lee Herbert, November 10, 1988.

16 Woody Woodrick, "55-Yard Loss Sets Up Prep Grid Victory," *Des Moines Register*, November 6, 1988. Woodrick was a assistant sports editor with the *Clarion Ledger/Jackson Daily News*, whose story was picked up by Gannett News Service. Like Will Kollmeyer on the television side, he helped the story "go viral" in an age before the Internet.

17 Gov. Ray Mabus, letter to David Lee Herbert, November 11, 1988.

Chapter 19

1 Littleton interview.

2 Powell interview.

3 Wm. E. Feeman, Letter to Coach Herbert, Nov. 6, 1988. (A follow-up letter dated November 30 thanked the Herberts for the photograph.

4 Brent Musburger, *NFL Today*, Nov. 6, 1988.

5 Hill phone interview.

6 Edmondson interview.

7 Dave Herbert interview, July 2018.

8 Lance Hollingsworth (former football player for David Lee Herbert), in conversation with the author, July 2018.

9 "Football Team History: Anguilla Wildcats." http://www.ahsfhs.org/MISSISSIPPI/teams/gamesbyyear.asp?year=1988&Team=Anguilla.

10 "Anguilla 22, Tishomingo 14," *Northeast Mississippi Daily Journal*, Nov. 12, 1988.

11 "Football Team History: Anguilla Wildcats," http://www.ahsfhs.org/mississippi/teams/gamesbyyear.asp?year=1994&Team=Anguilla. Accessed June 1, 2018.

12 Steven G. Watson, "Jags Were Once the Hawks and the Braves," *Madison County Journal* (Madison, MS), October 20, 2010.

13 "East Flora Playoff Results," Mississippi High School Football History, accessed July 10, 2018, http://www.ahsfhs.org/MISSISSIPPI/teams/playoffs.asp?Team=East%20Flora.

14 "Mississippi High School Football Head Coaches: Dwight Bowling," Mississippi High School Football History, accessed July 11, 2018. http://www.ahsfhs.org/MISSISSIPPI/coaches/coachestop.asp?Coach=Dwight%2BBowling.

15 Associated Press, "Former Football Coach Dwight Bowling Files Notice to Appeal Sentence," *Tuscaloosa News*, July 31, 2014.

16 Mallory Johnston, "Smithville Rebuilds despite Struggles," *Northeast Mississippi Daily Journal* (Tupelo, MS), May 5, 2017.

17 Ibid.

18 Adam Bruns, "Road to Redemption: One Year after an EF-5 Tornado Obliterated the Town, Things Are Looking Up in Smithville, Mississippi. | Site Selection Online," *Site Selection*, accessed July 11, 2018. https://siteselection.com/onlineInsider/road-to-redemption.cfm.

19 Bernard Blackwell, letter to David Lee Herbert, Dec. 9, 1988.

20 "Herbert Makes Hall of Fame," *Northeast Mississippi Daily Journal* (Tupelo, MS), Dec. 13, 1988.

21 Chris Burrows, *Northeast Mississippi Daily Journal*, Nov. 15, 1988.

22 Curley Hallman, letter to David Lee Herbert, July 24, 1989.

23 Mike Talbert, "Drewry Picks up Reins for Tishomingo," Northeast Mississippi Daily Journal (Tupelo, MS), July 13, 1989.

24 Jordan phone interview.

25 Dave Herbert interview, July 2016.

26 After a 2-7 season with Tishomingo in 1989, Jim Drewry returned to Booneville at the beginning of fall practice in 1990. There, he coaches another twenty seasons, winning three state titles and retiring as the winningest football coach in Mississippi history, becoming a member of state and national coaching halls of fame. At the time of Drewry's death in 2018, Bill Hurst of Centreville Academy and Ricky Black of Jackson Prep has passed his win total and were still active in the profession.

27 Hill phone interview.

28 Moore email.

Chapter 20

1 Bruce Heath (friend of David Lee Herbert), in conversation with the author, July 2018.

2 Linda Herbert interview, July 2017.

3 Linda Herbert interview, October 2018.

4 Burrows interview.

5　Kathy Haynes (Nurse and home health professional), phone conversation with the author, November 2018.

6　Taylor interview.

7　Rector interview.

8　Rector interview.

9　Ibid.

10　*Gleason,* directed by Clay Tweel (2016: Amazon Studios), Amazon Prime, https://www.amazon.com/gp/video/detail/B01I2BH93Y/ref=atv_dl_rdr.

11　Linda Herbert and Hollie Spellman interview, July 2017.

12　Ibid.

13　Ibid.

14　McClain interview.

15　Jo Leta Carpenter (cousin of David Lee Herbert), email conversation with the author, May 2019.

16　Linda Herbert interview, July 2017.

Chapter 21

1　"Getting a Free Ride," *Greenwood Commonwealth* (Greenwood, MS), November 5, 1995.

2　Haynes interview.

3　Linda Herbert and Hollie Spellman interview, July 2017.

4　Haynes interview.

5　Bowman interview.

6　Edwards interview.

7　Hollie Spellman interview. July 2018.

8　Ibid.

9　Whitfield interview.

10　Haynes interview.

11   Kollmeyer interview.

12   D.E. Wheeler, "The Rest... of the Tishomingo Story," *Northeast Mississippi Daily Journal* (Tupelo, MS), September 21, 2000.

13   Taylor interview.

14   Linda Herbert and Hollie Spellman interview. July 2017.

15   Whitfield interview.

16   Linda Herbert and Hollie Spellman interview. July 2017.

17   Bowman interview.

18   Linda Herbert and Hollie Spellman interview. July 2017.

19   Clayton interview.

20   Susie James, "Linda Herbert," *Greenwood Commonwealth* (Greenwood, MS). March 25, 2004.

21   Rector interview.

Chapter 22

1   Bowman interview.

2   Whitfield interview.

3   Rector interview.

4   Whitfield interview.

5   Holt interview.

6   Moore email.

7   Taylor interview.

8   McClung interview.

9   McKee interview.

10   Dave Herbert, interview, June 2017.

11   Randy Hogan, "Former Marvell Academy Coach, Headmaster Headed to Hall of Fame," *Sun-Times* (Heber Springs, AR), Aug 9. 2012.

12   Reans phone interview.

13   Royce Howie interview.

14 "God's Wonderful Game Plan—the Resurrection of Jesus," *Bible Center*, accessed April 18, 2019, https://www.biblecenter.com/sermons/godswonderfulgameplan.htm.

15 Jordan phone interview.

16 Bowman interview.

17 Haynes interview.

18 Rector interview.

19 Whitfield interview.

20 Derrick Brock and Ronny McKee interview.

21 Whitlock interview.

Epilogue

1 Stacy McClain Craig, in discussion with the author, March 2019.

In Their Own Words

Hollie Herbert

1 Hollie Herbert, "Behind Every Cloud There Is a Silver Lining," Nov. 24, 1992, paper presented at Tishomingo High School and in the author's possession.

2 Hollie Herbert Spellman, "My Dad's Story Is What Hope Means to Me: Courage, Determination and Faith," ALS Association, accessed June 11, 2018, http://www.alsa.org/about-als/aam-2014/stories/2013-aam-stories-428275506.html.

Linda Herbert

1 Linda Herbert, personal testimony, in the author's possession.

2 Frances de Sales, quoted in Charles E. Cowman, *Streams in the Desert*, (Basingstoke: Lakeland, 1985).

Joyce Herbert Bowman

1 Joyce Herbert Bowman, "A Legacy of Love," in the author's possession.

Lou Gehrig

1   Lou Gehrig, "Luckiest Man," National Baseball Hall of Fame, accessed June 11, 2018, https://baseballhall.org/discover-more/stories/baseball-history/lou-gehrig-luckiest-man.

CPSIA information can be obtained
at www.ICGtesting.com
Printed in the USA
BVHW061925170820
586600BV00003B/45/J